PEACE IN THE MIDDLE EAST?

Reflections on Justice and Nationhood

PEACE
IN THE
MIDDLE EAST?

*Reflections on Justice
and Nationhood*

NOAM CHOMSKY

VINTAGE BOOKS

A Division of Random House, New York

VINTAGE BOOKS EDITION, September 1974

All rights reserved under International and Pan-American
Copyright Conventions. Published in the United States by
Random House, Inc., New York. Distributed in Canada
by Random House of Canada Limited, Toronto. Originally
published by Pantheon Books, a Division of Random
House, Inc., in 1974.

Library of Congress Cataloging in Publication Data

Chomsky, Noam.
    Peace in the Middle East?

    1. Jewish–Arab relations—Addresses, essays,
lectures.   I. Title.
[DS119.7.C52   1974b]   320.9′56′04   74–5000
ISBN 0–394–71248–X

*Since this copyright page cannot accommodate
all acknowledgments, they can be found on
the following page.*

Manufactured in the United States of America

Acknowledgments

Portions of this book previously appeared in somewhat different form in *Liberation*, *The Arab World: From Nationalism to Revolution*, *Holy Cross Quarterly*, and *Ramparts*.

Grateful acknowledgment is made to the following for permission to reprint excerpts from previously published material:

The Christian Science Monitor: For material from "Japan Gets Blunt Choice on Oil," by Elizabeth Pond, from *The Christian Science Monitor*, January 24, 1974. Copyright © 1974 The Christian Science Publishing Society. All rights reserved.

Encounter Ltd.: For excerpts from "Who Is a Jew?" by Jacob Y. Talmon, from *Encounter*, May 1965.

Le Monde: For excerpts from material by Eric Rouleau (*Le Monde*—January 23, 1974; English translation in the *Guardian Weekly*, February 24, 1974) and by Yasir Arafat in *Le Monde*, February 20–26, 1969.

Macmillan Publishing Company, Inc.: For excerpts from *Israel Without Zionists*, by Uri Avnery (Macmillan, 1968).

Medina University Press International: For material from "A Radical Perspective," by Noam Chomsky, reprinted in *The Arab World: From Nationalism to Revolution*, edited by Abdeen Jabara and Janice Terry (1971).

The New Leader: For material from "The Geopolitics of Israel's Survival," by Hans Morgenthau, from *The New Leader*, December 24, 1973. Copyright © The American Labor Conference on International Affairs, Inc.

New Outlook: For excerpts from "The Palestine Challenge," by Shimon Shamir, from *New Outlook*, March–April 1969, page 14; and excerpts from "Al-Fatah's Political Thinking," by Ehud Yaari, *New Outlook*, November–December 1968 (*New Outlook: Middle East Monthly*, Tel Aviv, Israel).

CONTENTS

Foreword, by Irene L. Gendzier   ix

Introduction   1

CHAPTER 1   Nationalism and Conflict in Palestine   49
CHAPTER 2   A Radical Perspective   93
CHAPTER 3   Reflections on a National Conflict   105
CHAPTER 4   The Fourth Round   142
CHAPTER 5   The Peace Movement and the Middle East   153

About the Author   199

Foreword

I
Posing the Question

Any subject that affects people's lives in a profound way is urgent and inevitably controversial. This applies to the Arab-Israeli conflict, as anyone who has concerned himself with it can confirm. But this is, by any standard of human experience, an extraordinary conflict both in its roots and its dimensions. A product of recent history, it is wedded to a distant past. Of immediate consequence to those directly involved, it evokes passionate support from distant partisans. Few are indifferent to its outcome. And few are unaffected by its history and meaning. Small wonder that it is approached with difficulty and not a little trepidation. What makes it essential to reconsider the conflict at the present time is the continuation of the struggle and the danger it poses to those involved.

Those most immediately affected are, of course, Israelis and Palestinians. They have always been at the heart of the struggle. But it is one in which the ambition of Jews to re-create their homeland in Palestine and the equally adamant refusal of Palestinians to become a minority in their own land have always been complicated by the intervention of outside parties. Today, it is axiomatic that the Israeli-Palestinian conflict is effectively subordinated to Arab-Israeli and, even more, to United States and Soviet concerns. What will happen to individual Palestinians and Israelis in this process is a critical matter. The configuration of interests and forces which encapsulate the conflict are complicated enough. But they do not explain the ardor with which it is followed in those places where there are neither Israelis nor Palestinians, and where the convolutions of *Realpolitik* scarcely seem a subject of debate. To many who are physically removed from the Middle East, the conflict has little to do with the politics of the powers or the realities of the region. It is perceived as a struggle between Arabs and Jews. And this, in turn, is differently interpreted depending on one's history and society. To Westerners, the Palestinian and Arab identification of Israel with the West and its colonial tradition seems a distortion of an extraordinary pioneering adventure endorsed by historical necessity. To Palestinians and to Arabs in general, the constant refrain that discussion of Israel evokes, anti-Semitism and the experience of the Holocaust, is unrelated to what Zionism and Israel have meant in their experience. One cannot ignore the origins of these disparate views without guaranteeing distortion of some part of the problem. But it is no easy matter to transfer the experience of one people to another.

Westerners, in contrast to many Israelis who are more conscious of the immediate causes of the conflict, tend to view the State of Israel in ahistorical terms. It is not merely a nation but the revival of Biblical Israel, created because of and in spite of the long and agonizing history of anti-Semitism. From this perspective, Israel is the symbol of survival of Judaism and Jewry. Its existence needs no justification. What it requires is constant defense in the memory of earlier persecutions whose goal was well known. This view is held with varying degrees of sincerity by many whose personal experience is quite alien to that of the persecuted Jews of Europe. Some have claimed—and they are both self-conscious Jews and supporters of Israel—that this support is not only artificial but is a disguise for the guilt of indifference during World War II. Others decry the manipulation of sentiment that is designed to guarantee an uncritical support for Israel while prohibiting an analysis of its problems that is indispensable to the survival of Israelis. No one, however, who has any familiarity with the history of World War II and with the Nazi policy of genocide can be unaware of the vast, awesome dimensions of that mass-supported insane policy. Nor can one be oblivious to the impact it has had on those who survived and those who share, by choice or by experience, the collective memory of that period. But the definition of Israel that justifies all its policies by the memory of the Holocaust neither honors those who died nor protects those who live.

The historical link between anti-Semitism and Israel is part of the history of Zionism. It is the critical link that became, in effect, the motor force for the movement of modern Jewish nationalism. World War II confirmed the intensity of anti-Semitism and the fundamental amorality of nations, whose self-interest at all times took precedence over a concern with humanity, as immigration quotas for refugees after the war revealed. The war not only affected Jews in Europe; it was responsible for the emigration of large numbers of Jews to Palestine. This, in turn, affected the course of Zionism in Palestine and its relations with Great Britain and with the Palestinians. But the Palestinian aspect of Zionist experience, even at this juncture, cannot be understood solely in terms of what happened in Europe. This is a common misrepresentation of the Palestinian reality which distorts its history. For the most part Israelis understand this, since the difference between Palestine and Europe is dramatically clear. But it is an association that is often perpetuated in the West among those who know little of Middle Eastern history. From this perspective, Palestinians exist only insofar as they relate to Jews and Israelis. Their autonomous history is uneventful except as it touches on the current crisis. And since in that crisis, Palestinians are distinctly hostile to Zionism, the conclusion is that they are anti-Semitic. The history of anti-Semitism appears to repeat itself in this fashion.

Left-wing Zionists and binationalists of an earlier day, and some establishment and dissident figures among Israelis today, have acknowledged the roots of the present conflict in unmistakable terms. Their analysis is generally more lucid than that heard from their American supporters. This contrast is striking to anyone who has had the occasion to talk with Israelis and to hear debates as they are conducted in Israel. All such debates are hardly enlightened or rational, but getting to the central issues seems to be easier in the Middle East than in the United States. The intense acrimony engendered in the United States by the discussion of the conflict is symptomatic of the terms in which the origin of the conflict is presented. The most common assumption in such debates is that it is historically correct to subsume the struggle between Israelis and Arabs under the heading of anti-Semitic experience of world Jewry. Since criticism of such fundamental assumptions leads to a reconsideration of Palestinian history, it is often regarded as undermining and frequently presented as suspect. Those who persist in rejecting accepted interpretations are often classified as anti-Semitic, whether they are Jews or not. That their criticism may be directed at Palestinians and Arab governments as well as at Israel is irrelevant, as long as they are regarded as unsparing of Israel. These remarks apply to many circles of Zionist apologists in the United States, but anti-Zionists are not necessarily more faithful to past history. Circles that are "pro-Arab" often betray the same ignorance for a different set of reasons. Partisan in their views, responsive to their own interests—be they political or economic—such observers rarely provide a more adequate explanation of events in the Middle East. This is clearly not enough for those interested in the survival of Palestinians and Israelis, nor is it adequate as an explanation of the historical forces at work in the region.

Those who have resisted such facile classifications and who have tried to comprehend the experience of Zionism and Israel in Palestine in a less orthodox fashion have often been on the left. Their concern with justice and with alternatives to the present deadlock has a long tradition. Whether Jews, Israelis, Palestinians, Arabs, or Americans, they share common concerns. These preclude judging Israeli and Palestinian behavior according to a yardstick that confirms the humanity of the first while denying that of the second. For such people, particularly if they are Jews, the affirmation of one's religious identity is not predicated on the acceptance of a tolerated view of history. To give in to such pressure merely confirms the power of those who wish to deny a part of the truth at any price. It remains to be seen whose interests will be furthered by this.

An example of the definition of the conflict that effectively blocks discussion of its roots is the following statement that appeared some five months after the October war. Commenting on the complete Zionization of the American Jewish community, the author explains the erosion of all anti-Zionist and non-Zionist sentiment in this fashion: "Just as the refusal of the Arabs to accept the existence of a Jewish state in the Middle East turned the anti-Zionist position into a call for the massacre of Jews, it turned evenhandedness into an acquiescence in the same objective. For it was impossible to be evenhanded toward a dispute in which one party wanted to destroy the other, while the other wanted only to be left in peace." [1] The authors of *The New Anti-Semitism* are more pointed in ascribing motives to left-wing critics of Israel: "The Radical Left," Arnold Foster and Benjamin Epstein write, "comprising elements of the New and Old

Left, poses a threat to the Jewish people. It is committed to the liquidation of Israel."[2] Examples of this kind of censure would fill a volume. What is dangerous is that this attack, which is more vitriolic in most cases, as witness the reaction to Daniel Berrigan's address in the fall of 1973, is not limited to those on the left. The expression of evenhandedness has always been suspect from this perspective. This is so readily acknowledged that it is not surprising to see people censoring themselves. In a recent article on the use of antipersonnel weapons by Israeli forces in Syria in the October war, the writer felt it necessary to qualify his criticism by affirming Israel's right to exist, to be protected by secure borders, and to have continued American support.[3] This is a minor example which can be multiplied by many others.[4]

The assumption underlying these and other treatments of Israeli-Arab relations is that the "central aim of Arab countries is to destroy the State of Israel whenever they feel able to do so, while doing everything to harass and disturb its peaceful life."[5] This proposition is frequently echoed in the analysis of the crisis in the United States. It is instructive, however, to consider how differently the *origins* of that crisis are perceived in Israel and the United States. The most avowedly hawkish defendants of such a view in Israel, men such as former chief of military intelligence Yehoshofat Harkabi and former Defense Minister Moshe Dayan, are more honest in their explanations of the basis for Israeli-Palestinian hostility than many of their American supporters. Interviewed before the October war, Harkabi reflected on the nature of this confrontation: "Because we took the land," he noted, "this gives us the image of being bad, of being aggressive. The Jews always considered that the land belonged to them, but in fact it belonged to the Arabs. I would go farther: I would say the original source of this conflict lies with Israel, with the Jews—and you can quote me. But our attachment to this land is too powerful. The big problem, then, is not to start at the beginning but [to] find out 'Where do we go from here?' " [6] Dayan was reported to have told a group of high school students in Haifa in May 1973 that the establishment of the Jewish State had been at the expense and displacement of the Arabs.[7] In the same year, in a lecture he gave before the Israel Technological Institute in Haifa, he again noted: "We came to this country, which was already populated by Arabs, and we are establishing a Hebrew, that is, a Jewish state here. In considerable areas of the country we bought the land from the Arabs. Jewish villages were built in the place of Arab villages. You do not even know the names of these Arab villages, and I don't blame you, since these geography books no longer exist. Not only don't the books exist—the Arab villages are not there either." [8] At the time of the controversy over the villages of Ikrit and Biram, a journalist writing in the popular newspaper *Yediot Ahronot* observed that "it is a single truth that there is no Zionism, no settlement and no Jewish state without evacuation of Arabs and the expropriation and fencing of lands.' " [9]

These are not easy statements to make, and it is difficult to imagine what their impact must be on men and women who have been brought up to believe something quite different. But if Harkabi is correct in saying that the question today is where to go from here, he and Dayan are inadvertently performing an invaluable service in clarifying the deep roots of bitterness that divide Palestinians and Israelis today. To acknowledge the reasons for the conflict, while hardly a solution, at least serves to demystify Israeli-Palestinian relations. It must be noted that neither Dayan nor other Israeli officials have made comparable statements in their many fund-raising trips to the United States. This is regrettable but hardly surprising. If one wishes to preserve a conception of Israeli history in which the Palestinians appear as the personification of evil, it is necessary to camouflage a part of the truth. It is precisely this kind of caricature which so often seems to dominate the American treatment of the conflict. And this, in turn, has made Palestinian grievances appear to be fundamentally unsound and historically unjustified. As long as such an image persists, a resolution of the present deadlock seems difficult to conceive. In circles dedicated to the pursuit of peace in the Middle East, it is still possible to find descriptions of the Arab-Israeli struggle in which the legitimacy of the Palestinian national reality is held in doubt.

This is, of course, a major preoccupation in Israel at the present time. It is a unique characteristic of Golda Meir's government that at the very time its army was engaged in combat against the Palestinians, it continued to deny their existence. But there are people in the Israeli establishment who are not afraid to face the reality of Palestinian existence even if they have not resolved on how to deal with it. Arie Eliav, former secretary general of the Labor Party, writes: "Our relations with the Palestinian Arabs constitute the most important element of our relations with the Arab world as a whole." [10] He recognizes that "the Palestinian nation is identifiable as a national entity by national consciousness, by continuous territory where most of the Palestinians live, by a history of several decades replete with battles and wars, and a diaspora which maintains a link with the Palestinians' homeland." [11] These statements are impressive if one compares them with the abridged and edited versions of Palestinian realities that many Americans accept. They also suggest that Israelis have been taught to forget what an earlier generation could not deny.

II
Israel, the Arabs, and American Policy

The contrast between the statements of men such as Dayan, Eliav, and Harkabi and the guarded, conservative reactions of American commentators suggests that the American restatement of Israeli attitudes is often skewed. Yet the gap is even more severe when it comes to information on the Palestinians and the Arab world. It is not a question of favorable or unfavorable accounts, but of those that give us a sense of the reality of another society versus a stylized and partial view. The media normally restrict their coverage to crises, coups, or other dramatic events. Academics, with rare exceptions, seem largely preoccupied with the manipulations of ruling elites and their ability to guarantee stability. But what transpires below this bureaucratic surface is difficult to sense from the kind of information presented and the filter through which it is passed. It is an embargo of this kind that affects our understanding and that accounts for our unpreparedness in the face of the most diverse events. The war of October 1973, for instance, caught many Americans by surprise. It was regarded either as another example of the profound irrationality of the Middle East conflict or as an inexplicable catastrophe. There was little attempt to see it within the context of the continuing struggle between Israelis, Palestinians, and in this case, Egyptians and Syrians. But it was not possible to understand the meaning of October 1973 without analyzing what had occurred in the Middle East since 1967.

Although it is universally acclaimed as a major military triumph, the Israeli victory of the Six-Day War carried the seeds of its own undoing. By its conquest of the West Bank and the Gaza strip, Israel found itself in possession of what had been the territory of Mandate Palestine in 1922. It suddenly found itself ruling over a population of more than one million Palestinians whose presence posed the familiar question of Israeli-Palestinian relations. Jewish statehood was no longer an uncertain prospect as it had been in the Mandate period. The controversy over the Gaza strip and the West Bank nevertheless touched on "Israel's most sensitive nerve—the legitimacy of its statehood." [12] It also touched on the nature of that statehood. Arguments over whether Palestinians whose land was coveted should be integrated, separated, or assimilated into Israel largely revolved around this issue. Forced to face the troubling fruits of their conquest, Israelis reopened what is perhaps the most difficult question of their existence. By 1973, economic integration championed by Defense Minister Moshe Dayan was in effect. But few denied the importance of the objections raised by Finance Minister Pinhas Sapir. Emerging as a dove, Sapir in fact represented those concerned to keep Palestinians and Israelis separate in an effort to preserve the integral character of the Jewish state. Direct annexationists such as Israel Galili, however, ultimately won the support of the Golda Meir cabinet, and policy towards the West Bank before the October war was the Galili plan.

Israelis were surprised and saddened to discover that their six-year occupation, much heralded as the most liberal occupation policy in existence, had in fact not converted West Bankers to a sympathetic or a neutral position. Strikes, protests, and the expressions of support for the Palestine Liberation Organization heard after the October war revealed the futility of Israeli wishes. There had been dissenters among Israeli liberals and radicals who had consistently criticized occupation policy, but they had little effect in changing it. Denounced during the October war, a number of the professors "for peace and security" recanted and proclaimed their support for the government.[13] But the situation on the West Bank was not affected by these developments.

Before the October war it was not uncommon to hear

liberal Israelis and their American counterparts refer to the enlightened policy pursued by the Israeli government towards Israeli Arabs, the Palestinians who had remained in Israel after 1948. The implication was doubtless that the same opportune situation might eventually apply to or at least influence West Bank and Gaza inhabitants. A more honest exposition of the place of the roughly 400,000 Israeli Arabs in Israeli society suggests rather different conclusions. The second-class status of this minority had always been reinforced by suspicions of its collusion with Palestinians and Arabs outside the borders of Israel. Restricted by a variety of regulations, the Emergency Laws of 1949 and the Defense Laws of 1945, and by the expropriation of land that took place in 1947–1948 and after, Israeli Arabs were hardly in an ideal setting. While a severe critic of Israel's Arab policy has written that "it is not enough to say that nothing else was possible, and that the State of Israel could have been created in no other way," [14] it is doubtful whether something different was possible, given the definition of the state. The power of determining immigration policy and appropriate legislation for its citizens belongs to any sovereign state. But Israeli legislation has sanctioned the discrimination against the Arab population, thus making Israeli democracy largely a preserve of the Jewish majority.

When the occupation of the West Bank and Gaza territories occurred in 1967, it looked as though history was about to repeat itself. But the bulk of the population did not leave this time, nor was it given the option of becom-

ing a part of Israel. Instead, temporary occupation gave
way to permanent settlement and the inevitable wave of
repression crystallized a body of opinion increasingly
open in its opposition to the occupation. Aside from the
obvious effect it had on the Palestinian population of
the West Bank, the occupation seriously affected internal
life in Israel. The impact of the occupation on the conscience of the nation was a favorite theme among dov-
ish intellectuals. Other observers recognized the effect of
the influx of Palestinian workers on the economy. That
their wages were lower than those of Israeli workers,
though higher than they had been, did not diminish
their increasing importance as the new proletariat of Israel. Once again, those concerned with the preservation
of the character and principles of the state were heard to
object to the violation of the Zionist principle of exclusive Jewish labor. But the number of Palestinians working in Israel grew, as did awareness of the long-term
consequences of such an expansion. The October war
temporarily halted this process as the decision not to
work in Israeli industries and factories cut the Palestinian role in the economy.

Had Israel been free of internal problems not arising
out of the occupation, its situation might have differed.
But the occupation only served to aggravate tensions
that had not been resolved. These were not superficial;
they were rooted in Israel's Arab policy. The need for
immigration, for instance, a central preoccupation of the
state, coincided with the exodus of Soviet Jewry. This

coincidence, while generally a happy one for Soviet Jews, had mixed repercussions within Israel. On the one hand, the prospect of a sizable increase in population was encouraging to those aware of the permanent defense needs of the country and the population imbalance between Israel and its neighbors. On the other hand, the influx of Soviet Jews and the preferential treatment they received further depressed and angered Oriental Jewry, which constitutes roughly 60 percent of the entire population. Discriminated against in housing and employment, and more generally considered a threat by virtue of their origin, these "Levantine" elements have primarily been regarded as clients for assimilation. The emergence of the Panthers, a moderately militant organization reflecting Oriental Jewry's discontent, roused the Israeli ruling elite and forced a confrontation with this long-standing problem. Even more obviously affected by the October war was the economy. Israel was forced to turn with increased need to the United States and world Jewry, revealing the extent of financial and military dependence tying Israel to the United States. But the wartime economy was not a result of the October war. Israel's defense needs are predicated on a conception of Israeli-Arab relations which makes war a nearly permanent prospect. The roots of this tragic predicament lie in the history of Israel's relations with the Palestinians and the Arab states on its borders.

The October war, like the earlier wars between Israel and the Arabs, demonstrated the persistence of these tensions and the centrality of the Palestinian conflict. What was different in October 1973 was the dimensions of the conflict, and of course, its outcome and the ensuing diplomatic reshuffling among interested powers. Egypt and Syria had planned their coordinated attack with the dual purpose of retrieving their territory—Sinai and Golan—and forcing open the deadlocked diplomatic situation. That their military action "altered for years to come the balance of power in the Middle East," as Drew Middleton reported,[15] was due to the vastly improved fighting skills of both parties (Egyptian and Syrian), and the use of sophisticated Soviet weaponry.[16] But while tank clashes between combatants in the Sinai were described as surpassing anything "that occurred in 1967 or in the North African campaigns of World War II," [17] another politically more important confrontation was taking place. The oil embargo, engineered by Arab states in alliance with Egypt and Syria, dramatically revealed the extent of American, European, and Japanese dependence on Middle Eastern oil. It exposed the fragility of the Western alliance, and it prompted the independent initiatives of the Western European states and Japan in the Middle East. In the midst of these rapidly changing events, the United States and the Soviet Union tested their détente policy in order to effect a stabilization of the area. To a public shocked by the enormity of the casualties, the human cost of the war surpassed the news of dramatic strategic developments. In the United States, the revelation of Israel's utter dependence on American aid, followed by what appeared to be a change in the direction of American policy in the Middle East, seemed to be an alarming forecast of things to come. In fact, the United States' policy objectives did not change, although its allies in the area increased and their mutual relationship would necessarily differ in the future.

Contrary to what some believed, United States policy in the Middle East was never monolithic. While Israel was reputed to represent the "oldest direct interest" of the United States in the region, it was part of a larger commitment of equal if not more vital importance. The need for oil had become sufficiently clear by World War II so that appropriate arrangements were made between the United States and England in order to assure American oil companies a privileged position. The postwar period also witnessed the extension of the cold war to the Middle East. American policy was subsequently geared to the prevention of the emergence of any communist, procommunist, or neutralist regime. While attempts to introduce NATO-like pacts failed, the United States succeeded in establishing close relations with a number of states (Jordan, Saudi Arabia, Iran, and Turkey), more or less inheriting the role that Great Britain had been forced to abandon. Military as well as economic support for friendly states was instituted early. Between 1948 and 1973, American policy with respect to its appreciation of the potential interests of Israeli military strength evolved considerably. But it was primarily after 1967, and as a result of the conduct and outcome of the Six-Day War, that the United States began to rely more heavily on Israel in its over-all Middle Eastern strategy.

Israel has, therefore, indeed represented an important and at times critical pole of attraction for American support, but Arab states whose strategic locations and resources made them indispensable continued to receive outstanding support. Heavy supplies of economic and military aid were offered and provided to states that were, at times, at war with one another. This was demonstrated in 1973, when the United States not only armed Israel but continued to arm Jordan, Saudi Arabia, and Kuwait, along with Iran—which was not a belligerent. It is nevertheless correct to emphasize the special relationship, involving political and military coordination in the area, that marked American-Israeli relations after 1967, and to underline the fact that it was not regarded as threatening to other American interests in the region. It is this configuration of informal ententes and alliances, with Israel playing a privileged role, that was affected by the October war. But the objectives of United States policy have not changed, even if the sphere of American influence has been greatly expanded. It is in the new context of American influence in the region that Israel's extraordinary position, which resulted from her military superiority, has been altered though not dislodged.

Two areas may jeopardize these new developments: the intensification of Soviet-American competition in the Persian Gulf and local developments in that area, and the continued instability assured by the Palestine problem. The success of the United States' new détente with Syria and Egypt depends, in part, on its ability to bring about a satisfactory resolution of the Palestine conflict.

In terms of long-range interests, however, the Persian Gulf represents a more vital commitment. This was reflected in the extraordinary arms sales that marred exchanges between the United States and Saudi Arabia, Iran, and Kuwait in 1973. In the winter of 1973, the Defense Department stated that Iran had agreed to buy more than $2 billion worth of American weapons. In May of the same year, the Pentagon confirmed the agreement to sell advanced military aircraft to Saudi Arabia and Kuwait. The concern over the existing Soviet support system in the Indian Ocean has sparked an interest in extending our own bases in that area, which are in fact already being expanded. In comparison with these interests, which will determine American access to Middle Eastern oil, the United States' concern with the outcome of the Israeli-Palestinian conflict is secondary. But these interests are not mutually exclusive. The continued conflict of Israel and the Arabs would directly involve the Soviet Union and the United States, and those powers that successfully used the oil embargo earlier. It remains in the interest of the United States, then, to attempt to resolve this struggle as effectively as possible. Of all of the forces concerned, the Palestinians are the only ones that do not represent a state. They constitute the most difficult and potentially explosive factor.

In the period 1967–1973, while Israel's military superiority over its neighbors increased, there was a marked resurgence and transformation in Palestinian nationalism. The Palestine Liberation Organization, established in 1964, was largely discredited by the defeat of 1967 and by the role of its corrupt leadership. But the extent of defeat and the analysis of failure led to a revival of the organization. Although they did not share a unified ideology, the Resistance organizations that constituted the membership of the new PLO, under the leadership of Fatah leader Yasir Arafat, were committed to the restoration of Palestinian rights and to a new policy of self-reliance. They not only succeeded in changing the image of the Palestinian, who had previously been known exclusively as a refugee, but they sought to emphasize his independence from the host nations that supported them. As the Resistance organizations matured, they came to differ significantly in the nature of their analyses of the Middle East situation. Their revolutionary potential alienated Arab governments caught between the desire to endorse their goals and fear of the impact of their presence. Active Resistance politics furthermore promised Israeli retaliation. In 1970, the civil war in Jordan revealed the degree of tension between Palestinian organizations and the Jordanian state. Admittedly this was a special case, since half the population of Jordan was Palestinian and the Jordanian dynasty had been directly involved in the takeover of the West Bank in 1948. Jordan has always posed a special problem for Palestinians, but neighboring states did not miss the lesson.

In the wake of the tragedy that followed the September civil war, the resumption of terrorism by Black September, the sense of urgency surrounding the Palestine question was revived. Relations between the Palestinian organizations and the Arab states underwent a critical period. There was talk of the demise of the Resistance. There was a rumor that a Palestine entity might be supported on the West Bank. In fact, the Resistance organizations did not suffer final defeat and the idea of a Palestinian state was scotched by Israel and Jordan and the Palestinian organizations, all of whom opposed it for different reasons. In Israel, there had been talk of creating an independent West Bank leadership to provide a more moderate interlocuter for the Israelis. While there were some voices heard in support of this policy, the position of the government was, in the end, negative. The October 1973 war revived the idea of a Palestinian entity under circumstances that made it difficult to dismiss. This time, reactions of interested parties differed. While Golda Meir's government continued to reject the idea, other Israelis spoke up. Although far from having the support of the bulk of the population, the notion of a Palestinian state alongside Israel was gaining ground. Among Palestinians in the PLO, the subject forced the most intensive debate on long-term policy and strategy. Encouraged by the Soviet Union and by some of its Arab allies to join in the projected Geneva negotiations, the Palestinians were also urged not to reject the state idea out of hand. In Jordan, King Hussein was under pressure to defend his role as Palestinian spokesman, a role which many Palestinians rejected. Faced with the prospect of a Palestinian state independent of his own kingdom, he was forced to reckon with its impact on his future position. The outlook was hardly favorable. It is too early to know the details of the intricate negotiations that have transpired among all of these parties, but it is clear that the notion of a Palestinian state will seriously affect Palestinians, Israelis as well as Jordanians. The Palestinian question was left for last in the big-power agenda for the Middle East, an expression of tactical considerations as well as of the genuine difficulty which the subject would arouse.

In May of 1974, Syrian-Israeli negotiations appeared to be near the breaking point as a result of the resumption of terrorism. Palestinians, clearly struck by the apparent indifference to their fate which marked the activities of the major powers in the Middle East, resorted to the use of terror. Once again, the mood of anxiety that had gripped Israel after the October war and Palestinian despair at being ignored in the diplomatic shuttle converged in the now familiar pattern of violence and counterviolence. Awed by the seemingly endless series of wars, Israelis clamored for greater security and more adequate protection. But they also began to publicly question their government's policies. Protests marked the postwar period. It was not only on the left, a diverse group of dissident parties, that this occurred. It was a more pervasive phenomenon. What was at issue was nothing less than the need to redefine Israel's Palestinian policy, a redefinition that required examining the basic principles underlying that policy. In this atmosphere it was not surprising to hear questions raised about the past as well as the future. None was more crucial than whether or not there had ever been an alternative to the present situation of nearly permanent war between Israelis and Palestinians.

III
Binationalism and the Palestine Mandate

Finding an alternative to the deadlock of Israeli-Palestinian relations was not a new preoccupation. Before 1948 there were individuals and groups dedicated to the solution of this apparently intractable problem. They faced an uphill battle not only among their colleagues in the Zionist movement but in the larger context of Palestinian and Middle Eastern political life. The history of Mandate Palestine is part of the unhappy story of the Middle East after the end of World War I. Divided by secret treaties and commitments as seemingly contradictory as the Hussein-McMahon Correspondence (1915–1916) and the Balfour Declaration (1917), the Arab world was caught between nascent nationalist movements and the imperial interests to which they were tied. Great Britain, then in Egypt, used the promise of independence from Ottoman rule as a card in bargaining for Arab support. London also made complementary agreements with the French in 1916 and the Zionists in 1917. That this was satisfactory to other European powers who came in for a share of the partition plans was a reflection of successful imperialist practice. France and England had long histories of influence and involvement in the Middle East, and they understood the value of mutual cooperation. France was in North Africa at this period. England had been in Egypt since 1882, and both were concerned with the expanding interests of Germany and the exigencies of wartime. The imperialist tradition was to be challenged as a result of the transformation of the Middle East itself. No longer an inert vacuum to be maneuvered at will, it showed signs of unmistakably independent life. A number of events promoted this: Woodrow Wilson's Fourteen Points and the concept of self-determination; the Soviet disclosures of contradictory treaties entered into by the Entente Powers; the King Crane Commission designed to survey public opinion on the matter of Mandatory government and self-determination. The disillusionment in the Middle East after the war was not without cause. It arose out of the flagrant disrespect shown by the European powers towards those Arab states to whom independence had been promised. In Syria and Lebanon, in Iraq, and in Palestine, where the Balfour Declaration was not published until two-and-one-half years after its issuance, the sense of betrayal was evident. Under these circumstances, the history of the Mandate experience was necessarily troubled.

In Palestine, the Mandate was introduced with difficulty. In 1919 Jews constituted 9.7 percent of the population and Arabs, 91.3 percent. In 1936, the ratio was 29.5 percent for the Jewish population and 70.5 percent for the Palestinian Arab.[19] Zionism was not unknown in the Middle East. Its advocates circulated throughout the Ottoman Empire before the war in an effort to obtain support from Ottoman and Arab circles. Articles appeared in the local press arguing the pros and cons of

Zionism for the Arab world. The two issues that appeared most troublesome and were to remain critical throughout the Mandate were singled out early: immigration and the alienation of land. Under the British, the Balfour Declaration was introduced into the Mandate and Zionist efforts got under way. Well organized and virtually autonomous, the Jewish community grew and developed with the enormous energy and dedication that characterized its members. It was a well-knit community bound by a well-defined purpose. Relations with the British administration were not always simple or harmonious. While the first high commissioner, Sir Herbert Samuel, was a supporter of Zionism and a believer in its compatibility with Palestinian nationalism, he surrounded himself with aides who were less sympathetic to the Jewish community. This not only frustrated the efforts of the Yishuv; it revealed the contradictions in the British administration that only served to further complicate the running of the Mandate. In spite of this, the Jewish community did not abandon hope. Parties and plans mushroomed and the dream of a majority in Palestine protected by a benign British government was steadfastly nurtured.

Although poorly organized in comparison, and exhibiting considerably less cohesion as a community, Palestinian Arabs were not passive. Represented in their dealings with the British administration by a reactionary upper-class elite that dominated civil and religious offices, they consistently expressed their opposition to the Mandate on a variety of grounds: religious, political, economic, and demographic. The presence of the Jews was not the danger, they claimed. What was feared was the Zionist movement with its avowed aim of colonizing Palestine. Small as it was at first, the gradual increase in Jewish immigration and the highly organized practice of purchasing land affected the Palestinian community. Wealthy and often absentee landowners did sell their land, thus effectively displacing the Palestinian peasant, who was, more often than not, a sharecropper on someone else's land. At the end of the Mandate, however, Jewish holdings constituted no more than 7 percent of the total area of Palestine. As of 1936, 91.3 percent of the acreage purchased by the Jewish National Fund had been acquired from landowners, including 39.4 percent from those resident in Syria and Egypt, while only 8.7 percent had been purchased from the Palestinian fellaheen.[20] This leads to the conclusion that "some Arabs, especially the so-called feudalists, are directly and personally responsible for the alienation of the Palestinian patrimony, [but] the analyst should not ignore the fact that the overwhelming majority of Arabs did not sell their land." [21] The critical time in terms of acquisition of land came in the period of the 1948 war. By the armistice agreements of 1948–1949, Israel was in control of 77.4 percent of the area of the former Mandate,[22] and it was estimated that some 770,000 to 780,000 Palestinians had become refugees.

The contrast between the population figures of 1919 and 1948 does not tell the entire story. Nor is it possible, in so brief a space, to do any measure of justice to the

forces at work. Each community, though largely independent within itself, was caught in the larger net of
British dependence. The vulnerability of the Zionists
made them openly reliant on British support of the Balfour Declaration and the Mandate document that incorporated it. Palestinians continued to believe that Britain
would eventually honor its promises of independence
and self-government. Zionists and Palestinian Arabs who
saw their lives and mutual relations deformed by British
imperial interests strove without success to resist the di-
visive efforts of the British presence. But they were impeded in their efforts by a majority in their communities
and by forces beyond their control. Still, there were instances of Zionist attempts at diplomatic negotiation
with Arabs, often non-Palestinian. Chaim Weizmann
dealt a number of times with Abdullah of Transjordan,
who was anxious to open his country to Jewish capital
and who was willing to promote the transfer of Palestinians to his territory. Britain was as unwilling to allow
this kind of collaboration as it was to allow discussion
between Weizmann and Zaghlul Pasha, the Egyptian
nationalist leader, with whom Weizmann was prepared
to meet. For Weizmann, and for others in his position,
there was no real choice between British and Arab support. The Palestinians and other Arabs rejected Zionism.
Britain, the dominant power in the area, had guaranteed
the Jewish homeland. Zionism depended, therefore, more
on British than on Arab good will.

Palestinian and Arab perspectives were never identi-
cal. It is clear that there were Arabs with whom the

Zionists talked who were willing to consider arrangements, particularly if they were profitable. They were not directly affected by events in Palestine, and it was somewhat easier to deal with them. Aharon Cohen noted that "it was easier to solve the Arab-Jewish-Palestinian problem within a framework with the neighboring Arab countries than within the confines of the 27,000 kilometers of Palestine west of the Jordan." [23] For those Palestinians whose national aspirations superseded the prospect of private gain, the picture was discouraging. While Egyptian, Syrian, and Iraqi nationalists obtained important political concessions from their respective mandatory powers, the Palestinians were denied the same hope. Demands for the introduction of parliamentary government and self-determination were rejected on the grounds that these contradicted British commitments to the Zionists. As World War II approached, Britain became more conciliatory towards the Palestinian Arabs and the Arab world as a whole. But the war and the Nazi policy of genocide transformed the Palestinian situation. "The theory of catastrophic Zionism suddenly seemed vindicated and was soon to be confirmed in a way which even the gloomiest prophet could never have imagined." [24] The Jewish community joined to force open the doors of immigration in an effort to save Europe's Jews. Britain was caught by its desire to prove its control of the Jewish community and thereby assure the support of the Arab world. In 1942 the Biltmore program proclaimed the decision of the Zionist community in Palestine to form a Jewish state. Palestinians were therefore faced with increased Jewish immigration and the confirmation of Zionist plans for Palestine.

It is in the midst of such varied and conflicting events that efforts to arrive at a *modus vivendi* between Zionists and Palestinians must be considered. Although not all Zionists thought in terms of a state, with few exceptions all agreed on the need to create a Jewish majority in Palestine. Most Zionist leaders "were convinced that the real interests of the Jewish and Arab national liberation movements were compatible and complementary, and could therefore be realized harmoniously." [25] They overlooked the harsher vision of some members of the right-wing Revisionist Party, who warned that "never before in history have the native inhabitants of a country agreed of their own free will that their land should be colonized by foreigners." [26] There were deeply committed Zionists who believed they would not displace Palestinians but could work with them. For such people, the political objective was "the constitution of the Palestinian state in which should be formed a free Palestinian commonwealth composed of two peoples." [27] Convinced that there was no incompatibility between Zionism and Palestinian nationalism, they channeled their considerable efforts towards such an accommodation. None were more determined than the binationalists, who attracted support from a variety of political groups, some for tactical reasons and others out of sincere conviction. At different periods men such as Martin Buber, Judah Magnes, Chaim Kalvarisky, Moshe Smilansky, Chaim Arlosoroff, and even Chaim Weizmann and David Ben-Gurion supported binationalism. Left-wing parties such as Hasho-mer Hatzair and Mapai and other left-wing circles advo-cated the binationalist program. But a distinction must be made between the temporary support of some leading Mapai political figures and the consistent adherence to binationalist goals offered by other individuals and groups. Dedicated partisans of binationalism were al-ways a minority within the Zionist movement, although they may be said to have become its conscience on the Arab question. They were sensitive to signs of racism and superiority, and they rejected the notion of a Pales-tinian commonwealth as an outpost of European civiliza-tion in which the native population was to be civilized. Working in such associations as the Brit Shalom (1926), the Kedma Mizraha (1936), or the more ambitious and effective League for Jewish Arab Rapprochement and Cooperation (1939), binationalists attempted to recon-cile Zionist and Palestinian demands. Their conception of Zionism was affected by the realities of Palestinian life, and this was reflected in their program. They advo-cated the recognition of the legitimacy of two nations in Palestine, the Jewish and the Arab. They endorsed co-operation in a political structure that would guarantee the principle of nondomination of one community over another.

Arthur Ruppin, founder of the Brit Shalom, expressed the views of the binationalists when he declared that "one need not be a maximalist, i.e. demand mass immi-gration and a state, to be a faithful Zionist. . . . What was vital was a recognition that both nations were in

Palestine as of right." [28] In 1922, speaking before the Zionist Congress held in Karlsbad, the young statesman Chaim Arlosoroff affirmed that "the only possible course is the establishment of a common state in Palestine for Jews and Arabs as peoples with equal rights." [29] Three years later, Ben-Gurion said that "Palestine will be for the Jewish people and the Arabs living in it." [30] In 1927 he declared that "we have no right to discriminate against a single Arab child, even if thereby we attain everything we desire. Our work cannot be based on depriving anyone of his rights." [31] In 1931, Weizmann claimed that he had "no sympathy or understanding for the demand of a Jewish majority. . . . the world will construe this demand in only one sense, that we want to acquire a majority in order to drive out the Arabs." [32] Whether such statements were made out of tactical considerations or out of conviction depended on the circumstances as well as the man in question. Binationalists who believed in the long-term validity of their program realized that it was being exploited by others for short-term interests. They were aware of the fundamental resistance to their program even by those who, at times, spoke the same language.

On the Palestinian and Arab side, the efforts of men of good will were not ignored. In 1936, five influential Jews and Arab leaders "got together and by common consent, a draft of an agreement was formulated. This was to have been approved by the Jewish Agency and the Higher Arab Committee before the High Commissioner declared it illegal. . . ." [33] In 1940–1941, Adil Jabr, a member of the Jerusalem Municipal Council, drafted a proposal for a binationalist Palestine which looked forward to Jewish immigration into all countries of a proposed federation which was to include Palestine and Transjordan.[34] In November 1946, an agreement on cooperation and mutual help was signed by an Arab association called Falastin al-Jadida and the League for Jewish Arab Rapprochement and Cooperation.[35] The management of the Palestinian association was headed by Fauzi al-Hussaini, who declared himself in favor of the principle of nondomination and "the establishment of a binational state on the basis of political equality and full economic, social, and cultural cooperation between the two peoples." He recognized that immigration had become a political issue, but he also saw that it was not impervious to solution within a comprehensive accord. Al-Hussaini was not sparing of Palestinian sentiment and its reluctance to support binationalism. "The hour is late," he wrote, "and we must hurry. My friends and I know that we too will have great difficulty, the more so since political conditions have changed for the worse." He decried the growth of extremism in the Arab community, but he also recognized that outside forces impeded cooperation. "Imperialistic policy is playing with both of us, Arabs and Jews alike, and we have no choice but to unite and work hand in hand for the benefit of us both." Fauzi al-Hussaini was killed twelve days after the appearance of the joint declaration. The reactions in the Arab and the Jewish communities, particularly at the Zionist congress, were discouraging.[36]

There were other examples of Palestinian interest in binationalist efforts. But it would be an error to minimize the profound skepticism which binationalist ideas met with in the Palestinian community. Support was uncommon. It was not facilitated by the situation in the Zionist community. There, the obvious difficulty in obtaining a serious commitment from the Zionist Executive or the Jewish Agency hampered the efforts of the binationalists. "While Zionist leaders articulated the principles of non-domination, political equality, and accord between the two peoples, they formulated no concrete political proposals as a basis for effective negotiation." [37] Those sympathetic to such attempts expressed frequent distress at the absence of a clear-cut Jewish Agency policy towards the Arabs. It may not be correct to state that there was no such policy. The following statements suggest that a pessimistic line had evolved even among former binationalist supporters. In 1930, Arthur Ruppin challenged the notion that "the Jews would build their National Home without the impairment of the rights of the other inhabitants of the country." [38] Six years later he had "reached the conclusion that it has been decreed that we shall live in a state of perpetual war with the Arabs and there is no escaping casualties." [39] In the same year, Ben-Gurion argued that "an agreement with the Arabs is necessary for us, not in order to create peace in the country. Peace is indeed vital for us. It is not possible to build up a country in a situation of permanent war, but peace for us is a means. The aim is the complete and absolute fulfillment of Zionism. Only for this do we need an agreement. . . ." [40]

For binationalism to have succeeded would have required nothing less than the transformation of both Jewish and Palestinian Arab communities. It would have meant rechanneling the ambitions of each to create an independent state into a program for dual cooperation. It is important to question whether the maximalist demand of Zionism, the creation of an independent Jewish state, was indeed the accepted one from the beginning. If the goal was the establishment of a state and the creation of a majority in Palestine, then binationalism offered little more than a temporary diversion. From this point of view, if it had succeeded it would have impaired the achievement of the final goal. As it is, it would seem that binationalist attitudes and supporters were exploited by the Zionist Executive and the Jewish Agency, at those times when bitter confrontations between Jews and Arabs warned of the dangers ahead. Parity and non-domination were terms heard most frequently when the Jewish minority was small. For binationalists and for those who did not think in terms of a Jewish state, but rather of an Arab-Jewish commonwealth, there was perhaps some basis for collaboration. But the war and the Biltmore program made this more difficult. The former consolidated the power of Ben-Gurion and the Mapai party. They, in turn, used their efforts to obtain support for the Biltmore platform. As evidence of the overwhelming human suffering caused by the years of war became clear, Zionists and many who had not supported them earlier took action to save the remnants of European Jewry. Agonizing accounts of the imprisonment of Jews arriving from Europe, at the hands of the British in Palestine, only served to strengthen Zionist determination to end the arbitrary power of the Mandatory. Independence was supported by such realities.

It is, however, a shortsighted view that makes binationalists appear to be any less relevant under the circumstances. It was not less devotion that made binationalists refrain from claiming that total independence was the only solution. On the contrary, committed to Jewish life in Palestine, they believed that it could be secured only through Arab-Jewish cooperation. Their lesson for the present lies in this vision as well as in their failure to implement it. To those brought up on the axiom that Arab-Jewish cooperation is impossible, it is useful to recall the efforts of earlier Zionists who rejected this outlook. Yet one must also recognize the roots of their failure and the price that has been paid for it.

It is not possible to return to Palestine as it was before 1948. The 1967 war proved that. The October war of 1973 has resulted in a different configuration of forces. But a resolution of the Israeli-Palestinian conflict seems no closer. Still, as the powers effect a stabilization of the Middle East, it is urgent to question what future lies ahead for its peoples, and for Israelis and Palestinians among them. Certain realities have to be acknowledged in the formulation of any guiding principles. Chief among them ought to be that Palestinians and Israelis have the right to survive, and that neither will abandon this right at any cost. The survival of both peoples, and not of one at the expense of the other, must be the paramount principle. It is admittedly difficult to contemplate this in the midst of violence and counterviolence, and even more in the midst of the existing imbalance of forces between the two communities involved. But one may be allowed to hope that even in this atmosphere certain axioms may be accepted for the future. The recognition of the legitimacy of Palestinian self-determination is an imperative that is long overdue. The legitimacy and the permanence of Israelis in the Middle East are another prerequisite for a solution. For both peoples today, the contemplation of the other is undeniably painful and filled with bitterness. Yet these antagonists will one day have to meet, not as partisans in war, but as opposite numbers in the making of peace; this means Israelis and the representatives of the Palestinian people, which today is the Palestine Liberation Organization.

In the long run, however, if there is to be a resolution of the conflict that creates a situation different from the present one, it can only come about as a result of cooperation between both peoples. It is from Israelis and Palestinians that the new directions of a reconstruction in their relationship must come. How that is possible in the context of war or an imposed solution is difficult to imagine. But it is foolish to believe that a solution imposed from the outside, and not sustained by the genuine needs of the populations freed from the constraints of external force, can long survive. For something else to occur, forces within both communities will have to cooperate and struggle in a common effort. To believe that this is anything but the most difficult task is a dangerously naïve illusion. War and terrorism not only perpetuate the rift between the two peoples, they polarize sentiment in such a way as to strengthen the determination of each to survive at any cost. Even without an active war, it is not simple to transform society, its reigning ideology, and the years of fear and mistrust which accumulate. External forces rarely seem to intervene in the interests of the people concerned. Whether it is the superpowers that follow the direction of their own interests, or popular sentiment that perpetuates the polarization of sentiment from afar, the effect is detrimental to the peoples concerned.

No matter how involved one may be, the existential difference between the situation of a Palestinian and an Israeli—and they do differ—and that of an outsider is obvious. Under the circumstances, it is legitimate to ask whether one who is removed from the scene has the right to make any comment on this story. The assumption in this essay is that there exists not only a right but an obligation. And this because we are not free of involvement in this tragic affair, as its history so amply demonstrates. By its nature the conflict has affected those outside of the region, as it has been profoundly affected by events foreign to its land. To recognize this precludes indifference. There is another reason not to remain silent, and it is that silence today has become the most effective kind of complicity. If one rejects such passive collaboration, while acknowledging the limitations necessarily placed on outsiders, then the search for truth remains the most effective weapon in the struggle for reconciliation and justice.

For those unfamiliar with Noam Chomsky's writings on the Middle East, a few words may be in order. In the midst of a time and a place in which the Middle East is most often depicted in limited and emotion-laden terms that preclude rational consideration, few see beyond the drama of the present crisis. Chomsky must be counted among the few who are neither defeated by despair nor lulled by illusions of simple explanations for a conflict of unparallelled complexity. In the essays that follow, he has accomplished many things. He has analyzed the depth of American involvement in the Middle East and the national dimensions of the Arab-Israeli conflict itself. His argument on behalf of socialist binationalism is offered to Israelis and Palestinians with the recognition that, in the end, it is they who must and will decide their own fate. As to the discussion of the issue in the United States, Chomsky has challenged those who seek to suppress it in any but the most superficial terms. He has exposed the obstacles that lie in the path of those seeking a coherent understanding of the Arab-Israeli conflict, and in so doing, he has shown the domestic roots of this blockade of the truth. To anyone familiar with the lengthy and often sterile debates in the United States on the conflict, these essays come as a welcome and much-needed antidote. But beyond the critical level of providing knowledge, Chomsky has demonstrated his continued commitment to its purpose, justice wedded to truth.

One may disagree with what is offered, but none can fault the honesty and moral integrity of the effort.

Cambridge, Massachusetts
June 1974

Irene L. Gendzier
Associate Professor of History
Boston University

Notes

1. Norman Podhoretz, "Now Instant Zionism," *New York Times Magazine,* Feb. 3, 1974.
2. Arnold Foster and Benjamin Epstein, *The New Anti-Semitism,* McGraw-Hill Book Co., New York, 1974, p. 125.
3. Nick Thimmecsh, "Arab Civilians Suffer from Israeli Weapons," *Baltimore Sun,* Dec. 22, 1973.
4. See, for instance, Benjamin Taylor, "Journalist Says Arab Israelis Suffer Bias," *Boston Sunday Globe,* March 31, 1974, p. 35. To appreciate the meaning of Taylor's article, also see Alan Dershowitz, "Terrorism and Preventive Detention: The Case for Israel," in *Commentary,* vol. 50, no. 6, and the answer by Fawzi el-Asmar in vol. 51, no. 6.
5. Michael I. Handel, *Israeli Political-Military Doctrine,* Harvard Center for International Affairs, Cambridge, Mass., July 1973, p. 64.
6. Quoted in "Peace Won't be a Plane Ticket to Cairo," *Armed Forces Journal International,* Oct. 1973, p. 30.
7. As reported in *al-Hamishmar,* June 18, 1973.
8. *Ha'aretz,* April 4, 1969.
9. *Yediot Ahronot,* July 14, 1972.
10. Arie L. Eliav, *New Targets for Israel,* 2nd ed., E. Lewin Epstein Publishers, Jerusalem, 1968, p. 16.
11. *Ibid.*
12. Abraham S. Becker, *Israel and the Palestinian Occupied Territories: Military-Political Issues in the Debate,* Rand, Santa Monica, Calif., R882-1SA, Dec. 1971, p. iii.
13. See the letter signed by professors which appeared in the

New York Review of Books, Nov. 15, 1973, and the reply by Professor Daniel Amit of Hebrew University, reprinted in the *New York Review of Books,* Nov. 29, 1973.

14. Sabri Jiryis, *The Arabs in Israel,* Institute for Palestine Studies, Beirut, 1969, p. 179.

15. Drew Middleton, "Can Israel Afford Total Victory?" *New York Times,* Oct. 14.

16. Robert R. Rodwell, "The Mideast War: A Damned Close-Run Thing," *Air Force Magazine,* Feb. 1974, p. 39.

17. *Ibid.,* p. 41.

18. John Badeau, "The Middle East: Conflict in Priorities," *Foreign Affairs,* vol. 36, no. 2, Jan. 1958.

19. See Walid Khalidi, *From Haven to Conquest,* The Institute for Palestine Studies, Beirut, 1971, app. 1, pp. 841–3.

20. Aharon Cohen, *Israel and the Arab World,* Funk & Wagnalls, New York, 1970, pp. 199–200.

21. John Ruedy, "Dynamics of Land Alienation in Palestine," Association of Arab-American University Graduates, North Dartmouth, Mass., Information Paper no. 5, May 1973, p. 134.

22. *Ibid.,* p. 135.

23. Aharon Cohen, *op. cit.,* p. 265.

24. J. L. Talmon, *Israel Among the Nations,* Weidenfeld & Nicolson, London, 1970, p. 150.

25. Aharon Cohen, *op. cit.,* p. 221.

26. *Ibid.*

27. Susan Lee Hattis, *The Bi-National Idea in Palestine During Mandatory Times,* Shikmona Publishing Co., Haifa, 1970, p. 5.

28. *Ibid.,* p. 46.

29. Aharon Cohen, *op. cit.,* p. 245.

30. *Ibid.,* p. 248.

31. *Ibid.*

32. Hattis, *op. cit.,* p. 92.

33. Aharon Cohen, *op. cit.,* p. 266.

34. *Ibid.,* pp. 285–7. This is discussed at greater length in Chomsky's introduction below.

35. *Ibid.,* p. 351. Also see Chapter 1 below.

36. *Ibid.,* pp. 353–4. Also see Chomsky's introduction.

37. *Ibid.,* p. 249.

38. Hattis, *op. cit.,* p. 48.

39. *Ibid.,* p. 139.

40. *Ibid.,* p. 147.

PEACE IN
THE MIDDLE EAST?

Reflections on Justice and Nationhood

Introduction

The struggle that will determine the fate of Israel and the Palestinians takes place simultaneously in three arenas: local, regional, and international. Locally, there is a conflict between two national groups, Israeli Jews and Palestinian Arabs, each claiming rights in a territory of ambiguous boundaries that each regards as its national homeland. Questions of justice and human rights arise primarily in the context of this local conflict. Since 1948, the local conflict has been transformed into a broader regional conflict between Israel and the Arab states, with the Palestinian people generally playing a passive role: victims more than agents. Finally, the region has enormous strategic and economic importance for the great industrial powers. Shortly after the Balfour declaration committing the British government to support the creation of a Jewish National homeland in Palestine, Lord Balfour stated: "I do not care under what system we keep the oil, but I am clear that it is all-important that this oil should be available." Twenty-five years later, Secretary of State Hull emphasized that "there should be full realization of the fact that the oil of Saudi Arabia constitutes one of the world's greatest prizes." [1] During and after World War II, the United States took over the dominant role in controlling these resources, displacing Great Britain, and their value for the

industrial societies has never been greater than it is today. We may assume, with fair confidence, that the
United States will make every effort to ensure that this
great prize will be available, and to the extent possible,
under the control of American oil companies.

It has always been clear that if the parties to the local
conflict do not reach a stable and peaceful accommodation, then the superpowers will seek to impose a settlement in their own interests, a form of recolonization that
only by the merest accident will satisfy the needs and
interests of the people directly involved: Israeli Jews and
Palestinian Arabs. There is good reason to believe that
the primary objective of Egypt and Syria, when they
launched the October 1973 attack into territories conquered by Israel in 1967, was to create conditions that
would induce the United States to rethink its policies toward the region, and, in its own self-interest, impose a
settlement along the lines of United Nations Security
Council Resolution 242 (November 1967) as interpreted
in most of the world—that is, with Israel returning to essentially its 1967 borders, a peace treaty among the states
of the region, demilitarized zones separating potential
combatants, and perhaps a Palestine state in parts of the
West Bank and Gaza, subordinated to Jordan and Israel.

It has been suggested that the United States should
undertake "the relatively minor adjustment we would
be obliged to make in order to get along without Arab
oil" and become self-sufficient in energy supplies, so that
American policy for the region will be immune to any
pressures from the Arab states.[2] Such proposals are virtually irrelevant to the formation of state policy. The
problem is not merely access to Middle Eastern oil, but
also the profits of major American corporations, not only
the giant energy companies, but also others that are
looking forward to vast investment opportunities in the

Middle East. While the United States might reach self-sufficiency, Europe and Japan, for the foreseeable future, cannot. In one way or another, they will obtain access to the petroleum reserves of the Middle East, vast in quantity and lower in production cost than alternatives currently available. The result could be that United States industry, already barely competitive, would be priced out of world markets. The industrial systems of Europe and Japan, with independent resources of energy and raw materials, might surpass the United States in scale and productivity. It is hardly likely that the United States government will tolerate such prospects with equanimity.

If the Arab oil producers persist in some form of the current oil politics, then serious conflict is likely within the capitalist world system. The United States will insist on a "united front," which it can control. Its industrial competitors will continue to seek bilateral arrangements with the oil producers or perhaps will also move to co-ordinated efforts of their own. The real issues are clouded by rhetoric about "greed" and "cowardice." At the heart of the matter, however, are some quite substantial questions: Will the United States and United States–based multinational corporations continue to dominate the capitalist world system? Will the major oil companies be able to amass sufficient profits in the final period of petroleum-based energy to ensure their domination of the next phase (coal, nuclear energy)?

In the world of business and finance, there is now much concern that the European states and Japan are making "slow, but apparently inexorable, government inroads into the oil business," and that "national governments are even now beginning to negotiate direct deals with oil-producing countries."[3] "A rush of such deals is under way, with Japan, France, Britain, West Germany, and Italy either having signed, or still negotiating, the sale of arms, factories, and know-how to Iran and Arab states, in exchange for pledges of future oil," a bilateral approach that is "decried by Mr. Simon" (United States energy chief).[4] *Business Week* warns that "Americans may be left behind in the stampede for Arab business," quite apart from the "multibillion-dollar U.S. stake in oil," if there is "a backlash of Arab hostility towards the U.S."; "European and Japanese governments and private businessmen are practically falling over each other in a scramble to ingratiate themselves with Arab oil suppliers. . . ."[5] During the October 1973 war, Iraq awarded contracts totaling $260 million to European and Japanese groups, while continuing extensive American projects. It is feared that European and Japanese competitors may be preferred to United States bidders for further development projects.[6] In Egypt and other Arab states, American corporations continued their projects and negotiations through the October 1973 crisis, but the issue remains in doubt throughout the Middle East and North Africa.

The basic issues have been raised with particular clarity in the context of United States–Japanese relations. After World War II, the United States permitted Japan to industrialize with few constraints, while maintaining fairly tight control over Japanese energy resources. Well aware of these facts and their implications, the Arab oil producers are offering special inducements to Japan to make bilateral arrangements for Middle East oil. The Saudi Arabian oil minister, Sheikh Ahmed Zaki Yamani, put the matter clearly on a visit to Japan:

> For the time being, the American oil companies are dominating about 70 percent of the oil industry in the whole world. Whether you have an interest in this as Japanese or you don't, this is your decision . . . You do need oil. Oil will be in scarcity very soon, in the com-

ing few years, and therefore you can get much more than the others . . . bilaterally. . . . Now what you will have with us is oil as a quid pro quo for what you give —that's industry and technology.[7]

The Japanese Trade Ministry had already announced plans for extensive technical development projects in Libya, with the possibility of joint ventures in oil exploration. These steps raised

> the possibility of Japan's moving in, in partnership with the Arabs, to occupy the oil-development position long monopolized by the Western majors. Until now Japan has shied away from such a move for fear of offending both the Western majors and the U.S. government.[8]

As Sheikh Yamani pointed out further in Tokyo, there is an implied further cost in bilateral arrangements: "a less close relationship with the U.S.—and especially with the American oil companies." [9] The cost could be serious, not only to Japan but to United States–based corporations and the American government.

The long-range significance of independent European and Japanese initiatives is potentially very great, and there is little doubt that the United States government will be concerned to forestall them. The major oil producers, Saudi Arabia and Iran in particular, would doubtless prefer to remain in the American orbit, and can be expected to be cooperative if certain conditions are met. In the case of Saudi Arabia, it is unclear just what these conditions are. King Faisal's pronouncements might be understood as implying a return of Jerusalem to Arab rule and a regional settlement along the lines of the United Nations resolution. But it is not yet clear what he intends, or how seriously, or whether the United States would be willing to accept such demands. It is, however, most unlikely that the United States will simply tell the Arabs to keep their oil, as Kennan and others recommend. Rather, the United States will move to guarantee its access to, and control over, "one of the world's greatest prizes," insofar as this is possible.

Suppose that the Arab oil producers persist in the demands they formulated during the October war. Under these conditions, the United States would have several policy options. The most extreme would be invasion, either direct or through a surrogate. This possibility has been discussed, not only on the lunatic fringe, and the Pentagon has been taking no pains to conceal its military exercises in desert regions. Leonard Silk, financial correspondent for the *New York Times*, reported shortly after the October war that Klaus Heiss, Klaus Knorr, and Oskar Morgenstern of Mathematica, Inc., a Princeton research firm, had issued a study done for the Office of Naval Research which expresses their view (Silk's paraphrase) "that the major oil-exporting countries would be vulnerable to military power," though it is "highly unlikely that the industrialized oil-importing states will marshal the will to be tough and to act in unison." [10] There has been no lack of exhortations that the West should marshal the necessary will.

Irving Kristol notes philosophically that "insignificant nations, like insignificant people, can quickly experience delusions of significance . . . smaller nations are not going to behave reasonably—with a decent respect for the interests of others, including the great powers—unless it is costly to them to behave unreasonably." It is our duty to enforce this lesson. "In truth, the days of 'gunboat diplomacy' are never over. . . . Gunboats are as necessary for international order as police cars are for domestic order." Because of "the legalistic-moralistic-'idealistic' mold into which American foreign policy was cast after World War II," we haven't been manning the gunboats as we should (witness our unwillingness to use force in Vietnam). But perhaps this moral flabbiness can be overcome and we can enforce standards of reasonableness on the insignificant nations.[11]

Walter Laqueur, putting it more obliquely, suggests that Middle East oil "could be internationalized, not on behalf of a few oil companies but for the benefit of the rest of mankind." Furthermore, "Egypt could be encouraged to take over the Libyan oilfields." "Internationalization" is a polite term for invasion, but there should be no moral problem in this, since "all that is at stake is the fate of some desert sheikdoms." Laqueur goes on to suggest that "the internationalization of the Middle Eastern oil resources could be the major test for détente." That is to say, if the Russians do not support us in this humanitarian effort, it will prove that they are not serious about détente.[12] Laqueur's concern "for the benefit of the rest of mankind" does not, for some reason, extend to the natural conclusion that the industrial and agricultural resources of the West should also be internationalized. Nor do I recall that in the past he has urged punishment of the United States for its policies of economic boycott and blockade for many years, or condemned the policies of boycott of Arab labor and production that were a major factor in building a Jewish society in Palestine during the years when he was a journalist there.[13] Presumably the distinction, again, has to do with the relative "significance" of various nations.

Although a policy of direct invasion has its advocates, it is most unlikely, not only because of the inherent dangers and difficulties of execution, but also because there are simpler means available. A less costly and risky alternative would be a return to the Rogers Plan of 1970, which involves the return of Israeli forces to the 1967 boundaries, perhaps with "insubstantial alterations required for mutual security." [14] The basic logic of this proposal, which embodies the main ideas of the United Nations resolution as outlined earlier, is that the region should be converted into a kind of Latin America, with conservative Arab regimes allied to the United States and Israel embedded into the system.

It seems unlikely that there can be a peace settlement in the region that will leave Israel in control of substantial parts of the occupied territories. A stalemate of this sort might persist for some time, particularly if the Arab oil producers decide that their best interests lie in reconciliation with the United States at the expense of Egyptian and Syrian irredentism and Palestinian demands. But the local and regional conflicts will continue to simmer, and unpredictable developments within the Arab world might cause them to erupt at any moment. The likelihood of military confrontation in the region would remain high, and the international implications would remain threatening, even through periods of temporary stability. Next time, Israeli urban concentrations may not be spared. Even the possibility of a nuclear strike is not small. Sooner or later, it can be expected that the balance of international forces and the array of chance events will be such that Israel will be destroyed, and with it, probably much of the surrounding world. One cannot, of course, predict the course of such affairs with any confidence. But this forecast seems to me, nevertheless, a plausible one if no regional peace settlement is reached.

Under conditions of continued occupation and military confrontation, the prospects for the Palestinians are dim. They can look forward only to dispersal, suffering, and destruction.

If this analysis is more or less accurate, then the two most likely possibilities for the near future are (1) a stalemate with continued Israeli occupation of territories conquered in 1967, a no-war, no-peace arrangement that carries with it a high probability of eventual destruction for Israeli Jews and Palestinian Arabs, and beyond; or (2) an imposed settlement along the lines of the Rogers Plan and the United Nations resolution of November 1967. The latter outcome, while ugly in many respects, might be fairly stable. It would remove the immediate *casus belli* and set the stage for interstate relations that might gradually stabilize. It is likely that the security of Israel would be enhanced. Israel is as well protected by demilitarized zones on its borders, the reopening of the Suez Canal, the resettlement of Egyptian civilians,[15] and some sort of international guarantee, as by thinly defended areas that are a constant provocation. The same is true in the Golan region to the north. It was not considerations of security that motivated Israel to settle and begin to industrialize the Golan Heights (now virtually empty of Arabs, apart from the Druze), or to expel Bedouins from the Rafah region in the south, or expand the borders of Jerusalem, or undertake settlement and investment in the West Bank, the Gaza area, and Sinai. The annexation policy of the past years is to be explained on other grounds, to which I will return.

While a settlement along the lines of the Rogers Plan and the United Nations resolution might bring stability, I believe that it will perpetuate conditions that have prevented the realization of the just hopes and highest ideals expressed within each of the warring societies. In a Jewish state, *"klein aber mein,"* there can be no full recognition of basic human rights, and at best, only limited progress toward a just society. Such limitations are inherent in the concept of a Jewish state that also contains non-Jewish citizens. A Palestinian counterpart, founded on bitterness, frustration, and despair and dominated by its neighbors, will be a mirror-image, perhaps even a distorted image. Both will be subject to reactionary forces within and domination from outside. While speculation about such matters is naturally uncertain, still these seem to me reasonable estimates, for reasons to which I will return here and in the essays that follow.

These essays were written in the period 1969–1973, in the belief that Israeli Jews and Palestinian Arabs were pursuing self-destructive and possibly suicidal policies, and that, contrary to generally held assumptions, there were—and remain—alternatives that ought to be considered and that might well contribute to a more satisfactory outcome. These alternatives are by no means original. In fact, they are drawn from one important tendency in pre–World War II Zionism, a tendency which, I believe, acquired new relevance and potential significance after the 1967 war. These alternatives presuppose a willingness on the part of each of the local parties to recognize the essential element of justice in the demands of the other. I have neither the insight nor the presumption to offer a judgment on the respective merits of the counterposed demands and am frankly not overly impressed by the confident assertions I see on the part of others. Each set of demands is just and, in its own terms, compelling. An examination of these just demands suggests, to me at least, that they are not irreconcilable. This remains true under the changed circumstances brought about by the "fourth round" in October 1973.

I am well aware that to Palestinians and Israelis such discussion may seem hopelessly abstract, if not downright immoral. Palestinians may ask how it is possible to compare the rights of the oppressor and the oppressed, the foreign settlers and those whose homes they have taken. Israelis may contend that one cannot balance the simple desire to live in peace in the state established by decision of the United Nations against the demands of those who resort to violence and terror and who threaten the very existence of Israeli society. It is a simple exercise to construct a brief for each side. Some seem to take comfort in this fact, oblivious to the consequences of the positions that they advocate and refusing to comprehend the pleas of their adversaries.

To a Colonel Qaddafi, it seems entirely obvious that the European Jews should return to Europe. There are, after all, many European states, and there is no reason why the people of Palestine, who committed no crime, should be dispossessed by European settlers of the Mosaic persuasion. These should return to the states where hundreds of millions of Europeans already live, leaving the 3 million Palestinians and the "Arab Jews" in their own little slice of territory. To his precise counterparts in the American Jewish community, it seems equally obvious that the Arabs should stay in the Arab countries. There are, after all, many Arab states, and there is no reason why Israeli Jews should be denied their rights by Arabs who happen to regard themselves as Palestinians. The latter should be absorbed into the homeland of more than 100 million Arabs, leaving to the Jews and the Israeli Arabs in their midst the little slice of territory that is all they ask. It is a measure of the bias and irrationality of American opinion that Qaddafi is regarded as a fanatic, whereas his counterparts are considered moderates. It seems to me a plain fact that neither view can be adopted by people with any compassion or sense of justice.

Supporters of the just claims of each contending party who ignore the full complexity of the real situation bear a heavy responsibility. They have reinforced the tendencies of each toward self-destructive policies. Realists who stand above the conflict may note condescendingly that talk of reconciliation is naïve. It is useful to bear in mind analogies—not exact, but nonetheless suggestive—that have been drawn in the essays that follow and elsewhere. Realists of an earlier period understood that it was the highest duty of Germans to massacre Frenchmen and Englishmen, and conversely. There were, to be sure, a few people who failed to comprehend this elementary point. They were regarded with contempt and often bitterly denounced, or—as in the case of Karl Liebknecht and Bertrand Russell—imprisoned so that they would not corrupt others with their strange notion that people could live in peace and work together for social justice. History has a rather different verdict.

In the following remarks, I would like to outline briefly my own perception of the evolving situation, as a basis for the essays that follow.

The Jewish national movement, Zionism, was a product of European "civilization." Palestinian nationalism, as distinct from a more generalized Arab nationalism, was in large measure a product of Zionist success. Between the two World Wars, the local conflict intensified in bitterness and scale as Jewish immigration from Europe increased and the Jewish settlement, the Yishuv, took roots in Western Palestine, bringing economic development and material benefits while often dispossessing Arab peasants through land purchase and boycotting their labor and produce. The motives for the latter policies were complex. In part, they can be traced to chauvinism and an "exclusivist" ideology, but in part they also reflected the dilemmas of socialists who hoped to build an egalitarian society with a Jewish working class, not a society of wealthy Jewish planters exploiting the natives. The Yishuv was thus faced with a profound, never resolved contradiction. The most advanced socialist forms in existence, the germs of a just and egalitarian society, were constructed on lands purchased by the Jewish National Fund and from which Arabs were excluded in principle, lands that were in many instances purchased from absentee landlords with little regard for the peasants who lived and worked on them.

These contradictions did not pass without recognition. One of the earliest settlers wrote in the Hebrew periodical *HaShiloah* in 1907 that Zionism should "avoid a narrow, limited nationalism, which sees no further than itself. . . . Unless we want to deceive ourselves deliberately, we have to admit that we have thrown people out of their miserable lodgings and taken away their sustenance." Zionism should be based on "justice and law, absolute equality, and human brotherhood." He was reprimanded for his "Diaspora way of thinking" and told that "the main thing we should take into account should be what is good and effective for ourselves." Commenting on this interchange, Aharon Cohen observes, "Here we already have in embryo the essence of the debate that was to characterize discussions within the Zionist movement over the years." [16]

Between the two World Wars, it was possible to imagine a local accommodation throughout Western Palestine—or even the full territory of the British Mandate—that would be "based on the fundamental principle that whatever the number of the two peoples may be, no people shall dominate the other or be subject to the government of the other," in the formulation of Nahum Sokolov as he was elected president of the Zionist Organization in 1931. [17] But this admirable principle led to no constructive programs and met with little response from Palestinians.

Under the impact of the Nazi atrocities, the principle became—unfortunately, I feel—politically irrelevant. The United Nations' partition plan of 1947 led to civil war and then to intervention by armies of the Arab states the day after the Jewish state was proclaimed on May 14, 1948. In the course of the fighting, Israel made significant territorial gains. The terms of the local conflict were substantially altered as some 750,000 Palestinians fled or were driven from their homes. An approximately equal number of Jews took their place, about half being survivors of Hitler's massacres and most of the remainder being "Oriental" Jews who fled or were expelled from the Arab states. Of the approximately 400 settlements established after 1948, some 350 were on refugee property; about two-thirds of the cultivated land acquired by Israel had been Palestinian-owned.[18] Largely acquired by the Jewish National Fund, this land was exclusively for Jewish use, by law. By 1958, about 250,000 acres of land were expropriated from Palestinians who remained in Israel.[19] Thousands of Bedouins were expelled.[20]

In 1960, the Knesset (Israeli parliament) enacted the *Basic Law: Israel Lands*, extending to state lands the principles of the Jewish National Fund. According to official figures, 92 percent of the state's surface prior to June 1967 was thereby restricted to Jewish use, in perpetuity. Israeli Arabs were thus excluded by law from 92 percent of the territory of the state.

The "second round," the Israeli-British-French attack on Egypt in 1956, falls within the regional and international arenas of conflict, and the same is true of the 1967 war, which found the superpowers lined up in support of their respective client states.[21] By this time, however, there were the beginnings of an independent Palestinian involvement,[22] and in the aftermath of the 1967 war, Palestinian nationalism became a substantial element in the conflict. The war resulted in Israeli occupation of all of Western Palestine, the Golan Heights, the Sinai, and Sharm el-Sheikh. It also resulted in the flight or expulsion of several hundred thousand Palestinians from villages and refugee camps.

The newly emerging Palestinian organizations suffered a severe setback in 1970–1971 at the hands of the Jordanian army, backed by Israel and the United States. The 1973 war was, once again, primarily a regional conflict between Israel and the Arab states, with the superpowers giving massive aid to their respective clients and finally imposing a cease-fire.[23] Palestinian participation seems to have been marginal, and there is good reason to expect that the Palestinians will remain a minor factor in subsequent negotiations, if they materialize.

From 1970 to October 1973, after the "war of attrition" on the Suez Canal was ended by a cease-fire, Israel seemed firmly in control of the occupied territories. In August 1973, plans were announced for new settlements in these territories in addition to the dozens already established; new towns; expropriation of Arab lands; purchase of land in the occupied areas by the Jewish National Fund. The mayor of Jerusalem called for virtually doubling the jurisdictional area of the city, thus absorbing additional Arab lands. More significant, the governing Labor Party adopted an electoral program for the October elections that amounted to a form of annexation.[24] The leading Israeli newspaper, *Ha'aretz,* commented on September 4 that "the government gave its approval to [Dayan's] demand to set up settlements and towns within Judea and Samaria [the occupied West Bank] without annexation and without changing its status as an occupied area. . . . Through the initiative of Dayan, it will be possible to take over territories without annexing them and without granting their inhabitants, the Arabs, the rights of citizens in Israel." [25]

The plans went well beyond the West Bank; included were plans for an industrial town on the Golan Heights,[26] projects in the Rafah region near Gaza, and a deep-water port (Yamit) west of the Gaza strip.[27] These plans gave a stamp of approval to the gradual program of *de facto* annexation that had been under way since the June 1967 War (see chapter 3). The plans reflected the Israeli assessment that their military position was unchallenge-able, so that Arab and world opinion could be disre-garded.[28]

It is important to bear in mind that this was the elec-toral program of the governing party, the less expansion-ist of the two major political groupings. It may be that these programs were a factor in the timing of the Oc-tober war. They may also play a part in explaining the hostility to Israel on the part of the African states. While, in the United States, this is often described as capitula-tion to Arab pressure and bribery, the Israeli press has been more realistic. A. Salpeter, writing in *Ha'aretz* on the decision of Zaire to break relations with Israel, notes: "There is every reason to accept Mobuto's statement that our continued settlement of the territories conquered in 1967 is the main reason for his decision. . . . Changing borders by force of arms is, for reasons peculiar to Africa, received very negatively by African leaders. . . ." [29] The policy of annexation that had been taking shape with in-creasing clarity contributed to the diplomatic isolation of Israel, a development that poses extreme dangers, as became obvious during the October war. Countries that might have been willing to support Israel against direct aggression, even in the face of the Arab "oil weapon," were unwilling to extend themselves and suffer penal-ties in support of policies of which they disapproved.

As of September 1973, however, the policy of gradual annexation seemed a short-term success. It was widely believed that Israel might soon approach self-sufficiency in armaments, and Israeli military superiority seemed unchallengeable. General Dayan expressed the prevailing view when he explained to an economic conference in June 1973: "As long as we have Israelis as our soldiers, Americans as our suppliers, the Suez Canal as our military border, and the Arabs as our enemy, we should be alright." [30] Other generals gave more grandiose predictions (see chapter 4). The commander of the Israeli air force stated in July 1972 that Israeli air superiority over Egypt was increasing and "that, in effect, the Israelis had 'cracked' the Soviet-Egyptian missile defense system along the Canal." [31] Kimche, whose analysis draws heavily on Israeli government sources, concludes that this Israeli military supremacy was a major factor in leading Brezhnev to apprise Nixon in May 1972 "of the Soviet intention to disengage from the Egyptian-Israeli conflict." It partially explains, he contends, Soviet willingness to accept—he believes, to initiate—the expulsion of Soviet advisers from Egypt in July 1972.

By this time, the Russians had "decided to seek an accommodation with the United States in the Middle East and the Mediterranean at the price of abandoning the Soviet positions in Egypt and the military confrontation with Israel." What is more, Russia feared "the possible emergence of a new and powerful Middle Eastern alliance based on the two stronger military powers in the area—Israel and Iran." Israeli experts also expressed confidence in their growing industrial and technological superiority, and this confidence was shared by independent analysts. [32]

The United States government had every reason to regard its policy of tacit support for the Israeli occupation as successful. During the 1967–1973 period, the United States gave diplomatic support as well as substantial economic and military aid to Israel and Jordan, as well as to Iran, Saudi Arabia, and the Gulf oil producers.

Given the basic goals of American policy, outlined above, there was little reason to be dissatisfied with the status quo. From 1967 to October 1973, support for Israeli occupation of the territories was consistent with the general objectives of American policy, and of course, with the domestic needs of American administrations as well. A major threat to American interests is radical Arab nationalism. The oil producers and the United States had, and still have, a common interest in blocking any such force, and thus tacitly accepted the arrangements resulting from the 1967 war, rhetoric aside. In 1970–1971, this joint policy achieved a notable success when the Palestinian guerrilla movements were decimated.[33] At that time, United States government policy was vacillating between two options: the Rogers Plan and tacit support for permanent Israeli occupation. After the "war of attrition" and the crushing of the Palestinians, the Rogers Plan was dropped.

Considering the situation shortly before the October 1973 war, Kimche writes that "the decisive development" of the past fifty years is that "Israel had become the major military factor in the Middle East"; it could "strike at will with only the tacit approval of the United States government" and had thus become "indispensable to the United States," which was immobilized by the achievement of parity between the superpowers.[34] Israeli spokesmen expressed themselves in similar terms (see chapter 4). The belief that Israel might become the "watchdog" for the West [35] was by no means novel. It can be traced at least to Vladimir Jabotinsky's argument during World War I that "in the Middle East, nationalism will spread among indigenous populations; only the stable support of a nation that is foreign in culture and social forms from the other peoples in the region can serve as a prop for the British forces in this region." [36]

At one time, these were the views of reactionary extremists. By 1973, however, they had become the common coin of leading political and military figures—a most unhappy development.[37]

Some of those who shared the assessment of Israeli military and economic predominance nevertheless opposed annexation because of the "demographic problem." The latter phrase is used to refer to the problem posed by the existence of Arabs in a Jewish state. With a large and rapidly growing Arab population, the Jewish state, it was feared, could not achieve the "social cohesion" necessary for security, quite apart from other unpleasant internal consequences.[38] On these grounds, some Israeli doves rejected the policy of gradual annexation and suggested that there be an "autonomous Palestinian entity" with open borders to Jordan so that commercial relations could be maintained and so that those Palestinians "who will be unemployed may, eventually, emigrate to the oil-producing states of the Persian Gulf."[39]

Given the commitment to a Jewish state and the belief in Israeli military and economic supremacy, it is not surprising that there was no serious political challenge to the policy of incorporation of the occupied territories. Even some Israelis who were opposed to these policies felt that they were forced on Israel by the refusal of the Arab states to negotiate.[40] Implicit in this judgment is the belief that no Israeli initiative toward the Palestinians could provide the basis for security and regional peace. In fact, for many Israelis the question does not even arise. They simply adopt the position of Minister of Information Yisrael Galili: "We do not consider the Arabs of the land an ethnic group nor a people with a distinct nationalistic character." As Prime Minister Golda Meir put it:

It was not as though there was a Palestinian people in
Palestine considering itself as a Palestinian people and
we came and threw them out and took their country
away from them. They did not exist.[41]

On this assumption, the Palestinians "are not a party to
the conflict between Israel and the Arab states," as an
Israeli court ruled in 1969. Foreign Minister Abba Eban,
supposedly a dove, can thus insist that the Palestinians
"have no role to play" in any peace settlement.[42]

This is a convenient position for Israelis to assume,
since once it is adopted, moral issues vanish. In the context of a regional conflict with the Arab states, Israel's
moral position is strong—apart from the issue of the occupied territories, and problems here could be attributed
to the Arab refusal to negotiate. The problem of the Palestinians, on the other hand, is difficult to face honestly
and openly. Better to put it out of mind, as is commonly
done in the United States as well. This is particularly
easy when the Palestinians resort to terrorism as a last
resort, to impress their existence on popular consciousness. Then it is easy to dismiss them as a collection of
gangsters. Nagging doubts can be put to rest by propaganda about the flight of the refugees as a "tactical maneuver" on orders from the Arab armies.[43] Partisans of
national movements have never found any difficulty in
believing what has to be believed, regardless of the facts.

Much has been made in the West of the refusal of the
Arab states to settle the regional conflict through direct
negotiation with Israel, but it has less often been noted
that Israel has not only refused categorically to negotiate with the Palestinians—and still does—but has even
officially denied their existence as a national entity. In
the United States, even the use of the word "Palestinians" has called forth angry denunciations. Perhaps one

could expect nothing else. Israel is a state like any other; Zionism is a national movement like any other. As for the explanation, perhaps it is enough to quote Jon Kimche's observation on what he calls "this curious Israeli refusal to consider the Palestinian solution": "It was as if the assertion of a Jewish nation required the rejection of the existence of a Palestinian nation." [44]

Certainly, this is a view that has been expressed on the extreme right. Menahem Beigin once warned a Kibbutz audience of the danger inherent in recognizing a Palestinian people. Asked about this, he responded:

> My friend, take care. When you recognize the concept of "Palestine," you demolish your right to live in Ein Hahoresh. If this is Palestine and not the Land of Israel, then you are conquerors and not tillers of the land. You are invaders. If this is Palestine, then it belongs to a people who lived here before you came. Only if it is the Land of Israel do you have a right to live in Ein Hahoresh and in Deganiyah B. If it is not your country, your fatherland, the country of your ancestors and of your sons, then what are you doing here? You came to another people's homeland, as they claim, you expelled them and you have taken their land. . . . [45]

Since the Six-Day War of June 1967, such views have been expressed quite openly by advocates of direct annexation of the occupied territories, eliciting some sharp controversy in the Israeli press. The controversy renews, in contemporary terms, the debate over the essential meaning of Zionism discussed earlier (cf. p. 13). Clearly, this "curious Israeli refusal to consider the Palestinian solution" must be overcome if Israel is to adapt itself to the settlement that is likely to be imposed by the United States, or if initiatives are to develop within Israeli society that might lead to other, and I believe preferable, alternatives.

During the period 1967–1973, there were opportunities for a local accommodation that could have insulated Israel-Palestine from regional conflicts and perhaps—though this is more doubtful—from the machinations of the great powers. Had there been a local settlement, it is highly unlikely that the Arab states could have mobilized their populations for renewed military conflict, even if they had wanted to. Nor could they have achieved anything like the same diplomatic successes, even with the "oil weapon." But the preconditions, mentioned earlier, were never realized or even approached, on either side.

There have been groups in Israel that sought a way out of the impasse through recognition of Palestinian rights. The principles of Siah (Israeli New Left), approved by the Third National Conference in July 1972, begin with the statement that "Eretz Yisrael/Palestine is the territorial basis for the self-determination of two peoples," Jews and Palestinian Arabs, and call for a settlement on the basis of the June 4, 1967 borders with mutual recognition of two independent states and of the right in principle for Jews and Arabs to choose their homes within this region. But such groups and such programs were never able to challenge state policy so long as it seemed successful.

The intransigence of the Israeli government and the public in general on this issue was reinforced by the solid support it received in the United States, where a kind of hysteria almost made discussion impossible.[46] The predictable result was that the opportunities for a local settlement were lost, and the stage was set for the inevitable regional war. What came as a surprise was not the war itself, but rather its timing and the relative success achieved by Arab armies. Israel's General Sharon, now the hero of the 1973 Sinai campaign and a leader of the political right, states that "in a general way" the war came as no surprise: "It was obvious to me since the Six-Day War that if we do not reach some sort of solution with Egypt, there will ultimately be no escape from a new round" because of the "difficult situation" in which the Egyptians were placed, even though the situation remained satisfactory for the other three major actors: Israel, the United States, and the Soviet Union.[47] Thus it was not surprising that Egypt and Syria undertook "to conquer a part of the territories that Israel conquered in the Six-Day War," so as to achieve the primary political objective of "breaking the diplomatic deadlock." [48]

The annexation policy was not openly adopted and proclaimed. Rather, Israeli policy simply drifted in that direction. (Some of the early stages are described in chapter 3). It was only in August 1973, with the adoption of the Galili Protocols, that the governing party gave the policy a more or less official form. The argument, throughout, has been security. But a review of the facts suggests that the annexation policy is to be explained on other grounds. Consider, for example, the Sinai, where Israel is most likely to agree to some kind of compromise settlement. Sinai brings Israel a net income of some $400 million a year, an amount equivalent to about one-third of its export earnings, while Israeli occupation deprives Egypt of about $600 million a year.[49] Prospects for the future are bright, particularly if Dayan's plans for the deep-water port of Yamit are implemented. Apart from economic considerations, which are not insubstantial, the settlement and integration of "Judea and Samaria" (the occupied West Bank) are motivated by mystical attachments to the "historic land of Israel," invoked in official and other pronouncements (cf. chapter 3, p. 120). In the October 1973 war, Israeli settlements in the Golan Heights proved to be a liability from a military point of view, but Israel is nevertheless planning to double Jewish settlement there and to construct a new urban center.[50] A forced settlement along the lines of the United Nations resolution would be inconsistent with all such programs, but the issue is not primarily one of Israeli security.

Somewhat related conclusions have been drawn by Israeli doves. Professor Jacob Talmon has repeatedly deplored the fact that Israeli policy has been based

> on the assumption that we will be able to act as we wish, up to full annexation, while ignoring the opinions of other countries. In other words, we will have the power and opportunity to dictate our will to the whole world.[51]

In many articles, he has explained the fallacy in these assumptions and pointed to their grim consequences, an exercise in rationality that has earned him little applause on the part of partisans of annexation (cf. chapter 5, p. 179). Others have commented on the racist arrogance that led Israelis to believe that Arabs would never be able to contest Israeli force.[52] One of the most outspoken critics of the annexation policy, Reserve General Mattityahu Peled, outlined the three "myths" that led to the near-disaster in October 1973. The first myth was that Arabs were incompetent cowards who would never be capable of initiating an attack. The second was that Israeli air superiority guaranteed instant victory in the unlikely event of an Arab attack.

> The third myth, probably the biggest, was the tendency to believe—with an incredible arrogance that showed through in every domain—that we could force the Palestinians, all the Arabs and the whole world to accept a territorial status quo for the next 30 or 40 years. After

all, weren't we superior, infallible, unbeatable? And didn't we have Washington in our pocket thanks to a powerful Zionist lobby in the United States? Weren't we containing the Soviet Union and the communist bloc? What did it matter that Africa, Asia, and the Third World were hostile to us, since Mr. Nixon's veto at the United Nations had succeeded in taking the stuffing out of their anti-Israeli resolutions? In short, General Dayan and his cronies thought we were the undisputed masters of the Middle East and of history.[53]

It cannot be stressed too often that American Zionists who have supported these delusions and, with their cries of anti-Semitism and other hysterical abuse,[54] quite successfully suppressed any discussion of the dangers and alternatives, bear a measure of responsibility for the events of October 1973, a very close call for the State of Israel. Furthermore, the lesson has not been learned, as will be seen in chapter 5.

General Peled has explained over and over again that the new 1967 boundaries did not increase the security of Israel; quite the contrary, demilitarized zones might leave Israel in a better position from a strictly military point of view. Those who make a fetish of security, he argues, have been concerned "not with Israel's security but with her territorial dimensions." [55]

Although the intended message is quite different, some Israelis who tend toward the "activist" end of the spectrum on the issue of boundaries and security make essentially the same point. Michael Bar-Zohar rejects the argument of the doves that settlements on the Golan Heights served no useful security purpose (and, in fact, were an impediment to Israeli military operations there):

However, it is incorrect to maintain that the purpose of the settlements on the Golan Heights was for security. The Golan Heights settlements had hardly any security function to fulfill, just as no such function was to be attached to Kiryat Arba (in Hebron) or to the projected town of Yamit. The Golan settlements were of a purely political character. The purpose was to create facts in the area, to establish roots in a region we regarded as vital and to demonstrate our firm purpose not to retreat from that area. . . . Settlements on the Golan Heights were also intended to determine facts, which will be difficult to alter when the time comes. Under pressure, one can move a line on a map, one can move army units stationed in empty terrain—but it is far more difficult to uproot settlements and people who have struck roots in the land. That was the purpose of the Golan settlements—and not any notion of establishing a buffer of border-settlers. . . .[56]

Bar-Zohar does not go on to make the further observation that considerations of security have regularly been used to disguise the post-1967 policy of "creating facts" in the occupied areas, nor does he explore the purposes of the latter policy, perhaps because they are clear enough. Like many others, he argues that the October 1973 war demonstrated that Israel must retain the occupied territories, for if that war had been launched from the 1967 borders, the fighting would have taken place within settled areas. Putting aside the fact that Israel is intent on settling the occupied areas, this argument would be a rational response only to the proposal that the situation should revert to that of 1967. It does not even begin to deal with the actual proposal of the doves: that the occupied territories be demilitarized. Then no surprise attack can be launched from the 1967 borders, and there is no substance to the fears expressed by Bar-Zohar and others or to their arguments about "strategic depth." If the Sinai were demilitarized, the Israeli army would have ample foreknowledge of any

Egyptian penetration of this buffer zone and, as Peled and others have pointed out, would be in an advantageous position to counter it, as in 1967. Nor would there be any shelling of Israeli settlements from a demilitarized Golan Heights;[57] nor would Tel Aviv be in artillery range if the West Bank were demilitarized. By scrupulously avoiding the actual proposals of those who oppose continued "creeping annexation," the "activists" tacitly concede the accuracy of the assessment that security is being invoked simply as a disguise for territorial ambitions.

There is much loose talk about "security guarantees" that confuses these issues further. Thus it is claimed, correctly, that superpower guarantees are unreliable and that it is impossible to count on the United Nations. Therefore, it is urged, Israel must be in a position to guarantee its own security.[58] But in this world, Israel will never be in a position to guarantee its own security, no matter what its borders may be and no matter how massive its armaments. Guarantees of security do not exist. In the long run, Israel's security rests on relations with its neighbors. The policy of annexation rules out long-term security as unobtainable and thus virtually guarantees further military conflict and the ultimate destruction of a state that can lose only once. The annexation policy also maximizes the short-term threat, by stimulating irredentist forces in the surrounding states and gaining them international support. The short-term threat was regarded as slight in the past few years—mistakenly, as the October war revealed. It is easy to plead "security" to disguise very different motivations.[59]

In the essays that follow and elsewhere, I have argued that socialist binationalism offers the best long-range hope for a just peace in the region. Surely this conclusion is debatable, but not, so far as I can see, on grounds of security. A local accommodation between Israeli Jews and Palestinian Arabs would enhance the security of both. The barrier, within Israel, has not been the problem of security, but rather commitment to a Jewish state. Palestinians and their supporters also offered no acceptable basis for discussion and accommodation, with rare exceptions. In no case was the issue one of security.

It has been widely and, I think plausibly, speculated that the October war and subsequent events will gradually impel the United States to resurrect the Rogers Plan in some form (see chapter 4). There is every reason to expect that Egypt, Jordan, and Saudi Arabia will acquiesce (cf. note 14), whatever their longer-term goals may be. There will be extremely difficult problems, such as the status of Jerusalem, but one can at least imagine ways in which they might be resolved under superpower pressure. The Palestinian leadership, which is in any event powerless, seems to have reluctantly acceded to this program, apparently under Russian pressure.[60] Russian goals in the region seem to remain limited, and the Soviet Union continues to support the United Nations Security Council Resolution 242, with its likely consequence that Egypt will return to the American orbit along with Saudi Arabia and the Gulf oil producers. The crucial short-term question is whether Israel will submit to United States pressure and reverse the policies of the past few years. This would be a bitter pill, but Israel has successively cut off its options and now has little room to maneuver if the United States follows what seems a likely course of action, perhaps after the next stalemate collapses.

American moves in this direction would constitute a return to past policies. In 1953, Dulles suspended economic aid to Israel to compel it to end its project for unilateral diversion of Jordan water, and in 1956, Eisenhower compelled Israel to withdraw from the Sinai after the joint Israeli-French-British aggression against Egypt. A return to past policies would provoke a bitter political conflict in the United States. Since the overwhelming Israeli military victory of June 1967, American public opinion has been overwhelmingly sympathetic to Israel and its policy of *de facto* annexation. I return to this matter in chapter 5.

A forced settlement along the lines of Resolution 242 would enable Egypt and Saudi Arabia to revert to their preferred role as American client states; and Israel would remain the major military force in the region, with substantial arms production [61] and advanced industrial development. As such, it would remain a valued ally for the United States, which will continue to rely on Israeli and Iranian power to offset Russian influence and disruptive Arab forces. An Iranian diplomatic source explains that "without Israeli power in the Middle East, the Shah feels that the Arabs would be difficult to control and the Russians would very much gain an upper hand in the entire area." [62] Value judgments aside, there is plausibility to Senator Henry Jackson's observation that Iran, Israel, and Saudi Arabia "have served to inhibit and contain those irresponsible and radical elements in certain Arab states . . . who, were they free to do so, would pose a grave threat indeed to our principal sources of petroleum," and that "the Saudis understand . . . that Israel and Iran play a vital stabilizing role." [63] Like the United States, Saudi Arabia fears Russian influence, revolutionary movements in the peninsula (where Iran is already heavily engaged in counterinsurgency), the leftist regime of South Yemen, and future Qaddafis. It is likely to accept a powerful Israel, with more limited ambitions, within an American-based alliance. The same is true of Egypt. Even if the United

States were to impose a variant of the Rogers Plan, this would in no sense be interpretable, as some have argued, as "abandonment of Israel." [64]

Such a plan, if implemented, may lead to the reconstitution of what has been called "the triangle of 'gendarmes' consisting of Riyadh, Teheran, and Tel Aviv." [65] The internal disputes that will persist have their value for the imperial powers, which need Arab oil, but which must also find a way to reverse the flow of Western currencies to the Arab treasuries. [66] As has often been observed, "one very substantial way of doing this is to sell arms." [67] Iran is arming itself to the teeth, obviously with the intention of dominating the Persian Gulf. The oil boycott had barely been put into effect when it was reported that the United States air force and navy were "involved in an extensive program to strengthen the defenses of Saudi Arabia . . . with fighter planes, radar, and military advice," and with the sale of thirty Phantoms in the offing. [68] There is no contradiction here. The central concern of United States policy is that Saudi Arabia remain a loyal ally and that it be dependent on the United States for armaments and economic development. A certain tension in the region may even be conducive to the projected imperial settlement.

Russia requires Western currencies if it is to pursue its policies of détente, and can therefore be expected to try to maintain a major role in providing armaments to the Arab states, as will the European powers. [69] The gradual conversion of Israel into a military arsenal can be expected to continue under such an arrangement. About one-quarter of the Israeli work force is reported to be employed in armaments production, which already constitutes a major export industry and may soon become the major source of foreign exchange. [70] The interests of ruling groups and the imperial powers converge on the creation of a network of hostile states, jointly committed to repression of radical nationalism. Not a pretty picture, but a plausible projection, I am afraid. One might add that a system of Balkanization under the American aegis, while perhaps fairly stable, nevertheless contains explosive forces that might erupt into a major war.

If the emerging system includes a Palestinian state, there is every likelihood that it will be under the domination of Israel and Jordan, which will continue to pursue parallel policies as American allies. Since 1967, Israel has come to rely heavily on an Arab proletariat imported by day from the occupied territories. Shortly before the October War, the Israeli minister of commerce and industry, former army chief of staff Haim Bar-Lev, stated that Israel and the territories would remain "a single economic unit" under any political solution that might arise.[71] There can be no objection in principle to economic integration of Israeli and Palestinian societies—on the contrary, it would be most desirable under conditions of political parity and relative economic and social equality. But it is evident from the context of Bar-Lev's remarks and from the presupposed social and economic conditions that the "single economic unit" is to be controlled by Israel and Israeli capital. The same concept was expressed in the Galili Protocols. Israeli reliance on transient Arab labor from the "Palestinian state" might well continue under the kind of settlement that seems now to be under consideration, along with other forms of economic integration and Israeli investment. The Palestinian state is likely to be a kind of Bantustan, a reservoir of cheap labor, thus overcoming the fears of Israeli liberals that annexation would erode the Jewish character of the state, while perpetuating conditions of economic dependence.

Under any arrangement that can be imagined for the

near future, Israel will remain a Jewish state—that is, a
state based on the principle of discrimination. There is
no other way for a state with non-Jewish citizens to remain a Jewish state, as all but the most irrational must
concede. Very likely, the policies of expropriation, expulsion, establishment of pure Jewish settlement areas,
exclusion of Arabs from state lands, and repression of
independent political activity that challenges the basic
exclusivist ideology will all continue (see chapters 3 and
5). It is hard, even under the best of circumstances, to
see how conditions might be otherwise.

Israel will continue to be a state where "the moment
the magic word *security* is uttered, the wheels of the
machine of Justice slow down . . . even when these security reasons cannot convince a reasonable man," as in
the case of the uprooted people of the villages of Biram
and Ikrit, "illegally evicted from their homes." [72] This
exploitation of "security reasons" will persist alongside
high levels of justice and democracy (by world standards) for the privileged majority. Israel will be a garrison
state, surrounded by hostile neighbors, though probably
more secure than before, since further regional wars will
no longer be inevitable. It will also, quite likely, remain
a state with a strong element of religious coercion. Jacob
Talmon has observed:

> In Israel today, the Rabbinate is rapidly developing
> into a firmly institutionalized Church imposing an ex-
> acting discipline on its members and facing the general
> body of laymen as a distinct power. This is not a reli-
> gious development, but, ironically enough, the outcome
> of the emergence of the State. The latter has given birth
> and legitimacy to an established Church.[73]

He also points out that none of this has roots in Jewish
tradition. The theocratic elements in Israeli society, without parallel in the industrial world, are often explained

in terms of the problems of coalition politics, but the reasons seem to me to lie deeper. Such a development is not very surprising in a society in which some basis must be established—in ideology, cultural attitude, and law—to distinguish the privileged majority from the non-Jewish citizens.

For similar reasons, one can expect the Palestinian state, if it comes into being, to develop on the same model. The Palestinian movement is sometimes described in the West as a movement of revolutionary socialists, but this is far from an accurate characterization.[74] Radical and libertarian elements in the movement will not have a bright future in a Palestinian state dominated by its neighbors, with discriminatory structures that may even be exaggerated in reaction to hopelessness and subordination.

In this way, history will perhaps realize the worst fears of early Zionist leaders, such men as Arthur Ruppin, who was in charge of colonization in the 1920s and who warned just fifty years ago that "a Jewish state of one million or even a few million (after fifty years!) will be nothing but a new Montenegro or Lithuania." He warned that Zionism must no longer pursue Herzl's "diplomatic and imperialist approach" and must recognize that "Herzl's concept of a Jewish state was possible only because he ignored the presence of the Arabs."[75] He was not alone in this view. Berl Katznelson, addressing a Mapai conference in 1931, said:

> . . . I do not wish to see the realization of Zionism in the form of the new Polish state with Arabs in the position of the Jews and the Jews in the position of Poles, the ruling people. For me this would be the complete perversion of the Zionist ideal. . . .[76]

Our generation has been witness to the fact that nations aspiring to freedom who threw off the yoke of subjugation rushed to place this yoke on the shoulder of others. Over the generations in which we were persecuted and exiled and slaughtered, we learned not only the pain of exile and subjugation, but also contempt for tyranny. Was that only a case of sour grapes? Are we now nurturing the dream of slaves who wish to reign? [77]

It seems to me not impossible that after the experience of building and living in new Montenegros and Lithuanias, Jews and Arabs may turn to a better way, one which has always been a possibility. It will be based on the fundamental principle, already cited, "that whatever the number of the two peoples may be, no people shall dominate the other or be subject to the government of the other." Each people will have the right to participate in self-governing national institutions. Any individual will be free to live where he wants, to be free from religious control, to define himself as a Jew, an Arab, or something else, and to live accordingly. People will be united by bonds other than their identification as Jews or Arabs (or lack of any such identification). This society, in the former Palestine, should permit all Palestinians the right of return, along with Jews who wish to find their place in this national homeland. All oppressive or discriminatory structures should be dismantled, and discriminatory practices should be condemned rather than reinforced. The society will not be a Jewish state or an Arab state, but rather a democratic multinational society.

Many schemes can be imagined that would conform to such general principles as these. To cite just one—not the only one:

> The regime in Palestine must at all times assure both the Jews and the Arabs the possibility of unhampered development and full national independence, so as to rule out any domination by Arabs of Jews, or by Jews

of Arabs. The regime must foster the rapprochement, accord, and cooperation of the Jewish people and the Arabs in Palestine . . . [which will be] . . . a federal state, comprising an alliance of cantons (autonomous districts), some with Jews in the majority, and some with Arabs; national autonomy of each people, with exclusive authority in matters of education, culture, and language; matters of religion: under the control of autonomous religious congregations, organized as free statutory bodies; the highest body of the state: the federal council, consisting of two houses—(a) one representing nationalities in which Jews and Arabs will have equal representation, and (b) one in which representatives of the cantons will participate in proportion to their respective populations. Any federal law and any change in the federal constitution can be enacted only with the agreement of both houses.

This was not the suggestion of an idle visionary or utopian dreamer remote from the social and political struggle, but of David Ben-Gurion, in an internal party discussion in October 1930.[78] There are those who argue that such proposals were put forth hypocritically, as a tactic at a particular moment. I think that the circumstances and manner in which these proposals were made, and an analysis of the social conditions at the time, support a different interpretation. I think that the proposals of Ben-Gurion, Pinhas Rutenberg,[79] and others reflected a commitment to justice and a clear understanding of what a new Lithuania or Montenegro would become. These proposals, I think, were the honest expression of men who did not want to be the Poles in a new Poland in which the Arabs would be the Jews. It should be recalled, in particular, that these were years of class struggle as well as "nation building" in Palestine. In opposing the Revisionist demand for a Jewish state in the 1930s, Ben-Gurion, a labor leader as well as a spokesman for

Jewish nationalism, was also expressing a very different conception of what kind of society the new Palestine was to be (see chapter 1).

There was, to be sure, a significant change in the positions taken by Ben-Gurion and others through this period. In 1931, speaking before the Seventeenth Zionist Congress, Ben-Gurion stated:

> We declare before world opinion, before the workers' movement, and before the Arab world, that we shall not agree, either now or in the future, to the rule of one national group over the other. Nor do we accept the idea of a Jewish state, which would eventually mean Jewish domination of Arabs in Palestine.[80]

And before the Royal Commission in 1937, he testified as follows:

> If Palestine were uninhabited we might have asked for a Jewish state, for then it would not harm anyone else. But there are other residents in Palestine, and just as we do not wish to be at the mercy of others, they too have the right not to be at the mercy of the Jews.[81]

In 1940–1941, an Arab member of the Jerusalem Municipal Council, Adil Jabr, after consultation with Palestinian and other Arab leaders, drafted a proposal for a binational Palestine based on full equality within a broader federation of autonomous states.[82] The proposal was presented to Ben-Gurion by Haim Kalvarisky, a long-time advocate of Jewish-Arab cooperation. According to Kalvarisky, Ben-Gurion rebuffed the offer with "unrestrained anger," describing it as "an abomination" and refusing to deal with the document at all. Cohen comments:

> The bottleneck was Jabr's fourth proposal suggesting a bi-national Palestine, based on parity in government. Ben-Gurion's unwillingness to agree to parity (which

he had ostensibly favored since 1931), and not the oft-heard complaint that "there is no one to talk to in the Arab camp," was the real obstacle on the way to accord.

Jabr's own reaction to the negative response on the part of Moshe Shertok (later Sharett) when the proposal was offered was, according to Kalvarisky, that "as long as talk on accord is vague, the Jews would be found to be very agreeable to accord and peace, but when matters progressed to the stage of concrete proposals they will put all kinds of obstacles in your path and cause its failure." The event lends support to the argument that the socialist binationalism of centrists such as Ben-Gurion was merely rhetorical. Intervening events provide, I believe, a more plausible explanation: the complex internal strife in Palestine in 1936–1939 (see chapter 1), World War II, and the realization of the meaning of Nazi success for the Jewish communities in Europe.

Whether driven by events or drawn by opportunity, the centrist socialists in the Zionist movement had abandoned any interest in a solution based on political parity by the early 1940s, and the Revisionist demands became the official position of the Zionist movement. Opposition to a Jewish state continued in the left wing of the Histadrut (the Jewish labor movement) and among intellectuals such as Judah Magnes, Martin Buber, and others who formed the Ihud. There were many reasons why earlier plans for a political solution based on the principle of equality and nondomination failed. It is not necessary to relive that history, though it is important to understand it. It seems to me that at this moment it is important for such alternatives to be considered and debated, and furthermore to be implemented by Jews and Arabs who will be repelled by the imperial settlement and will seek a more decent life.

If this comes about, it will be as part of a broader movement struggling for social justice. There must be a basis for cooperation. It will take place only among people who find that they are united by bonds that transcend their nationalist associations. If there is to be a return to the Zionist principle of 1931, that "whatever the number of the two peoples may be, no people shall dominate the other or be subject to the government of the other," it will only be within the context of an effort to create a socialist society. Within Israel, this will mean a return to the egalitarian ideals and libertarian social structures of the Yishuv. It will mean a return, under the new conditions of an advanced industrial society, to the principle expressed by the Jewish labor movement in 1924, that "the main and most reliable means of strengthening friendship, peace, and mutual understanding between the Jewish people and the Arab people is . . . the accord, alliance, and joint effort of Jewish and Arab workers in town and country." [83] Socialist binationalism is a possibility; binationalism without domination is otherwise an empty formula.

These essays are motivated by a conviction that some form of socialist binationalism offers the best hope for reconciling the just and compelling demands of the two parties to the local conflict in the former Palestine and that, however dim the prospects may seem, it is important to keep that hope alive until such time as popular movements within Israeli and Palestinian society, supported by an international socialist movement that does not now exist, will undertake to make such a hope a reality.

I have introduced no changes of substance in editing the essays for publication here. Each one attempts an assessment of the situation existing at the time of writing.

Any such assessment is always hazardous and involves a fair amount of speculation. I therefore cited the best sources I could find and gave what seemed to me, at the time, the most reasonable evaluation of existing conditions. Changing events have led to a reassessment in a number of respects, and there can be little doubt that this will continue to be the case. But the basic argument remains.

A few final remarks on the origin of the essays. Chapter 1 is based on a talk given at MIT in a general forum organized by Arab students in March 1969. It appeared in *Liberation*, November 1969, and in Herbert Mason, ed., *Reflections on the Middle East Crisis* (Mouton, The Hague, 1970). Chapter 2 was an invited talk before the Third Annual Convention of the Association of Arab-American University Graduates, held in Evanston, Illinois, October 29–November 1, 1970. As noted in the introductory remarks, I did not keep to the assigned title, retained here. The text appeared in Abdeen Jabara and Janice Terry, eds., *The Arab World: From Nationalism to Revolution* (Medina University Press, Wilmette, Illinois, 1971). Chapter 3 is in two parts. The first part is the approximate text of a talk given at Holy Cross College, Worcester, Massachusetts, in February 1971, in a symposium on the Middle East. The second part was added in June 1972. The two parts appeared in the *Holy Cross Quarterly*, Summer 1972. Chapter 4 was written in October 1973, immediately after the cease-fire went into effect, and appeared in *Ramparts*, January 1974. Chapter 5 has a different focus. It is concerned with attitudes toward the Arab-Israeli conflict in the United States and the curious ways in which the peace movement and the American left have been brought into this issue. It was written in January 1974, as was this introduction.

Notes

1. Cited by Jon Kimche, *There Could Have Been Peace,* Dial Press, New York 1973, pp. 223, 226.
2. George F. Kennan, "And Thank You Very Much," *New York Times,* Op-Ed page, Dec. 2, 1973.
3. *Business Week,* Dec. 22, 1973.
4. Harry B. Ellis, business-financial correspondent of the *Christian Science Monitor,* Jan. 29, 1974.
5. *Business Week,* Oct. 20, 1973; Dec. 22, 1973.
6. *Business Week,* Nov. 3, 1973. On tendencies toward state capitalism and nonalignment in Iraq (incidentally, the only oil-producing country where Russian influence is substantial), see the report by Robert Graham of the London *Financial Times* in *Middle East International,* Oct. 1973.
7. Elizabeth Pond, "Japan Gets Blunt Choice on Oil," *Christian Science Monitor,* Jan. 29, 1974, reporting from Tokyo.
8. Elizabeth Pond, *Christian Science Monitor,* Nov. 19, 1973.
9. Elizabeth Pond's paraphrase; cf. note 7.
10. *New York Times,* financial pages, Nov. 14, 1973.
11. Irving Kristol, "Where Have All the Gunboats Gone?" *Wall Street Journal,* Dec. 13, 1973. Neither Kristol's interesting interpretation of recent history nor the moral level of his recommendations should lead the reader to dismiss this article as without significance.
12. Walter Laqueur, "Détente: What's Left of It?" *New York Times Magazine,* Dec. 16, 1973.
13. Laqueur is identified in the *New York Times* as "director of the Institute of Contemporary History in London and chairman of the Research Council of the Center for Strategic and International Studies in Washington," i.e., a neutral expert. The principle of "truth in packaging" might suggest that further information be provided when he writes about Israel and the Middle East.
14. The wording is that of Secretary of State Rogers, Dec. 9, 1969; cited in a discussion of possible United Nations initiatives by John Reddaway, *Middle East Internatonal,* Oct. 1973. The Rogers Plan was made public on June 24, 1970, and accepted by Nasser on July 23. Cf. John K. Cooley, *Green March, Black September,* Frank Cass, London, 1973, p. 110. On the Israeli reaction, which was evasive but basically quite negative, see Kimche, *op. cit.,* pp. 286f. The Rogers Plan implied acceptance of the existence of the

State of Israel as a sovereign state within recognized borders.

15. A plan to establish a demilitarized belt along both sides of the Suez Canal, so that the canal could be reopened and the cities in the canal zone rebuilt, was suggested to the Israeli cabinet by Moshe Dayan in the fall of 1970, but rejected. Cf. Kimche, *op. cit.*, pp. 294f.

16. Aharon Cohen, *Israel and the Arab World*, Funk & Wagnalls, New York, 1970, pp. 67–9. This valuable work, now available in English, gives a voluminous record of attempts to lay a basis for Arab-Jewish cooperation in Palestine.

17. *Ibid.*, p. 261.

18. Halim I. Barakat, "The Palestinian Refugees: An Uprooted Community Seeking Repatriation," *International Migration Review*, vol. 7, 1973, p. 153, citing estimates by Don Peretz.

19. Barakat, *op. cit.*, citing the detailed analysis by Sabri Jiryis, *The Arabs in Israel*, Institute for Palestine Studies, Beirut, 1969.

20. Cf. General E. L. M. Burns, *Between Arab and Israeli*, Institute for Palestine Studies, Beirut, 1969, p. 93; Kennett Love, *Suez*, McGraw-Hill, New York, 1969, pp. 11, 61–2. Love notes that the "worst single Arab reprisal committed in Israel," the "ambush-massacre" of eleven Israelis on a Negev bus on March 17, 1954, was carried out by members of a Bedouin tribe expelled from the al-Auja region of the Sinai in September 1950. On the interaction of terrorist initiatives, see chapter 1, below. Expulsion of Bedouins continues. See note 72 and chapter 3, section II, below. For some estimates of the scale over the years, see Janet L. Abu-Lughod, "The Demographic Transformation of Palestine," in Ibrahim Abu-Lughod, ed., *The Transformation of Palestine*, Northwestern University Press, Evanston, Ill., 1971, pp. 149, 156, 161.

21. It is widely believed that although "it is unlikely that the Soviet Union wanted a war at that stage," nevertheless "it decisively contributed towards its outbreak through some major errors (at best) of judgment" (Walter Laqueur, *The Struggle for the Middle East*, Macmillan, New York, 1969, p. 78). Jon Kimche argues that military and intelligence relations between the United States and Israel in the years prior to the war were so close as to amount virtually to joint military planning and that a United States–Israeli army understanding of late May in effect "cleared the way for the 5 June initiative" (*op. cit.*, pp. 251–8). For a useful discussion of the military background, see Geoffrey Kemp,

"Strategy and Arms Levels," in J. C. Hurewitz, ed., *Soviet-American Rivalry in the Middle East*, Proceedings of the Academy of Political Science, vol. 29, no. 3, 1969. On the backgrounds of the war as seen by the Israeli military command, see below, pp. 22–3; chapter 3, section II, p. 124; chapter 5, pp. 182–3; and references cited there.

22. On earlier Palestinian precedents in the pre–World War II period, see Cooley, *op. cit.*, p. 37; also chapter 1, p. 63, below.

23. According to United States government reports, the United States air force flew 22,300 tons of military equipment, ammunition, spare parts, and medical supplies to Israel from October 13 to November 14, including tanks, helicopters, and heavy artillery. United States intelligence estimates that the Soviet Union carried 200,000 to 225,000 tons of matériel to Syria and Egypt by sea during a comparable period (Drew Middleton, *New York Times*, Nov. 28, 1973). Total estimates of sea and air transport are conflicting, but there is no doubt that the scale was immense.

24. For details from the Israeli press, see *Viewpoint*, P.O. Box 18042, Jerusalem, Sept. 15, 1973; *Israleft News Service*, P.O. Box 9013, Jerusalem, Sept. 17, Oct. 2, 1973. Cf. chapter 4.

25. Cited in *Viewpoint, loc. cit.*

26. The site of the city has been reported in *Maariv*. According to this report, the town is to be a regional industrial center with a population of several tens of thousands. Cf. *New York Times*, Dec. 10, 1973.

27. *Viewpoint, loc. cit.*

28. For some discussion, see chapters 3 and 4. The former was written on the assumption that these assessments were more or less accurate, so that the military threat to Israel was not immediate, though evidently the long-term threat of destruction remained; it is, plainly, implicit in the policy of repeated confrontaton with an enemy that cannot be finally defeated. The immediate threat, under the given assumptions, was that of internal corrosion, as Israel proceeded to incorporate territories with a substantial Arab population that must be deprived of rights, given the ideological commitment to Jewish dominance. The October 1973 events revealed that the assumptions were dubious and that the "long term" may not be too long. After the October war, the Labor Party revised the August electoral program described above. Without explicitly repudiating the Galili Protocols, which laid the basis for annexation of the territories, the new

program nevertheless does not reiterate them. Cf. *Davar*, Nov. 29, 1973, reprinted in *Israleft*, Dec. 1, 1973.

29. *Ha'aretz*, Oct. 7, 1973. For extensive quotes, see *Israleft*, Nov. 15, 1973.

30. Cited by Robert Graham, *Middle East International*, July 1973.

31. Kimche, *op. cit.*, p. 338.

32. See chapter 3, below.

33. On these events, see Cooley, *op. cit.*

34. Kimche, *op. cit.*, pp. 237–8.

35. The expression is that of Gershom Schocken, editor and publisher of *Ha'aretz*, Sept. 30, 1951. For a lengthy excerpt in which this view is developed, see Arie Bober, ed., *The Other Israel*, Doubleday, New York, 1972, pp. 16–17.

36. Cited in Cohen, *op. cit.*, p. 128, from the *Chronicles of the Haganah*. For discussion of the position of the "Zionist extremists" led by Jabotinsky, from the point of view of a Zionist historian, see Ben Halpern, *The Idea of a Jewish State*, 2nd ed., Harvard University Press, Cambridge, Mass., 1969, pp. 32f. See Samuel Katz, *Days of Fire*, Doubleday, Garden City, N.Y., 1968, for defense of Jabotinsky and criticism of the Zionist leadership from his point of view. Katz was a member of the High Command of the Irgun Zvai Leumi. On the role of the latter organization, see chapter 1, below; and for some of Jabotinsky's views, note 21 of chapter 1.

37. On the gradual emergence of right-wing extremist positions as basic Zionist policy, see chapters 1 and 3. While the causes may be debated, the fact is quite clear.

38. Cf. Saul Friedländer, *Réflexions sur l'avenir d'Israël*, Éditions du Seuil, Paris, p. 143. Friedländer is a well-known historian and academic dove, a professor of contemporary history and international relations at the Hebrew University in Jerusalem and the Institut Universitaire des Hautes Etudes Internationales in Geneva.

39. *Ibid.* Such an arrangement, Friedländer argues, would solve the "demographic problem" from the Israeli point of view. One might recall the status of the Jews in Eastern Europe before World War II. The eminent Israeli historian Jacob Talmon describes it in these terms: "And indeed, knowing themselves to be undesirables, conscious of the determination of the government and majority population to make conditions so unbearable to them that they would be forced to emigrate, with economic opportunities constantly shrinking, with no access to government posts, public works, and

services, no wonder the Jewish youth of those countries felt that their existence was unreal, transitional, a kind of preparation for some future reality—redemption through Zion or through the coming World Revolution" (*Israel Among the Nations*, City College Papers, no. 9, New York, 1968). "Plight without ideology," Talmon writes, "would have reduced the Jews of Central and Eastern Europe to a mob of wretched refugees, whereas ideology gave them the dignity of a hard-pressed nation on the march." Similar observations may well apply to the Palestinians. Cf. chapter 1, below.

40. Cf. Friedländer, *op. cit.*, pp. 104f.

41. *Sunday Times*, London, June 15, 1969. A longer excerpt appears in Cooley, *op. cit.*, pp. 196–7. Galili's statement, before a Kibbutz conference in 1969, elicited an important response from Talmon. Cf. Cooley, *ibid.*, pp. 205–7.

42. Cooley, *op. cit.*, p. 197.

43. Cf. Chapter 5, p. 170, and the reference of note 23, chapter 5. On the facts of the matter, see also John H. Davis, *The Evasive Peace*, John Murray, London, 1968, ch. 5. (As commissioner general of UNWRA, Davis was in charge of Palestinian refugee programs.)

44. Kimche, *op. cit.*, p. 264.

45. *Yediot Ahronot*, Oct. 17, 1969. Cited in Bober, *op. cit.*, p. 77.

46. Cf. my "Israel and the New Left," in Mordecai S. Chertoff, ed., *The New Left and the Jews*, Pitman, New York, 1971, and chapter 5, below. As discussed there, more was involved than just the affairs of the Middle East. Though small in scale by comparison, the support given by some segments of the left to Palestinian movements has been no less mindless, in my opinion, than the general support for Israeli intransigence. See chapter 2. In this case too, those who advocate that others undertake a suicidal and self-destructive course of action might do well to reflect, quite apart from any judgment as to the rights and wrongs of the case.

47. Reproduced in *Siah*, Nov. 15, 1973, from *Davar*. Characteristically, Sharon speaks only of the problem of settlement with Egypt.

48. Itzhak Rabin, *ibid*. General Rabin (former chief of staff and ambassador to the United States) adds that if the Arab states had achieved greater initial success, they would have exploited it for further military goals, and Jordan might have joined seriously in the war.

49. Oil economist Thomas R. Stauffer of the Harvard University

Middle East Center, *Christian Science Monitor*, Jan. 10, 1974.

50. Pinhas Sapir, *Maariv*, Nov. 1, 1973.

51. *Ha'aretz*, Nov. 30, Dec. 7, 1973.

52. Yehuda Gotthalf, *Davar*, Oct. 26, 1973; Boaz Evron, *Yediot Ahronot*, Oct. 10, 1973. Translated in *New Outlook*, Oct.–Nov. 1973.

53. Eric Rouleau, *Le Monde*, Jan. 23, 1974; translated in *Le Monde* English section, *Guardian Weekly*, Feb. 2, 1974.

54. Cf. chapter 5. As noted there, these efforts to suppress discussion persist, though with much less success, given the reassessment of United States government policy since October 1973. The examples discussed in chapter 5 may be dismissed as extreme and untypical. Perhaps a personal experience may help convey the mood of these years. In late 1970, I tried to persuade a group of American Jewish professors (liberals and socialists) to sponsor tours in the United States by Israeli doves (writers, professors, journalists) to help make Americans aware of some of the range of opinion in Israel. They refused, though they generally agreed with the views of the Israelis I suggested that they invite. I could only take this to reflect the fear that expression of these views might cause doubt and controversy. To cite one further incident, when Knesset member Uri Avneri visited the United States, a directive was sent to all Hillel foundations on American campuses urging that he not be permitted to speak. (To their credit, several Hillel rabbis disregarded this appeal.) The efforts to limit discussion are wrong in themselves, but also, I believe, harmful to the people of Israel and their security, for reasons I have been discussing.

55. *Maariv*, Dec. 7, 1973, cited in *Viewpoint*, Jan. 1974.

56. *Yediot Ahronot*, Nov. 23, 1973. Translated by *Jewish Liberation Information Service*, Jan. 1974, P.O. Box 7557, Jerusalem. Dr. Bar-Zohar is a well-known political scientist and journalist, very critical of Israeli doves.

57. It is sometimes overlooked that the Syrian shelling followed Israeli encroachments into the demilitarized zones for agricultural development and water-diversion projects. References to the unreliability of a United Nations force commonly overlook the fact that Israel refused appeals to permit the United Nations force to operate on its side of the border, as well as on the Egyptian side. The situation is complex, considerably more so than the casual reader of the American press might believe. It is also well to bear in mind that

Arabs, too, have reason to fear shelling from the Golan
Golan Heights since the war of 1967" (*Christian Science*
by Israeli air attacks and artillery shelling from the nearby
of Irbid, "nearly 100 people have been killed or wounded
Heights. John K. Cooley reports that in the Jordanian city
Monitor, Jan. 30, 1970).

58. It is less often noted that the Arab states surrounding Israel
also have a "security problem," not to speak of the Palestinians. Thus the United States is party to a tripartite agreement guaranteeing that no territories in the region will be
taken by force. The value of this guarantee for Egypt, Syria,
and Jordan since 1967 is obvious enough, but rarely discussed.

59. For some examples, see the discussion in chapter 5.

60. Cf. the report by Eric Rouleau, *Le Monde*, Nov. 6, 1973.
There have been continuing reports since of debate within
the leadership of the Palestine Liberation Organization over
this matter, but their options seem fairly limited.

61. See below, p. 30.

62. *New York Times*, Dec. 30, 1973.

63. May 21, 1973. The text appears in *War/Peace Report*, July–
Aug., 1973.

64. For example, Hans Morgenthau. See chapter 5, note 48.

65. Ibrahim Sus, "L'Offensive diplomatique de l'Arabie Saoudite,"
Le Monde diplomatique, Oct. 1973.

66. It is commonly argued that these vast funds would permit Arab
rulers to disrupt the international monetary system and that
the funds would be "excessive," considering the domestic
needs of the Arab states. On the hypocrisy of these attitudes, see Marwan Iskandar, *The Arab Oil Question*, 2nd
ed. Jan. 1974, Middle East Economic Consultants, International Book Services, Inc., Portland, Ore. He points out
that the projected oil revenues over the coming thirteen
years for 150 million Arabs amount to less than three-fourths
of the annual United States national income. One might argue that this income is unlikely to be distributed properly,
but then the plea should be for more equitable development, not for reversing the flow of funds to the Western
world, where there are also some problems of distribution.
Iskandar also points out that during the 1960s the West
obtained an implicit subsidy (he estimates $31.5 billion)
from the oil producers as a result of its ability then to drive
down prices, with no complaints about the unfairness of
all of this. Investigation of trade and aid reveals many similar examples. For the justification, we can return to Kristol's

insightful distinction between the "significant" and "insignificant" nations.

67. Graham, *op. cit.* See note 30, above.

68. Drew Middleton, *New York Times*, Nov. 18, 1973. The oil-producing countries already devote 20 to 50 percent of their budgets to military purchases. See Iskandar, *op. cit.*

69. It is, incidentally, curious to read the denunciations of the European states (France in particular) for attempting to cut into the American arms trade—another example of their irresponsible bilateralism. Cf. pp. 3–5, above.

70. See Sheldon Kirshner, "Report on Israel's Budding Arms Industry," *New Outlook*, Sept. 1973.

71. *Maariv*, Aug. 29. 1973.

72. Amnon Rubinstein, *Ha'aretz*, Aug. 10, 1973, in *New Outlook*, Sept. 1973. To cite another case, the Bedouin tribes evicted by force from the Rafah region in 1972 appealed to the courts that the alleged "security grounds" were fraudulent. The High Court rejected their appeal, on grounds that the courts cannot interfere with such decisions on the part of the military commander. But local Jewish settlements continued to employ Arab workers who had been expelled from their homes. Moshe Dayan warned them to cease this practice, since by doing so they were undermining the plea of the military before the High Court that the Bedouins were evicted for security reasons: "If the settlers continue employing as labourers those same Bedouins that lived on this land and were removed for security reasons, they are just taking away the grounds for our claim and are closing the area for further Jewish settlement" (Ehud ben Ezer, *Ha'aretz*, Aug. 13, 1973). On the court decisions, see articles from the Israeli press translated in *Israleft*, June 21, 1973.

73. "Who Is a Jew?", *Encounter*, May 1965, cited in Georges R. Tamarin, *The Israeli Dilemma*, Rotterdam University Press, Rotterdam, 1973, p. 37. The latter work gives some striking examples of the impact on children's attitudes of life in a "warfare state." On the matter of the religious role in the Israeli state and society, see also Norman L. Zucker, *The Coming Crisis in Israel*, MIT Press, Cambridge, Mass., 1973.

74. Cf. Cooley, *op. cit.* Also Gérard Chaliand, *La Résistance palestinienne*, Éditions du Seuil, Paris, 1970; trans. *The Palestinian Resistance*, Penguin Books, Baltimore, 1972.

75. Cited in Amos Elon, *The Israelis*, Holt, Rinehart & Winston, New York, 1971, p. 178.

76. Cf. note 39.

77. Cited in Cohen, *op. cit.*, p. 260.
78. *Ibid.*, p. 260.
79. *Ibid.*, pp. 267–9. This detailed plan was presented in a per-
    sonal note submitted to the Jewish Agency in 1936 and
    was unknown until reported by Moshe Smilansky in 1953
    in his autobiography.
80. *Ibid.*, p. 291.
81. *Ibid.*
82. *Ibid.*, pp. 285–7.
83. *Ibid.*, p. 258.

CHAPTER 1

Nationalism and Conflict in Palestine

These remarks are based on a talk delivered at a forum of the Arab Club of MIT. I am grateful to many Arab and Israeli students for their helpful comments and criticism. From many conversations with them, I feel that they are much closer to one another, in their fundamental aspirations, than they sometimes realize. It is this belief that encourages me to speculate about what may appear to be some rather distant prospects for reconciliation and cooperative effort. There can be few things more sad than the sight of young people who are, perhaps, fated to kill one another because they cannot escape the grip of fetishism and mistrust.

Before discussing the crisis in the Middle East, I would like to mention three other matters. The first has to do with my personal background and involvement in this issue. Secondly, I would like to mention reservations I feel about discussing this topic on a public platform. And finally, I want to stress several factors that limit the significance of anything I have to say. Ordinarily, these matters might be out of place, but in this case I think they are appropriate. They may help the reader to place these comments in a proper context and to take them as they are intended.

To begin with some personal background: I grew up with a deep interest in the revival of Hebrew culture

associated with the settlement of Palestine. I found myself on the fringes of the left wing of the Zionist youth
movement, never joining because of certain political disagreements, but enormously attracted, emotionally and
intellectually, by what I saw as a dramatic effort to
create, out of the wreckage of European civilization,
some form of libertarian socialism in the Middle East. My
sympathies were with those opposed to a Jewish state
and concerned with Arab-Jewish cooperation, those who
saw the primary issue not as a conflict of Arab and
Jewish rights, but in very different terms: as a conflict between a potentially free, collective form of social organization as embodied in the Kibbutz and other socialist
institutions on the one hand, and, on the other, the auto-
cratic forms of modern social organization, either capitalist or state capitalist, or state socialist on the Soviet
model.

In 1947, with the United Nations partition agreement,
this point of view became unrealistic, or at least unrelated to the actual drift of events. Prior to that time it
was perhaps not entirely unrealistic. And again, I think,
today this may be a realistic prospect, perhaps the only
hope for the Jewish and Arab inhabitants of the old Palestine.

I should say, at the outset, that my views have not
changed very much since that time. I think that a socialist binationalist position was correct then, and remains
so today. Implicit in this judgment are certain factual
assumptions regarding the prospects for Arab-Jewish cooperation based on an interpretation of interests along
other than national lines. These assumptions are not solidly grounded and are surely open to challenge, as is the
implicit value judgment concerning the desirability of a
socialist binational community as compared to a sub-
division of Palestine into separate Arab and Jewish states

or the establishment of a single Jewish or Arab state in the whole region that would preserve no form of communal autonomy. These are the questions that I would like to explore, quite tentatively, and subject to reservations that I will mention.

Returning to my personal experience, the partition plan seemed to me at best a dubious move, and perhaps a catastrophic error. Of course, I shared the general dismay over the subsequent violence and the forceable transfer of populations. A few years later I spent several very happy months working in a Kibbutz and for several years thought very seriously about returning permanently. Some of my closest friends, including several who have had a significant influence on my own thinking over the years, now live in Kibbutzim or elsewhere in Israel, and I retain close connections that are quite separate from any political judgments and attitudes. I mention all of this to make clear that I inevitably view the continuing conflict from a very specific point of view, colored by these personal relationships. Perhaps this personal history distorts my perspective. In any event, it should be understood by the reader.

Let me turn next to certain reservations that I have about discussing the topic at all. These reservations would be less strong in an Israeli context, where my point of view might at least be a reasonable topic for discussion, though it would not be widely shared, I presume. The American context is quite different. In general, the spectrum of political thinking in the United States is skewed sharply to the right as compared with the other Western democracies, of which Israel is essentially one. Interacting with the narrow conservatism that dominates American opinion is an ideological commitment to a perverse kind of "pragmatism" (as its adherents like to call it). This translates into practice as a system of techniques for enforcing the stability of an American-dominated world system within which national societies are to be managed by the rich in cooperation with a "meritocratic elite" that serves the dominant social institutions, the corporations, and the national state that is closely linked to them in its top personnel and conception of the "national interest." In this highly ideological country, where political commitments often border on the fanatic, the question of cooperation in the common interest can barely be raised without serious miscomprehension. Specifically, there is little likelihood of a useful discussion of the possibilities for Arab-Jewish cooperation to build a socialist Palestinian society when the terms are set by the conservative coercive "pragmatism" of American opinion.

It is, furthermore, characteristic of American ethnic minorities that they tend to support the right-wing forces in the national societies to which they often retain a cultural or economic connection. The American Jewish community is no exception. The American Zionist movement has always been a conservative force within world Zionism, and tended toward maximalist and strong nationalist programs at a time when this was by no means typical of the Palestinian settlement itself. To cite just one case, the Zionist Organization of America was, I believe, the first organized segment of world Zionism to formulate as an official doctrine "that Palestine be established as a Jewish commonwealth" and to condemn any program that denies these "fundamental principles," even the program of the politically rather conservative Ihud group in Palestine, which was specifically repudiated (October 1942).[1] At the Basel Congress of the World Zionist Organization in 1946, the first after the war, Chaim Weizmann was impelled to condemn the nationalist extremism of the American delegation.[2] Today, it seems to me that this general conservatism and nationalist extremism are harmful to the long-range interests of the people of Israel as well as to the search for a just peace; in any event, they have helped create an atmosphere in the United States in which discussion and exploration of the basic issues is at best quite difficult.

An Israeli writer like Amos Oz, for whom the abandonment of the Jewish state "is a concession we could not make and shall never be able to make," can nevertheless appreciate the absolute validity of the right of the Palestinian Arabs to national self-determination in Palestine: "This is our country; it is their country. Right clashes with right. 'To be a free people in our own land' is a right that is universally valid, or not valid at all." He sees the conflict as a tragedy, "a clash between total justice and total justice. . . . We are here—because we can exist nowhere but here as a nation, as a Jewish state. The Arabs are here—because Palestine is the homeland of the Palestinians, just as Iraq is the homeland of the Iraqis and Holland the homeland of the Dutch." The Jews have no objective justification other than "the right of one who is drowning and grasps the only plank he can." The Palestinian Arabs understand the meaning of Zionism only too well, he says; they regard themselves "as the despoiled owners of the whole country, with some reluctantly accepting the situation and some not accepting it at all." [3] Similarly, General Moshe Dayan speaks quite clearly of the justice of the Arab position: "It is not true that the Arabs hate the Jews for personal, religious, or racial reasons. They consider us—and justly, from their point of view—as Westerners, foreigners, invaders who have seized an Arab country to turn it into a Jewish state." [4] Speaking at the funeral of a murdered friend, just before the Sinai campaign of 1967, Dayan said: "We must beware of blaming the murderers. Who are we to reproach them for hating us? Colonists who transform into a Jewish homeland the territory they have lived in for generations." [5] In a pro-Zionist Israeli journal, a senior official of the government of Israel can propose that formal sovereignty should be ceded to a binational Palestinian Union ("a constitutional monarchy headed by the present ruler of the Kingdom of Jordan," "a union of Jewish and Arab settlement areas, each of which will be guaranteed autonomy in matters of culture, education, religion, and welfare"). [6]

I mention these examples, which can be multiplied, to illustrate a significant difference between the Israeli and the American Jewish communities. In the latter, there is little willingness to face the fact that the Palestinian Arabs have suffered a monstrous historical injustice, whatever one may think of the competing claims. Until this is recognized, discussion of the Middle East crisis cannot even begin. Amos Oz introduces his essay by deploring the fact that "anyone who stands up and speaks out in these days risks being stoned in the market place and being accused of Jewish self-hate or of betraying the nation or desecrating the memory of the fallen." To the American Jewish community, these words apply quite accurately, more so than to Israel, so far as I can determine. This is most unfortunate. Political hysteria benefits no one. The barriers that have been raised to any serious discussion of the issues will only diminish what meager possibilities may exist for peaceful reconciliation.

Finally, I want to emphasize that I approach these questions with no particular expert knowledge or even intimate contact, nothing more than what I have just described. Nor do I have any specific policy recommendations in which I, at least, would place much confidence. Specifically, I doubt very much that any American initiatives are likely to be helpful. As to initiatives by the American government or other great powers—these might well prove disastrous.

With all of these reservations, I feel that the problem must still be faced, and with a sense of considerable urgency. The reasons for this sense of urgency are put very well by Uri Avneri, in one of the most important of the recent books on the Middle East crisis:

> An uneasy cease-fire prevails along the frozen fronts of the recent war, a cease-fire fraught with dangers, broken by intermittent shots. The armies confronting each other across the cease-fire lines are arming quickly. A new war is assumed by all of them as a virtual certainty, with only the exact timing still in doubt. But the next war, or the one after it, will be quite different from the recent one, so different, in fact, that the *Blitzkrieg* of June 1967, will look, in comparison, like a humanitarian exercise.
>
> Nuclear weapons, missiles of all types, are nearing the Semitic scene. Their advent is inevitable. If the vicious circle is not broken, and broken soon, it will lead, with the preordained certainty of a Greek tragedy, toward a holocaust that will bury Tel Aviv and Cairo, Damascus and Jerusalem.
>
> Semitic suicide is the only alternative to Semitic peace.
>
> A different kind of tragedy is brewing in Palestine itself. If no just solution is found soon, the guerilla war of organizations like al-Fatah will start a vicious circle of its own, a steep spiral of terror and counter-terror, killing and retaliation, sabotage and mass deportation, which will bring undreamt-of miseries to the Palestinian people. It will poison the atmosphere and generate a nightmare that will make peace impossible in our lifetime, turning Israel into an armed and beleaguered camp forever, bringing the Arab march toward progress to a complete standstill, and perhaps spelling the end

of the Palestinian-Arab people as a nation—the very people for whose freedom al-Fatah fights in vain.

Cease-fire—this is not a passive imperative. In order to cease fire, acts of peace must be done. Peace must be waged—actively, imaginatively, incessantly. In the words of the psalmist: "Seek peace and pursue it." The search can be passive—the pursuit cannot.[7]

General Dayan speaks with equal realism, in the remarks from which I have already quoted: "As long as we have to fulfill our aims against the will of the Arabs, we shall be forced to live in a permanent state of war."

I do not see any way in which Americans can contribute to the active pursuit of peace. That is a matter for the people of the former Palestine themselves. But it is conceivable that Americans might make some contri-channels of communication, by broadening the scope of discussion and exploring basic issues in ways that are not easily open to those who see their lives as immediately bution to the passive search for peace, by providing threatened. It cannot be said that anything serious has been done to realize these possibilities.

I suspect that the major contribution that can be made in the United States, or outside the Palestine area, is more indirect. The situation in the Middle East, as elsewhere, might be very different if there were an international left with a strong base in the United States that could provide an alternative framework for thinking and action,[8]—an alternative, that is, to the system of national states which, under the circumstances of the world today, leads to massacre and repression for the weak and probable suicide for the strong. I am thinking of an international movement that could challenge the destructive concept of "national interest," which in practice means the interests of the ruling groups of the various societies of the world and which creates insoluble conflicts over issues that in no way reflect the needs and aspirations of the people of these societies, an international left that could represent humane ideals in the face of the powerful institutions, state and private, that dominate national policy and determine the course of international affairs.

In the specific case of the Palestine problem, such a new framework, I think, is desperately needed, and I can imagine no source from which it might derive other than a revitalized international movement that would stand for the ideals of brotherhood, cooperation, democracy, social and economic development guided by intrinsic, historically evolving needs—ideals that do belong to the left, or would if it existed in any serious form. Perhaps the most significant contribution that can be made to reconciliation in Palestine by those not directly involved is to work for the creation of an international movement guided by these ideals and committed to a struggle for them, often in opposition to the national states, the national and international private empires, and the elites that govern them.

It is perfectly possible to construct an "Arab case" and a "Jewish case," each having a high degree of plausibility and persuasiveness, each quite simple in its essentials. The Arab case is based on the premise that the great powers imposed a European migration, a national home for the Jews, and finally a Jewish state, in cynical disregard of the wishes of the overwhelming majority of the population,[9] innocent of any charge. The result: hundreds of thousands of Arab refugees in exile, while the "law of return" of the Jewish state confers citizenship, automatically, on any Jew who chooses to settle in their former homes. The Zionist case relies on the aspirations of a people who suffered two millennia of exile and savage persecution culminating in the most fantastic outburst of collective insanity in human history, on the natural belief that a normal human existence will be possible only in a national home in the land to which they had never lost their ties, and on the extraordinary creativity and courage of those who made the desert bloom. The conflict between these opposing claims was recognized from the start. Arthur Balfour put the matter clearly, as he saw it, in a memorandum of 1919:

> . . . in Palestine we do not propose even to go through the form of consulting the wishes of the present inhabitants of the country, though the American [King-Crane] Commission has been going through the form of asking what they are. The four great powers are committed to Zionism and Zionism, be it right or wrong, good or bad, is rooted in age-long tradition, in present needs, in future hopes, of far profounder import than the desires and prejudices of the 700,000 Arabs who now inhabit that ancient land.[10]

The Arabs of Palestine may be pardoned for not sharing this sense of the priorities.

Not only can the Arab and Jewish case be formulated with power and persuasiveness; furthermore, each can be plausibly raised to the level of a demand for survival, hence in a sense an absolute demand. To the Israelis, the 1948 war is "the war of liberation." To the Arabs, it is "the war of conquest." Each side sees itself as a genuine national liberation movement. Each is the authentic Vietcong. Formulated within the framework of national survival, these competing claims lead inevitably to an irresoluble conflict. To such a conflict there can be no just solution. Force will prevail. Peace with justice is excluded from the start. Not surprisingly, the image of a crusader state is invoked by men of the most divergent views: Arnold Toynbee, Gamal Abdul Nasser, Itzhak Rabin, and many others.

The likely evolution of the conflict should be particularly evident to the Israelis, given the Jewish historical experience. The exile of the Palestinian Arabs is taking on some of the characteristics of the Jewish Diaspora. There are similarities between the emerging national movement of the Palestinian Arabs in exile and the Zionist movement itself. In "an open letter to the occupiers of my homeland," a Palestinian refugee writes these words:

> Theodore Herzl once said the Jews must go to Palestine because it was "a land without people for a people without land." I cry, I sorrow, for that land was mine. *I* am people, the *Palestinians* are people, and you who have suffered such persecutions, have *forced* us to pick up your ancient cry: *"NEXT YEAR, JERUSALEM."* [11]

It is unlikely that the sentiments expressed in this letter will diminish in intensity. Rather, it is reasonable to expect that each Israeli victory will strengthen the forces of Palestinian Arab nationalism. Whatever agreements may be reached between Israel and the Arab states—and any agreements seem, for the moment, quite unlikely—these forces will no doubt persist. Israel is incapable of conquering the Arab hinterland, it is partially dependent on Western support (a weak reed, at best), and it can lose only once. The prospects are not attractive.

Many Israeli spokesmen believe that the terrorism of the Arab movements (from the Arab point of view, the resistance to the occupying forces) can easily be contained, that it is an unpleasantness on the order of traffic accidents. I am in no position to judge, but it is far from certain. Eric Rouleau cites an Israeli spokesman who told him "that the commandos had considerably improved their equipment, technique, and fighting spirit." He cites a statement by Moshe Dayan that it is wrong to think of the fedayeen only as criminals, that in fact they are "inspired by a patriotism and idealism that should not be underestimated." [12] There are reports indicating growing sympathy for the fedayeen in the occupied territories,[13] where an Israeli journalist describes the attitude of the Arabs as now ranging "from passive dislike to open hatred." [14] Some knowledgeable Israeli observers sense, furthermore, that "growing numbers of Israeli Arabs, torn between conflicting loyalties, are being drawn into the unrest," noting correctly that this development is "more alarming from Israel's point of view" than the terrorism itself.[15] Yet it appears an inevitable development. Under the existing conditions, the Palestinian Arabs will inevitably be regarded as a potential fifth column and treated as second-class citizens.[16] It would be most remarkable if they did not react, ultimately, in such a way as to fulfill these fears. Furthermore, it is unimaginable that these fears will abate, so long as the threat of extermination remains. The likely consequences are all too clear.

Israel asks only peace, normal relations with its neighbors, and its continued existence as a state. But when the Arab-Israel conflict is posed in the terms of national conflict, it is quite unlikely that these aims can be achieved. Israel can hardly hope to make peace on its terms with the Arab states for the simple reason that these terms do not make provision for the rights of the Arabs of Palestine, now largely in exile or under military occupation, as they see their rights. The Palestinian Arabs are increasingly becoming an organized force, certain to press their demands in conflict with the Arab states and with Israel as well. This force cannot be overlooked, nor can its claims be lightly dismissed. The major consequence of the Six-Day War may prove to be the consolidation of the Palestinian Arabs, for the first time, as a serious political and paramilitary force. If so, then the framework of national conflict is indeed a prescription for Semitic suicide.

Eric Rouleau speaks of "the classical chain reaction—occupation, resistance, repression, more resistance." There are other links in this chain. The Israeli journalist Victor Cygielman writes: "One thing is sure, terrorism will not succeed in wrecking Israel, but it may succeed in ruining Israeli democracy."[17] He is speaking of the demoralizing effect of "such measures of collective punishment as the blowing up of houses, administrative arrests and deportation to Jordan," and he comments that "the arrest of several citizens of Taibe and Haifa [i.e., within the territory of Israel itself] on the charge of having tried to establish *El Fatah* cells on Israeli soil, may show a developing trend." Other Israeli intellectuals have voiced similar fears.

Still other dangers are pointed out by the Israeli Middle East expert Shimon Shamir:

> Perhaps the highest price that Israel might have to pay for a prolonged political domination of the Palestinian Arab society would be in the field from which Israel derives its strength—the spirit of its citizen-army. It can be doubted whether a society whose institutions have been engaged for a long time in frustrating the political demands of a large Arab population could again manifest the same spirit of absolute solidarity, of fighting with one's back to the wall, of raging resistance to threats of extermination.[18]

In part, this "high price" is a consequence of the occupation. But the occupation is unlikely to be abandoned until security is guaranteed, and there is no way for security to be guaranteed within the framework accepted by both sides.

It is natural to think that security can be achieved only through strength and through the use of force against a threatening opponent. Perhaps so. But those who adopt this course must at least be clear about the likely dynamics of the process to which they are contributing: occupation, resistance, repression, more resistance, more repression, erosion of democracy, internal quandaries and demoralization, further polarization and extremism on both sides, and ultimately—one shrinks from the obvious conclusions. It is not evident that security is to be achieved through the use of force.

There is some historical experience on which we can draw. My impression—I stress again the limitations of my knowledge—is that by and large, the effect of coercion and force is to create a strong, vigorous, often irrational opponent, committed to the destruction of those who wield this force. There is an exception, of course, namely, when the opponent can be physically crushed.

It seems clear that the current exercise of force is having just this effect. Terroristic attacks on civilians simply consolidate Israeli opinion and drive the population into the hands of those who advocate the reliance on force. If this process does succeed in destroying Israeli democracy and turning Israel into a police state, the Palestinian Arabs will have gained very little thereby. Similarly, collective punishment, razing of houses and villages, detention, and exile, surely have the effect of strengthening the hands of those in the Palestinian Arab movement who see the physical destruction of Israeli society as the only solution.

In the past, I think that much the same was true. Prior to 1948, the Jewish community in Palestine in general tried to avoid the use of force and coercion and to refrain from a policy of reprisal in response to physical attacks and terror. The policy of *Havlagah*—restraint—in the late

1930s was not only a moral achievement of the highest order, but was also, it seems, reasonably effective as a tactic. There were groups in the Jewish settlement that did believe in the resort to terror against the Mandatory authorities and reprisals against the Arab revolt (itself largely directed against the Mandatory—"a furious but futile revolt against Great Britain" [19]). These were the groups of the extreme right—chauvinist, anti-Arab, anti-labor, with their social roots among the Zionist bourgeoisie and the associations of private farmers. Tensions between these groups and the Socialist-Zionist settlers "erupted in a miniature Jewish civil war early in the 1940s." [20]

As to the policy of anti-Arab reprisal, instead of my trying to assess its effects, let me simply present the words of the political arm of the terrorist organizations:

> Out of the humiliated souls of Palestine Jewry, the Irgun Tsevai Leumi (National Military Organization) was born. It was created by a few dynamic spirits within the national youth and was inspired by Jabotinsky's untiring propaganda for Jewish self-defense—propaganda that for years had been stigmatized by official Jewish leaders as "Fascist," "militarist," and "reactionary." [21] In September, 1937, the Irgun struck. During the first week of that month, the Arabs killed three Jews. The Irgun executed thirteen Arabs for the crime. In panic-stricken fury, the Arabs derailed a train, ambushed one Jewish bus and bombed another—claiming the lives of fourteen more Jews. For two months, Arab terrorism flamed again with murderous violence.[22]

Evidently, a great tribute to the effectiveness of the reprisal policy. The document goes on to explain how the Irgun "avenged the murder of every Jew," while "the flustered Jewish Agency publicly denounced the actions of the Irgun 'which (it said) are marring the moral record of Palestine Jewry, hampering the political struggle and undermining security.'" The accuracy of the charge is illustrated by the continuing account of Irgun actions— for example, of how the Irgun fearlessly invaded Arab settlements on the occasion of an Arab parade celebrating the 1939 White Paper, "transform[ing] the day of victory into a day of mourning," and so on.

It was semifascist elements such as these that were largely responsible for the reprisals, which had the effects just indicated. The same, I believe, was largely true at the time of the partition agreement. Let me quote a report from the *Bulletin* of the Council on Jewish-Arab Cooperation, a group that emphasized "the possibilities for independent political action by workers as a class, as contrasted to reliance on decisions of any of the big powers":

> The role of the Jewish terrorist bands (Irgun Zvai Leumi and the Stern group) in the recent fighting can be seen from a listing of their activities. Dec. 7—they threw a bomb into the Arab market place in Haifa. Dec. 11—they bombed Arab buses in Haifa and Jerusalem, killing and wounding many, and shot two Arabs in Jerusalem. Dec. 12—bombings and shootings in Haifa, nearby Tireh, Gaza, Hebron and other cities, killing many Arabs. Dec. 13—Irgun agents bombed Arab buses, killing 16 and wounding at least 67 Arabs. Jewish terrorists carried out a series of assaults on Dec. 15, attacking Arab buses, Arab pedestrians and random personnel of the Transjordan Frontier Force.

These actions began precisely at the time when it appeared to newspaper correspondents and to the *Bulletin* correspondents in Palestine that Arab attacks were subsiding, or when, after enduring much hardship from Arab terrorist dominance, Arabs took initiative to effect formal understandings with Jewish neighbors against all armed terrorists. At no time did the Jewish terrorists even claim to be attacking the Mufti's bands or to be making any differentiation among Arabs. The special attention to Haifa, a workers' city where the Arabs had committed almost no attacks, indicates the intention to arouse Arab workers to anti-Jewish reprisals.[23]

During these and following months, Arab terrorists, both Palestinian and infiltrated, were responsible for widespread murder and destruction, giving substance to the statements of men like Azzam Pasha, secretary general of the Arab League, who announced "a war of extermination and a momentous massacre which will be spoken of like the Mongolian massacre and the Crusades." [24]

One cannot fail to note, throughout this period, the similarities of intent on the part of the terrorists on both sides, and still more strikingly, the impact of each in strengthening the influence of the other and increasing the general polarization and drift toward irresoluble national conflict. Perhaps the conflict was unavoidable. In any event, the policy of terror and reprisal made a major contribution to intensifying it and embittering relations among people who must cooperate, ultimately, if they are to survive in some decent fashion.

Reprisals have a certain logic within the framework of national conflict. One who sees a national conflict between all Arabs and all Jews might well argue that any terrorist act by any Arab or Jew can properly be the occasion for a reprisal against any Jew or Arab. In this way, the terror continues on its upward spiral, and the use of force is given new legitimacy within each of the polarizing societies.

Even from a narrow point of view, one can raise the factual question of the actual effects of the reprisal policy. I have already noted two occasions when its effect on security was at best dubious. Let me turn to a third,

a few years later. I quote from Nadav Safran, a well-
known Harvard Middle Eastern scholar with pro-Israel
sympathies. Commenting on the Israeli attack on the
Gaza strip in 1955, the first major reprisal against Arab-
held territory by the Israeli army, he has this to say:

> The Egyptian authorities tended at first merely to wink
> at infiltration undertaken for all sorts of purposes from
> the Gaza strip under their control. But after a murder-
> ous Israeli retaliatory raid on Gaza in February 1955,
> the Egyptian government responded defiantly by
> launching a deliberate raiding campaign from Gaza and
> Jordan. . . . Israeli retaliatory attacks only increased the
> defiance of the Egyptian authorities and the murderous-
> ness of the raids, until finally Israel took advantage of
> a favorable conjuncture to launch an all-out invasion
> of Sinai and the Gaza strip in October 1956.[25]

Once again, the policy of forceful reprisal had rather
dubious consequences, from the point of view of security.
Safran goes on to say that since the 1956 war the border
has been quiet (prior to the Six-Day War), so that the
1956 attack was a success from the Israeli point of view,
as he sees it. But Safran's analysis—which is highly professional and informative—suffers from a fundamental
defect typical of the "realist" political science of which
his work is a good example. He disregards the people of
Palestine and considers only the relations among national
states and the interplay among them at the level of coercive force. This choice of framework, which is quite
explicit, is appropriate for the study of some aspects of
the problem, but one who focuses on "the manipulation
of various forms of coercion in the service of policy, and
of policy in the service of enhancing the means of coercion" (Safran) will no doubt miss a great deal. Safran,
by virtually eliminating from consideration the Arab
population of Palestine, seriously underestimates the rise

of Palestinian Arab nationalism. In particular, he fails to see the significance of the rise of al-Fatah, which many observers believe to be a genuine expression—the first—of the national consciousness of the masses of Palestinian Arabs.[26]

The moderate Lebanese journalist Ghassan Tueini described "the formation of *Fatah* [as] the single most significant event in the Arab World for 50 years." [27] There is a fair amount of evidence that this represents the thinking of many Palestinian intellectuals, who might agree with a teacher in East Jerusalem that the "Palestinians had to take matters into their own hands," that they have captured "the imagination of the Arab masses . . . thanks to the Israeli policy of retaliation as well as a strenuous effort on their part." [28] The explicit goal of al-Fatah is to involve the masses in struggle, now that they have recognized the futility of looking to the Arab states for salvation. "In our view, any liberation activity that does not try to involve the masses properly is doomed to failure, since it ignores the most important element influencing the struggle." [29] It is clearly recognized that this may draw the Arab countries into war. The prospect is welcomed, even if the result is a defeat, which will lead to an extended occupation and further opportunities for growth of the liberation movement. In the article just quoted, Nasr (see note 28) continues: "No Arab-Israeli settlement (even one sponsored by Nasser) is worth the paper it is written on without fedayeen agreement." This seems plausible, given the growth of al-Fatah as an expression of Palestinian Arab national consciousness.

If these assessments are accurate, as the information available to me suggests, then Safran's analysis of the interstate conflict is of only marginal relevance.

Returning to the matter of force and security, Safran argues that though the 1955 reprisal and subsequent retaliatory attacks increased the Egyptian support for terrorism, nevertheless after the 1956 war the level of violence subsided. However, from another point of view that takes in a somewhat longer time span, the 1956 war contributed significantly to violent confrontation. The 1956 war apparently provided the immediate impulse for the formation of al-Fatah, and, as just noted, this counts as a rather questionable gain from the point of view of Israeli security. According to Chaliand (see note 26), until 1961 the organization was occupied with establishing the nucleus of a political organization among the Palestinian intelligentsia, and then for several years proceeded to develop a paramilitary organization. Its first casualty was suffered at the hands of a Jordanian soldier in 1965, and until the Six-Day War it was strictly controlled by the Arab states. The catastrophic defeat of June 1967 left a political and military vacuum that was quickly filled by al-Fatah, now relatively free from the constraints formerly imposed and solidly based in the Palestinian population.

Most observers agree that the Israeli retaliatory attack on Karama in March 1968 "marked a turning point in the evolution of the Palestine armed resistance movement." [30] It enormously increased the strength and prestige of al-Fatah (which claimed a victory and was believed, whatever the facts may be) among the Arab masses and, as a result, with the Arab states, which, no doubt reluctantly, are forced to grant to the Palestinian resistance considerable latitude. The organization now claims to be unable to absorb the volunteers flocking to it. [31]

As I have already noted, some Israeli commentators concede that the movement exhibits considerable élan and vitality, though few regard it as a true military threat. Ehud Yaari (see note 29) is probably fairly representative of informed Israeli opinion when he writes:

> Even its most vigorous critics cannot deny Al-Fath its character as an ideological movement, as well as an active military organization. The skeleton of the new theory has already been set up; only actual experience can show whether it will put on flesh and blood. The fundamental difference between the wave of terror that preceded the Sinai Campaign in 1956 and the wave that has been growing since 1965 lies in the fact that in contrast to the murderous groups acting for revenge or profit, Israel now faces a terrorist organization with a specific political theory; terror one of a number of elements.

In short, it seems accurate to say that Israel now faces a liberation movement modeling itself consciously on others that have proven successful. Many differences can be noted. However, still taking the narrow view of Israeli security, the evolution from predatory bands to a conscious mass-based liberation movement hardly counts as a success for the policy of security through force.

Israeli retaliation is seen by al-Fatah leadership as a major weapon in their arsenal. The Fatah leader Yasir Arafat says:

> Thank God for Dayan. He provides the daily proof of the expansionist nature of Zionism. . . . After the 1967 defeat, Arab opinion, broken and dispirited, was ready to conclude peace at any price. If Israel, after its lightning victory, had proclaimed that it has no expansionist aims, and withdrawn its troops from the conquered territories, while continuing to occupy certain strategic points necessary to its security, the affair would have been easily settled with the countries that were the victims of the aggression.[32]

Other Fatah spokesmen have expressed similar views. One, quoted by Hudson (see note 31), advocates violence because it "forces the Israelis to retaliate desperately and indiscriminately against the surrounding Arab countries, but in so doing Israel only diminishes its reputation in the international community and forces the Arab governments into even greater solidarity with the Palestinians," who will themselves, it is expected, be drawn into resistance in reaction to the harsh reprisals in the occupied areas or the neighboring countries.

How accurate this analysis may be I am in no position to judge. I suspect that it is fairly realistic. It relies on factors often overlooked by the "realist" analysts who think only in terms of national states that monopolize the instruments of coercion and use them to achieve the "national interest" as conceived by their respective elites. What is overlooked is the dynamics of a popular national movement. With all the differences that have so often been stressed, there still remains an analogy to Vietnam, where American force, applied on an enormous and horrifying scale, led to a tremendous upsurge of Vietcong strength.[33] In this respect, the situation in Palestine may be similar. A story has it that Dayan once advised that the Israeli military study the American policy in Vietnam carefully, and then do just the opposite. This advice is difficult to follow for an occupying power, operating within the framework of national conflict.

It seems to me that something like the foregoing is what is suggested by the history of the past years. The policy of reprisal, wisely shunned by the socialist masses in Palestine in earlier years, has, not surprisingly, become national policy with the establishment of the state. As noted, it has a certain logic within the framework of national conflict. It is the logic of despair and ultimate disaster.

One might argue that it is rather cheap, from 5,000 miles away, to urge the advantages of a policy of conciliation in preference to the harsh tactic of repression and reprisal (or a combination of the carrot and the stick). How else are we to defend ourselves from the terrorist attacks? Or, from the other side, how are we to liberate our homeland except through violent resistance? Each reproach is legitimate, in its own terms. Still, certain questions must be faced: What are the actual consequences of violence, on either side? Is there an alternative to the framework of national conflict, the relentless pursuit of "national interest" through force?

With regard to the first question, I can only repeat that each side seems to me to be locked into a suicidal policy. Israel cannot hope to achieve peace on its terms by force. Rather, it will simply build the forces that will lead to its eventual destruction by force, or to a permanent garrison state, or, perhaps, to some form of colonization of the area by the great powers to enforce their form of stability—not too unlikely if nuclear weapons and missiles enter the picture.[34] Unless it achieves a settlement with the Palestinian Arabs, or crushes them by force, Israel will no doubt be unable to reach any meaningful agreement with Egypt or the other Arab states. There will be a constant temptation to undertake pre-emptive strikes, which, if successful, will simply reconstitute the original conflict at a higher level of hostility and enhance the power of those who demand a military solution. For Egypt, an acceptable long-term strategy may be "to reduce the margin of Israel's military superiority to the point when Israel can no longer win battles except at great human cost." [35] The internal effects in Israel might be such as to destroy whatever was of lasting human value in the Zionist ideal. Perhaps it is appropriate to recall the warning of Ahad Ha-am, quoted by Moshe

Smilansky in expressing his opposition to the Biltmore Program (see note 1):

> In the days of the House of Herod, Palestine was a Jewish State. Such a Jewish State would be poison for our nation and drag it down into the dust. Our small State would never attain a political power worthy of the name, for it would be but a football between its neighbors, and but exist by diplomatic chicanery and constant submission to whoever was dominant at the time. Thus we should become a small and low people in spiritual servitude, looking with envy towards the mighty fist.[36]

Parallel comments apply with respect to the Arab states and the Arab liberation movements. There is no possibility that the Jewish population of Israel will give up its cultural autonomy, or freely leave, or abandon a high degree of self-government. Any plan of liberation that aims at these goals will lead to one or another form of massacre, or perhaps to recolonization by the great powers. In this case, too, whatever is of lasting human value in the movement for Arab liberation can hardly survive such policies, and will be submerged in reaction and authoritarianism.

Within the framework of "national interest," of the conflict of "Jewish rights" and "Arab rights," the problem cannot be resolved in terms that satisfy the just aspirations of the people of what was once Palestine.

In principle, there is a very different framework of thinking within which the problem of Palestine can be formulated. How realistic it is, I am not competent to judge—though I might add that I am not too impressed by the "realism" of contemporary ideologists, including many who masquerade as political scientists, historians, or revolutionaries. The alternative is ridiculously simple, and therefore no doubt terribly naïve. It draws from one part of the historical experience and the expressed ideals of the Zionist and Arab nationalist movements, from currents that can barely be perceived today, after two decades of intermittent war, but that are nonetheless quite real.

The alternative to the framework of national states, national conflict, and national interest, is cooperation among people who have common interests that are not expressible in national terms, that in general assume class lines. Such alternatives are open to those who believe that the common interest of the great masses of people in Palestine—and everywhere—is the construction of a world of democratic communities in which political institutions, as well as the commercial and industrial system as a whole, are under direct popular control, and the resources of modern civilization are directed to the satisfaction of human needs and libertarian values. There is little reason to suppose that these interests are served by a Jewish state, any more than they are served by the states of the Arab world. Feeling this way, I read with some slight degree of optimism such statements as this by a spokesman for one of the Palestinian Arab organizations:

> It is not enough simply to wear khaki and shoot to have a revolution, and the Palestinian youth are not giving their lives just to restore the oppressive rule of landlords and big businessmen in Palestine.[37]

Such comments bring to mind the position of the Left Front of Histadrut, which won 20 percent of the vote in the August 1944 elections, on a platform that included this statement:

> The Left Front will fight for the construction of Palestine as a joint homeland for the Jewish people returning to its land and for the masses of the Arab people who

dwell in it; for setting up of a state form for Palestine in the spirit of the brotherhood of peoples, non-
domination, and national fraternity—in accordance with
the national, social, and political interests of the two
peoples, and looking forward to the creation of a socialist Palestine.[38]

A social revolution that would be democratic and socialist, that would move both Arab and Jewish society in
these directions, would serve the vital interest of the
great majority of the people in Palestine, as elsewhere.
At least, this is my personal belief, and a belief that was
surely a driving force behind the Jewish settlement of
Palestine in the first place. It is quite true, I believe, that
"Zionism, being the outcome partly of Jewish and partly
of non-Jewish enlightenment, and being also a secular
reaction to Jewish assimilation . . . conceived the Jewish
national revival more in terms of the realisation of a
harmonious 'just society' than in terms of the realisation
of Jewish political independence." [39] Or, to be more exact, this was a major element in the prewar settlement.

This tendency is given little emphasis in the predominantly political and military histories. It is presented and
analyzed in such works as the Esco Foundation study
(see note 1), or in Aharon Cohen's massive study of
Jewish-Arab cooperation and conflict (see note 19), with
its extensive documentation of efforts—abortive, but not
hopeless—to create a binational Palestinian community
in which the vital interests and just goals of Jews and
Arabs might be met. The problem, as he formulates it,
has always been this: "how to weave together concrete
interests and high aspirations, to create the conditions
for cooperative and compatible efforts, to exploit the
given objective possibilities and to strengthen the forces
working to advance the common good, both material and
spiritual." The greatest obstacle has been "the failure to

understand the true significance of this task, narrowness of vision and insufficient effort." As Cohen correctly observes: "In the absence of the intellectual and moral courage to face this failure honestly, there is no hope of repairing that which demands repair . . . no hope of breaking out of the magic circle: an increase in the Jewish constructive effort in Israel, an increase in its strength —and along with it, an increase in the dangers that threaten all of these achievements. . . ."

This is, I believe, the proper standpoint from which to approach the problems of today, as it was a generation ago. Then it represented, I think it is fair to say, a significant position in the Palestinian Jewish community—a matter to which I will return. Ben-Gurion once wrote that only an insane person could attribute to Zionism the wish to force any of the Arab community from their homes: "Zionism has not come to inherit its place or to build on its ruins. . . . We have no right to harm a single Arab child, even if with this we could achieve all that we wish." [40] It can never be too late to try to recapture this vision.

A movement to create a democratic, socialist Palestine —optimally, integrated into a broader federation—that preserves some degree of communal autonomy and national self-government is not beyond the bounds of possibility. It might build on what, to my mind, is the outstanding contribution of the Zionist movement to modern history—the cooperatives, which have proven to be an outstanding social and economic success and point the way to the future, if there is to be a future for the human race. The long-standing position of the left wing of the Kibbutz movement was "that the kibbutz was not simply a form of settlement but a way of life, the *raison d'être* of Zionism." [41] One of the consequences of the partition —to my mind, an extremely unfortunate one—has been the relative decline in importance of the collectives within Israel. Perhaps this trend could be reversed if the national struggle were to be transcended by a movement for social reconstruction of a revitalized Arab-Jewish left. Admittedly, the possibilities seem slight. But there are some historical precedents that are hopeful. One thinks at once of Yugoslavia, where in the course of a successful social revolution, "the old conflict-provoking ethnic ties (Serb, Croat, and so forth) give some evidence of being less 'irrational' and less binding, with more individuals thereby willing to think of themselves quite simply as individuals operating within a broad Yugoslav context." [42]

If the Arab and the Israeli left are to develop a common program, each will have to extricate itself from a broader national movement in which the goals of social reconstruction are subordinated to the demand for national self-determination. One can imagine a variety of possibilities for binational federation, with parity between partially autonomous communities. A common political and social struggle might take the place of national conflict—as meaningless, ultimately, as it was to those who slaughtered one another for the glory of the nation at Verdun.

National ties are strong, and any steps toward cooperation must build upon them. True cooperation can only be for common goals, and between equals. In this respect, the formation of al-Fatah might prove to be a significant step toward peaceful reconciliation. A shattered, fragmented society cannot come to terms with a well-organized, technologically advanced counterpart. The Israeli left can lose nothing, and can perhaps gain a great deal, by trying to relate itself in some way to the newly consolidating Palestinian Arab community, particularly its left-wing elements. To do so, it will have to see the other side of the coin (as Aharon Cohen has put it on several occasions) and offer a positive and meaningful program for cooperation, even one with long-range and perhaps still distant goals. Given the present constellation of forces, it is reasonably clear that the initiative must come from this source. It is not for me to suggest concrete steps—in fact, the bare beginnings perhaps already exist.[43] To extend them and build upon them should be the major preoccupation of those concerned to create the conditions for a just peace.

Might there be any Arab response to such initiatives? From the information available to me, it seems that there might very well be a response. Consider, for example, the following remarks in a recent editorial in the official organ of the Arab Socialist Union, the only functioning political organization in Egypt.[44]

> . . . the new society [in Palestine] must be open to all Jews, Moslems, and Christians without exclusiveness or discrimination between first and second-class citizens; and this non-racist nature of the new state must impose its implications and principles, by necessity, on its constitution and laws, and on the rights and duties of the citizens. . . . [This strategy] must be crystallized into a "dynamic organization" that will strengthen all Arabs and Jews antagonistic to imperialism, Zionism, and all forms of racism on the local and international levels. . . . In my opinion, the first step in building this front, which will completely change the balance of power, is the joint responsibility of the Palestinian Resistance on the one hand, and of the Jewish local and world masses antagonistic to imperialism and Zionism, on the other. This front, by undertaking such a progressive program, which represents the will for liberation from imperialism and racism, will not be serving the interest of the Arab and Jewish masses . . . alone, but will serve humanity's movement in advancing towards a new world

free of colonialism, imperialism and aggression, and free of the dangers of a total destructive war which is the situation in the Middle East today, one of the world's most explosive regions.

The editorial is said to be "the fruits of a positive discussion which I had the opportunity to conduct at consecutive meetings with a number of the leaders of Fatah and the Popular Front in addition to some Arab friends among revolutionaries and intellectuals." Fatah statements repeatedly call for "the destruction of the Zionist and racist structures [of the state of Israel and the establishment of a] secular and democratic Palestine reaching from the Mediterranean to Jordan" [45] (I presume this means including Jordan).

Y. Harkabi, who quotes a number of statements of this sort (see note 26), observes that "the Arabs' objective of destroying the state of Israel (what may be called a 'politicide') drives them to genocide," since "Zionism is not only a political regime or a superstructure of sorts, but is embodied in a *society*." This is a possible, but not an absolutely necessary, interpretation of such proposals.[46] The Israeli left might well give a different interpretation, first, to the aspirations of Zionism, and correspondingly, to the intention of these statements. By so doing, it may help to give substance and reality to a more sympathetic and constructive interpretation.

The goal of a democratic socialist community with equal rights for all citizens and the goal of "a federative framework with the Kingdom of Jordan and the Palestinian people, based on cooperation in the fields of security and economics" [47] do not, on the face of it, appear to be incompatible. There may, then, be room for fruitful and perhaps eventually cooperative effort between the Arab and the Israeli left. I suspect that the fundamental stumbling block to any agreement will prove to be the

Israeli "law of return," which Ben-Gurion 'has described as "the peculiar sign that singles out the State of Israel and fixes its central mission, the Zionist-Jewish mission . . . the foundation scroll of the rights of the Jewish people in Israel." [48] It is primarily by virtue of this law that Israel is a "Jewish State." It is hard to imagine that the Arabs of Palestine will consent to a law which, in effect, prevents them from returning to their homes on the theory that the Jews of the word have a more pressing need and a greater right to settle in this land. I have seen no sign that any substantial segment of Israeli opinion is willing to consider the abandonment of the principle embodied in the "law of the return." [49]

It seems to me that the situation of today is more like that of 1947 than of any intervening period. Furthermore, there have been twenty years of experience from which, perhaps, something has been learned. Both international and domestic factors are more conducive to a peaceful resolution of the conflict than has been the case for some time.

As to the international situation, the possibilities of great power conflict are quite real, and insofar as their leaders are rational, neither of the great powers can conceivably fail to fear such a conflict.[50] It is also possible that the great powers have learned that even in their narrow self-interest, attempts to organize the Middle East within an imperial system are not likely to be successful. Dulles's Baghdad Pact led to the Nasser-USSR arms deal, which significantly increased the flow of weapons and the level of tension in the Middle East. Attempts to intervene in Syria, Lebanon, and Jordan in 1957–1958 ranged from the ludicrous to near-disaster. Safran describes them as "the final failure in the succession of unsuccessful British, British-American, and American attempts since the end of World War II to organize the Middle

East heartland in the frame of the Western alliance system." [51] The Soviet attempt to intervene, for example in Iraq, was no less of a catastrophe. [52] Perhaps, then, the great powers might be willing to keep hands off, even to permit some form of genuine socialist development in the Middle East outside of the framework of competing imperialisms, if it has substantial domestic roots.

A sensible American policy would encourage Israel to break free of Western influence. Out of a felt need to rely on the Western powers, Israel has been unable to support anticolonial forces in North Africa and the Middle East—for example, the Algerian FLN. Such a policy must, naturally, be harmful to the development of decent relations with the Arab countries and their peoples. A different Western policy might, in principle, permit options that would, no doubt, be more congenial to much of the Israeli population itself. It might also, in principle, include the kind of economic assistance that actually contributes to development—in this case, to help close the economic and social gap between Arab and Jewish populations, a prerequisite to any real cooperation. The chances that such a policy will be undertaken are no doubt slight.

Far more important are the domestic factors, no longer what they were twenty years ago. In 1947, the Palestinian Jewish community was traumatized by the holocaust. It was aware that no world power would be willing to lift a finger to save the miserable remnants of European Jewry, no more than they were at the international conferences of Evian in 1938 or Bermuda in 1943. Furthermore, it was psychologically impossible to contemplate the resettlement of these tortured victims in a new diaspora. The Palestinian Jewish settlement acted accordingly and did succeed in settling 300,000 Jewish refugees in a Jewish state, but at a fearful cost.

An approximately equal number of Jewish refugees
reached Israel after having been expelled from the Arab
countries in the wake of the 1948 war, and hundreds of
thousands of Arab refugees fled, or were driven from
their homes in the new state of Israel. For those Arabs
who remained, living standards have no doubt improved,
but there is much evidence that many were dispossessed
of homes, land, and property, and deprived of the right
of free political organization.[53]

Today the situation is very different. The Nazi massacre, though unforgettable in its horror, no longer de-
termines the choice of action. Rather, it is the living
death of the refugee camps and the steady drift toward
further misery yet to come that set the terms for policy.

From the perspective of twenty years, I think we can
see the extent to which the war jarred the Zionist movement into a new and somewhat different course, which
might still be modified without an abandonment of its
fundamental aims. The concept of a Jewish state is not
so deeply rooted in the history of the Jewish settlement
of Palestine as one might be led to believe, judging by
the temperament that has prevailed in recent years. I
have already mentioned that the first official formulation
of the demand for a Jewish state was in 1942, when the
war was under way and the center of World Zionism
had shifted to the United States. After an extensive
analysis, the Esco Foundation report concluded: "It is
not too much to say that the position of the Zionist leadership from the Twelfth Carlsbad Congress in 1921 [the
first to convene after the Balfour declaration] to the
Twenty-First Congress in Geneva in 1939 was strongly
tinctured with bi-nationalism." [54] At the Congress of
1931, Weizmann insisted that security could be achieved
only by establishing friendly relations with the Arabs of
Palestine on the basis "of complete parity without regard

to the numerical strength of either people." [55] Ben-Gurion spoke in similar terms in testifying before the Peel Commission in 1937.[56] Even Jabotinsky insisted only that "the Jewish point of view should always prevail" in a state that had "that measure of self-government which for instance the State of Nebraska possesses," [57] and his nationalist extremism caused him to leave the Zionist organization several years later. Many others—Kalvarisky, Arlosoroff,[58] Magnes, Smilansky—labored incessantly to establish a dialogue with Palestine Arabs that would lead to Arab-Jewish cooperation within a binational framework.

Their efforts were not so unsuccessful as is often claimed.[59] In the early 1920s several Arab peasant parties called for Arab-Jewish cooperation against exploiters, and in Haifa, largely a working-class city, the former Arab mayor (who had been removed by the British) was a member of an upper-class Moslem society that spoke of the need for Arab-Jewish cooperation.[60] A number of conferences of Jews and Arabs took place, some that appeared to offer some promise, though no serious efforts were made by official bodies to carry matters further. There were joint strikes and demonstrations of Arab and Jewish workers until 1947, and among agricultural communities there was undoubtedly much friendly contact, persisting beyond the establishment of the state.

Many of the Arabs who attempted to maintain friendly relations were assassinated, as were some who combatted the politics of the Arab leadership. One example, just prior to the partition agreement, was the case of the Arab labor leader Sami Taha, who was murdered after an attempt to form an Arab "workers' party," free from the control of the Arab Higher Committee.[61] He had called for a democratic Palestinian state in which Jews and Arabs would have equal rights. He was a supporter of

Musa al-Alami, who had been involved in earlier discussions with Weizmann and others and was regarded as a spokesman for the rights of Arab workers and peasants.[62] It seems fair to say that there was an unwritten unholy alliance of sorts among the Jewish and Arab right-wing terrorist organizations and segments of the British forces, all engaged in terroristic attacks that polarized the two societies and killed a number of those who attempted reconciliation (see note 20).

Perhaps the most significant case was that of Fawzi al-Husseini, who was assassinated in November 1946. He was the nephew of the Mufti, Haj Amin al-Husseini. He had taken part in the 1929 riots and had been imprisoned by the British during the 1936–1939 revolt. Later, he became convinced of the necessity for Arab-Jewish cooperation, and just a few weeks before he was killed, he signed an agreement in the name of a new organization, Falastin al-Jadida (New Palestine), with the League for Arab-Jewish Rapprochement that had been founded in 1939 and was headed by Kalvarisky. The document expressed the desire of each organization "to support the activities of [the other] and to assist it in all possible ways to make them a success." [63]

In the months before his death, he had spoken widely in support of such a view. Some of his remarks deserve fuller quotation:

> There is a way for understanding and agreement between the two nations, despite the many stumbling-blocks in this path. Agreement is a necessity for the development of the country and the liberation of the two nations. The conditions of agreement—the principle of non-domination of one nation over the other and the establishment of a bi-national state on the basis of political parity and full cooperative effort between the two nations in economic, social and cultural domains.

Immigration is a political problem and within the framework of general agreement it will not be difficult to solve this problem on the basis of the absorptive capacity of the land. The agreement between the two nations must receive international authorization by the UN, which must guarantee to the Arabs that the bi-national independent Palestine will join a federation with the neighboring Arab states.

These principles were written into the agreement between the League and Falastin al-Jadida.

At a meeting of Jews and Arabs at the home of Kalvarisky in Jerusalem, Fawzi al-Husseini lauded Kalvarisky's long-term efforts in the cause of Arab-Jewish cooperation, noted their partial success, and announced his intention to undertake similar efforts among the Arab population. He expressed his belief that, despite the support of the Mandatory authorities for the Arab leadership of Jamal al-Husseini and the Mufti, his efforts would meet with success if they received moral, organizational, and political support from the Jewish community and if cooperative efforts showed concrete results.

These efforts did receive a hopeful response in the Arab community, according to Cohen, but were cut short by Fawzi al-Husseini's assassination. The mood of World Zionism is indicated by the reaction at the Zionist Congress in Basel, when a spokesman for Hashomer Hatzair, Y. Chazan, spoke of the murder. According to the report in *Davar:* "Laughter and hilarity were caused by the story (of Chazan) about one Arab, a Zionist sympathizer, who was killed in Jerusalem because he believed in Jewish-Arab agreement and favored immigration. From the Revisionist rows someone commented: 'So this one Arab was killed, and now no one remains.'"

Such people as Chaim Kalvarisky and Fawzi al-Husseini existed. Many of them paid with their lives for the efforts to bring about reconciliation and peace. Because the support for them was insufficient, many, many more have been killed and maimed and driven from their homes, to empty, wasted lives, to hatred and torment. And the story has not yet come to an end.

I would like to conclude these remarks with an excerpt from an editorial statement in the *Bulletin* for Jewish-Arab cooperation in January 1948, just at the outbreak of the Twenty-Year War. I think that these words were appropriate then, and that they are again appropriate today:

A major obstacle to bringing about peace in Palestine is the prevailing view that most Jews have of what they want from the Arabs. *What they would essentially prefer is that the Arabs be passive in respect to the Jews.* They want the Arabs not to object to Jewish immigration and construction, not to be too closely involved in the Jewish economy, and currently not to attack Jews or to harbor the attackers. In return, the Arabs would get economic benefits from the neighboring Jewish economy, would be gradually modernized economically and politically, and would on their part not be attacked by the Jews. *The weakness of this view is that people are not passive.* They may appear passive in that they accept the controls and ideas of relatively static upper classes. But when economic and social changes take place about them, they react to them. When the Arab upper class tries to direct the population into anti-Jewish attitudes, the Jewish workers cannot counter this by asking the Arab population not to react at all and to leave the Jews alone. They can only offer the Arabs an alternative way of reacting, one more useful to the Arab peasants and workers.

The only practicable alternative to war is therefore not peace but cooperation. In a long-range political sense, we can say that the only alternative to a war

between nations is not a static peace . . . but a war between classes, between ruled and ruler, of the Jewish
and Arab worker and peasant against the two upper
classes, against the fascist parties of both nations, and
the British or other outside interests that want to control the area.

These remarks, I repeat, were made in early 1948. They
have a certain relevance to the situation of today. In
particular, I think it is important to consider the idea
that the only practicable alternative to war is not peace
but cooperation—the active pursuit of peace—and that
cooperation cannot exist in the abstract, but must be
directed to the satisfaction of real human needs. In the
Middle East, as elsewhere, these needs can be perceived
as they are reflected—caricatured, I believe—in terms of
"national interest." This way, it seems to me, lies tragedy
and bitterness. Other ways are open, and they might
provide a way to a better life, not only in Palestine, but
in every part of this tragic and strife-torn world.

Notes

1. See Esco Foundation, *Palestine: A Study of Jewish, Arab and
   British Policies*, Yale University Press, New Haven, Conn.,
   1947, vol. 2, pp. 1087, 1100. The 1942 program is generally
   referred to as the "Biltmore Program."
2. See Christopher Sykes, *Crossroads to Israel*, William Collins,
   London, 1965, for a description of this occasion.
3. "Meaning of Homeland," *New Outlook*, Dec. 1967.
4. *Le Monde*, weekly selection, July 9–16, 1969.
5. *Ibid.*, July 16, 1969.
6. Zalmen Chen, "A Binational Solution," in *New Outlook*, June
   1968. See also the discussion among the editors, March–
   April 1968. This journal has, for more than ten years, provided sane and highly informative commentary on the Palestine problem.

7. Uri Avneri, *Israel Without Zionists*, Macmillan, New York, 1968.

8. For a preliminary effort in this direction see *Eléments*, journal of the Comité de la Gauche pour la Paix négociée au Moyen-Orient, nos. 2–3, May 1969, 15 rue des Minimes, Paris 3°.

9. Population estimates vary. The Esco Foundation study (*op. cit.*, vol. 1, p. 321) gives these figures: for 1920, 67,000 Jews out of a population of 673,000; for 1930, 164,796 Jews out of a population of 992,559.

10. Quoted in Christopher Sykes, *op. cit.*

11. The letter appears in *The Middle East Newsletter*, May–June 1969, an anti-Zionist periodical published in Beirut.

12. *Le Monde*, weekly selection, July 10–16, 1969 (Rouleau's paraphrase).

13. See for example the eyewitness report of Amnon Kapeliuk in *New Outlook*, Nov.–Dec. 1968.

14. Ze'ev Schul, *Jerusalem Post Weekly*, reprinted in *Atlas*, August 1969.

15. Shmuel B'ari in *New Outlook*, March–April 1969.

16. See the statement by the Israeli journalist Nissim Rejwan in *New Outlook*, March–April 1968. He writes that: "The official view . . . has been repeatedly explained by the Prime Minister's present Adviser on Arab affairs. It is that one cannot expect loyalty from the Arabs of Israel 'since they belong to another nationality.' As long as such a view prevails we will not in honesty be able to claim that we treat our non-Jewish citizens as equals."

17. *New Outlook*, Feb. 1968.

18. *Ibid.*, March–April 1969.

19. Amos Perlmutter, *Military and Politics in Israel*, Frank Cass, 1969, London, p. 19, a highly expert study by an Israeli scholar. John Marlowe describes the rebellion as "in fact a peasant revolt, drawing its enthusiasm, its heroism, its organisation and its persistence from sources within itself which have never been properly understood and which now will never be known" (Sykes, *op. cit.*). The Esco Foundation study concluded: "While the bands undoubtedly included genuine sympathizers with the Arab national cause, they also contained many recruits from the lower elements in the towns who were attracted by the pay and the chance of robbery. . . . Acts of terror were committed not only against government officials and Jews, but also against Arabs who did not fall in with the policy of the Mufti party." This is borne out by the casualty figures for 1939: "69 British,

92 Jewish and 486 Arab civilians, besides 1,138 rebels killed" (vol. 2, pp. 876–80). According to figures from official sources cited by Aharon Cohen (*Israel and the Arab World*, Sifriat Poalim, in 1964; Hebrew—translations mine throughout) twice as many Arabs were killed by Arabs as by Jews in the period 1936–1939, "because of friendly relations with Jews (village Mukhtars, Arab guards, Arab workers who worked with Jews, and so on), or because of their political opposition to the Mufti and his associates" (p. 204). (Cohen's book has since been translated; see introduction, note 16.)

20. Perlmutter, *op. cit.*, p. 42. For example, Sykes reports that "in January, 1942, the Sternists murdered two officials of Histadruth, and when they fought the police they concentrated their vengeance on the Jewish personnel." The Esco Foundation study (vol. 2, p. 1040) reports the murder of a member of Hashomer Hatzair by members of Betar who had invaded a meeting in 1944.

21. With justice. It is enough to read the "Ideology of Betar," written by Jabotinsky. Betar is a party "founded upon the principles of discipline. . . . For it is the highest achievement of a mass of free men, if they are capable to act in unison, with the absolute precision of a machine. Only a free, cultured people can do so. . . . Discipline is the subordination of a mass to one leader"—the *Rosh Betar*, Jabotinsky. Continuing: "We have decided that in building a State, we must utilize the means at hand, be they old or new, good or bad, if only we will thus attain a Jewish majority." Among the means was strike-breaking: "An unjust and State-disintegrating strike must be mercilessly broke [sic], as well as any other attempt to damage the Jewish State reconstruction. . . . it is the right and duty of Betar itself to decide as to the justice or unjustice of a conflict, help the former, and break up the latter." Revisionist spokesmen in the 1930s expressed their admiration for Mussolini, Franco, and the murderers of Liebknecht and Luxemburg. According to Perlmutter, they also made "attempts to collaborate with the Fascists and Nazis in Eastern Europe, during World War II" (p. 45). He believes that the Irgun "constituted far more of a threat to the Yishuv than . . . toward the Mandatory" (p. 27). As already noted, they were responsible for attacks on Jews as well as Arabs. (In this respect, they were comparable to the terrorists of the Arab right.) Their best-known exploit was the Deir Yassin massacre in 1948 (largely an operation of the Irgun Tsevai Leumi—the Revisionist paper

HaMashkif, in August 1948, applauded this "dazzling display of warfare" because it was a main factor in causing the flight of Arab refugees). David Ben-Gurion was perceptive when in 1933 he entitled an article "Jabotinsky in the Footsteps of Hitler." The strong antagonism of the Palestinian Jewish settlement to the Revisionists and their various outgrowths is very much to its credit; the relatively good press they have received in the United States is largely a result of ignorance, I suspect.

22. *This Is Betar*, undated, early 1940s. Betar was a youth group founded by Vladimir Jabotinsky, the head of the Revisionist wing of the Zionist movement, which has now become, in effect, the Herut Party in Israel.

23. Vol. 3, no. 12, Dec. 1947. I should emphasize that my own point of view was heavily influenced by this group and a number of the people associated with it.

24. Cited in Rony Gabbay, *A Political Study of the Arab-Jewish Conflict*, Librairie E. Droz, Geneva-Paris, 1959. This is an excellent and detailed study of the period from 1948 to 1958.

25. Nadav Safran, *From War to War*, Pegasus, New York, 1969, pp. 45–6.

26. See particularly the important study of Gérard Chaliand, "La Résistance palestinienne entre Israël et les états arabes," *Le Monde diplomatique*, March 1969. For a recent journalistic account, see Mervyn Jones in *New Statesman*, June 13, 1969. He is "wholly convinced" (admittedly, on brief exposure) that al-Fatah is the "authentic expression" of a new "coherent and militant nation." Chaliand suggests an analogy to the early Kuomintang, and feels that if it fails, it may be supplanted by a more revolutionary mass movement, as in China or Vietnam. He notes that small Marxist groups exist which seem to him to share more directly in the daily life of the refugees (specifically, the FPLP). There is a detailed analysis by the former Israeli chief of military intelligence, Y. Harkabi: *Fedayeen Action and Arab Strategy*, Adelphi Papers, no. 53, Institute for Strategic Studies, London, Dec. 1968. He is rather disparaging and regards the organization more as a nuisance than a threat. His belief that it has suffered a serious setback in "its failure to establish bases in the occupied territories" seems questionable. See note 13.

27. Quoted by Desmond Stewart in *Encounter*, June 1969.

28. Joseph Nasri Nasr, "Palestinians Want a New Elite," *New Outlook*, Feb. 1969.

29. A spokesman for al-Fatah, quoted by the commentator on

Arab affairs for *Davar*, Ehud Yaari, in "Al-Fath's Political Thinking," *New Outlook*, Nov.–Dec. 1968.

30. Abbas Kelidar, "Shifts and Changes in the Arab World," *The World Today*, Dec. 1969.

31. According to the American political scientist Michael Hudson, in an unpublished paper ("The Palestinian Resistance Exists"), before the Six-Day War "al-Fatah numbered no more than 200–300 men; by the time of the Karamah battle it had increased to around 2,000; but in the three months following the Karamah battle it had burgeoned to 15,000." His account is based on three months of intensive investigation in Israel and the Arab states.

32. *Le Monde*, weekly selection, Feb. 20–26, 1969.

33. In 1965, the first year of intensive bombardment of South Vietnam, local recruitment of the Vietcong tripled, according to American military sources.

34. On these possibilities, see Geoffrey Kemp, *Arms and Security: The Egypt-Israel Case*, Adelphi Papers, no. 52, Institute for Strategic Studies, London, Oct. 1968.

35. *Ibid.*

36. Esco Foundation study, vol. 1, p. 583. See note 1. The original essay is entitled "The Jewish State and the Jewish Problem," 1897.

37. Quoted by Hudson. The spokesman is from the FPLP. See note 26.

38. Quoted in the *Bulletin* of the Council on Jewish-Arab Cooperation, Jan.–Feb. 1946.

39. Unpublished lecture by the Israeli scholar Dan Avni-Segré, Oxford, Jan. 1969.

40. 1925, 1927. Quoted in Cohen's study, pp. 231–2. Some regard such statements as hypocritical, but I think that is an error.

41. Perlmutter, *op. cit.*, p. 28, commenting on the views of Yitzhak Tabenkin, expressed in an article of 1937.

42. George Zaninovich, *Development of Socialist Yugoslavia*, Johns Hopkins Press, Baltimore, 1968, p. 105.

43. See in particular the symposium to which I have already referred in *New Outlook*, March–April 1968.

44. Loutfy Al Khowly, "An International Arab-Jewish Front Against Imperialism and Racism," *Al-Tali'a (The Vanguard)*, April 1969. I am indebted to James Ansara and Dennis Kfoury for bringing this to my attention and providing a rough translation. The translators inform me that the word translated throughout as "racism" refers as well to religious and cultural domination, in a sense which has no exact English equivalent.

45. Yasir Arafat, *Le Monde*, weekly selection, Feb. 20–26, 1969.

46. It might also be argued that the many Fatah statements formulating the goal of a democratic Palestine with equal rights for all citizens are merely intended for propaganda purposes. Harkabi, who has undertaken an exhaustive analysis of Fatah material and whose view, as noted, is highly unsympathetic, concludes that "it should be acknowledged that there is little difference between what they say for external and what is intended for home consumption."

47. The formulation of Haim Darin-Drabkin in the symposium referred to in note 43.

48. *Jewish Agency Digest*, Aug. 24, 1951. Quoted in John H. Davis, *The Evasive Peace*, John Murray, London, 1968, p. 84.

49. An exception is the Matzpen group, a socialist anti-Zionist party that numbers several hundred members.

50. For an evaluation of the situation, see Curt Casteyger, *Conflict and Tension in the Mediterranean*, Adelphi Papers, no. 51, Institute for Strategic Studies, London, Sept. 1968.

51. Safran, *op. cit.*, p. 119.

52. For discussion of all these events, from 1948 to the present, see Safran and also Maxime Rodinson, *Israel and the Arabs*, Pantheon Books, New York, 1968.

53. For an Arab view, documented largely from Israel sources, see Sabri Jiryis, *The Arabs of Palestine*. The Institute for Palestine Studies, Beirut, 1968. It should be read by those who wish to see "the other side of the coin." An account from a pro-Israeli view is given by Ernest Stock, *From Conflict to Understanding*, Institute of Human Relations Press of the American Jewish Committee, New York, 1968. See also the excellent study by Don Peretz, *Israel and the Palestinian Arabs*, Middle East Institute, Washington, D.C., 1956. The extensive study *Israeli Society* by S. M. Eisenstadt, Basic Books, New York, 1967, devotes 18 out of 424 pages to the Arabs of Israel.

54. Esco Foundation study, vol. 2, p. 1124.

55. *Ibid.*, p. 747.

56. *Ibid.*, p. 801–2.

57. *Ibid.*, p. 621. The date was 1929.

58. He was murdered in 1933, it is generally assumed, by Revisionist assassins, not long after the conclusion of a conference that he had organized among Jewish and Arab leaders to consider problems of Jewish-Arab cooperation. The conference is discussed by Cohen (*op. cit.*, pp. 235–7),

who believes that it "might have opened a new chapter in
Arab-Jewish relations in Palestine."

59. The best sources of information are Cohen's detailed and ex-
    tensive book and the Esco Foundation study, the former
    considerably more sanguine as to the possibilities for success.
60. Esco Foundation study, vol. 1, pp. 485–6.
61. Cohen, *op. cit.*, p. 351.
62. A contemporary account is given in the *Bulletin* of the Coun-
    cil on Jewish-Arab Cooperation, Nov. 1947.
63. The text is presented in Cohen, *op. cit.*, p. 328. I follow his
    account.

CHAPTER 2

A Radical Perspective

Let me begin by entering a disclaimer. What I have to say will not be particularly radical. I will be satisfied if it is somewhat realistic and more or less humane. There may be, some day, a program of action in the Middle East that is both radical and realistic. However, it seems to me that that day is still remote.

I would like to distinguish very clearly between predictions and recommendations. A plausible analysis of the present situation leads, I am afraid, to unpleasant conclusions. I frankly expect them but do not recommend them. It is possible to recommend more attractive alternatives. It may even be possible to work toward them. One can only be skeptical, however, as to whether such efforts will succeed.

The participants in the Palestine tragedy of the past half-century perceive it as a national conflict: Jews against Arabs. To such a conflict—or better, to a conflict so perceived—there is no solution except through force.

This conclusion is, of course, not unique to the Arab-Israeli conflict. Rather, it is typical of national conflicts. Consider the Franco-German conflict in World War I. Those who spoke out against that meaningless slaughter were regarded as traitors. When Karl Liebknecht opposed war credits, he was denounced as a lunatic, a fanatic. These traitors and lunatics were right, of course. Both sides were following a losing strategy. Again, this is typical of national conflicts, which rarely serve the interests of those who are slaughtering or threatening one another.

In the present case, I think that each side is pursuing a losing strategy. Israel is, at the moment, the more powerful military force by a large margin. It is capable of striking far more serious blows. The fate of the city of Suez is a sufficient example. According to recent reports, Israel is the only Middle Eastern power possessing medium-range surface-to-surface missiles that can be fitted with conventional or nuclear warheads. From inside Israel they could reach Cairo and Alexandria. It seems likely that Israel is on the verge of producing nuclear weapons and may, in fact, already be doing so.[1] Israel has been hoping that, by exercising military force, it can bring the Arab states to the negotiating table on its terms and can get them to suppress the Palestine guerrilla movement. Such plans are not likely to succeed. The Israeli scholar Y. L. Talmon writes that "Israel may be able to win and win and go on winning till its last breath, win itself to death. . . . After every victory, [it faces] more difficult, more complicated problems. . . . The abyss of mutual hatred will deepen and the desires for vengeance will mount." [2] Though Israel has military superiority, it cannot administer a crushing blow. Such a capability might well lead to Russian intervention, destruction of Israel, and perhaps a nuclear war.

For example, those Israelis who believe that the way to achieve security is through military strength were pleased when the United States supplied Israel with Phantom jets, which the Israeli air force used in deep-penetration bombing raids on Egyptian targets. The result was a Russian intervention that re-established the earlier military "balance" at a much higher level of force and potential danger. In general, each military success

simply reconstitutes the struggle at a higher level of bitterness and hostility, a higher level of military force
(compare 1948, 1956, 1967, and 1970), a higher level of
potential danger to all concerned. From the Israeli point
of view, this is a losing strategy. Israel can win every
conflict but the last. Sooner or later, it is likely that at
some moment the international situation will be unfavorable. That moment, if it arrives, will be the end of Israel,
though the catastrophe will probably be far greater in
scale.

Even in the short run, it is a losing strategy. Israeli
democracy can hardly survive with 1 million Arabs in
the occupied territories who cannot become citizens with
equal rights because Israel insists on a dominant Jewish
majority. The army will plausibly argue that the territories cannot be abandoned for reasons of security.
Present Israeli policy speaks of secure and guaranteed
borders. Everyone knows, of course, that there is no such
thing as a guarantee of security. If Israel were to write
the peace treaty itself and everyone were to sign on the
dotted line, this would not guarantee security. The result
is a hopeless impasse.

Furthermore, Israel is forced to be increasingly dependent on the world powers, in particular, the United
States. It is common these days to hear Israel described
as a tool of Western imperialism. As a description this is
not accurate, but as a prediction it may well be so. From
the point of view of American imperial interests, such
dependence will be welcomed for many reasons. Let me
mention one that is rarely considered. The United States
has a great need for an international enemy so that the
population can be effectively mobilized, as in the past
quarter-century, to support the use of American power
throughout the world and the development of a form of
highly militarized, highly centralized state capitalism at

home. These policies naturally carry a severe social cost and require an acquiescent, passive, frightened population. Now that the cold-war consensus is eroding, American militarists welcome the threat to Israel. The Joseph Alsops, with supreme cynicism, eagerly exploit the danger to Israel and argue that only the American martial spirit and American military power are capable of saving Israel from Russian-supported genocide. This campaign has been successful, even in drawing left-liberal support.

The Arabs are also following a losing strategy. Egypt, for example, has taken terrific punishment because of Israeli air superiority, and there is no reason to doubt that this will continue. It is likely that the technological gap will increase rather than decline. Similarly, the Palestinian movement cannot succeed in its present form. Israel is not Algeria. Its inhabitants will not be driven out or freely leave or abandon a high degree of self-government. Any policy directed to these ends will lead to continued destruction, to a strengthening of the reactionary and repressive forces on all sides, and perhaps to a form of recolonization by the great powers—in any event, to increasing dependence on the imperial powers, which have their own interests in maintaining such dependence.

The tragic irony is that each side, in fighting for national independence, is losing it in the course of the struggle. Since 1947, arms expenditures alone have surpassed $25 billion and are increasing. This in itself is a kind of recolonization, which may be followed by more direct forms. All of this can only be described as an enormous tragedy for the people of the Middle East. One recalls a warning of Rosa Luxemburg: "In the era of rampaging imperialism, there can be no more national wars. [The assertion of] national interests can only serve as a means of deception, of betraying the working masses of people to their deadly enemy, imperialism."

The situation of the Palestinian Arabs is at the heart of the Arab-Israeli impasse. Their problems, their demands, their rights and prospects have not been seriously discussed in the West and are cynically disregarded. In fact, the Palestinians are at best an annoyance and an embarrassment to every powerful group in the Middle East and to the great powers as well. I think it is no exaggeration to say that all of the national states directly involved in the area are united in the hope, open or secret, that the Palestinians will somehow quietly disappear. Correspondingly, their efforts not to disappear as a political or social force lead them into conflict with the great powers and most of the Middle Eastern states. It is not surprising, therefore, that their national movement, or at least some elements in it, seems to be moving in a revolutionary direction. The development of this movement, which is a matter of enormous significance for the future of the Middle East, will also very largely determine the possibilities for a just peace.

It is difficult to be optimistic when considering the possibilities for a just peace in the Middle East. Peace and justice, though surely interlinked, are very different. At least we know what we mean when we speak of peace. When we speak of justice, matters are not so simple. There are, as I have noted, apparently just demands of conflicting national groups, demands that appear to be quite incompatible. But it is, nevertheless, surely true that the search for justice transcends national lines; some would argue that it requires abolishing and overcoming national divisions. For the left, in particular, the problem of justice is inextricably linked to the problem of radical social transformation in every existing society. For this reason alone—it is not the only one—the left has been deeply concerned with the evolution of the Palestinian movements.

The Palestinians have suffered a severe historical injustice in that they have been deprived of a substantial part of their traditional home. I believe that this much, at least, can be conceded by any reasonable person. This injustice is—if we are to be honest—irreversible, except through means that are impossible to execute, given the present realities. Even if such means were practical and realistic, they would be intolerable to civilized opinion. The Palestinian groups that have consolidated in the past few years argue that this injustice could be rectified by the establishment of a democratic secular state in all of Palestine. However, they frankly acknowledge—in fact, insist—that this would require elimination of the "political, military, social, syndical, and cultural institutions" of Israel. I am quoting here from the May 6, 1970 program of the Unified Command of the Palestinian Resistance Movement, which included all the Palestinian organizations. The same program enunciates the principle that no basic change in Israeli institutions can be achieved by forces within Israel so that the elimination of these institutions must be achieved through armed struggle.

I am not concerned here with the legitimacy of this position, but rather with its implications. Given the assumptions, the conclusions no doubt follow. Furthermore, acceptance of the conclusions as the basis for action guarantees that the major assumption will remain true—that is, all elements of Israeli society will be unified in opposing the armed struggle against its institutions. Therefore, no basic change in Israeli institutions will be carried out by forces within Israel acting in concert with Palestinians with similar aims. The further consequences are those I have already mentioned. Specifically, the struggle will be a suicidal one for the Palestinians, who have already suffered miserably. Even if, contrary to fact, the means proposed could succeed—I repeat and emphasize, even if, *contrary to fact,* these means could succeed—they would involve the destruction by force of a unified society, its people, and its institutions—a consequence intolerable to civilized opinion on the left or elsewhere. In my opinion, no one who has any concern for the Palestinians would urge such a course upon them.

George Habash has recently described a disagreement in the Palestinian movement as to whether the principal concern should be the struggle over Israel or whether the movement should concentrate first on overthrowing the reactionary Arab governments which have indirectly prevented the liberation of Palestine. It is possible that events may have resolved this disagreement and that the strategy of the left—devotion of more energy to overthrowing the reactionary Arab governments—may predominate. This will be an extremely difficult course; as I noted earlier, one can expect virtually unanimous opposition from the established states of the region, as well as from the great imperialist powers—in particular, the United States and the Soviet Union. Nevertheless, there are some possibilities of success, perhaps along the Vietnamese model, though one should not push the analogy too far.

Suppose that the first stage of the struggle succeeds, as it may, and a revolutionary government is established in Amman or, perhaps, elsewhere. Then what is proposed is the slogan "an Arab Hanoi in Amman." But consider the implications. If what is suggested is that the revolutionary regime of Jordan will be a rear base for a popular resistance in the occupied territories, then the slogan is, arguably, appropriate in principle, though one may question its realism. But if it suggests that the Arab Hanoi will be a rear base for the liberation of what is now Israel, then the analogy is wholly inappropriate. It would be appropriate only if one accepted the American government's propaganda line that the war in South Vietnam was exported from the North. For, apart from any judgment of right or wrong, the fact is that the Jewish population of Israel would be unified in opposing this armed struggle. It would, therefore, in no sense be a war of liberation on the Vietnamese model, but rather a war between states that are legitimate in that they receive the overwhelming support of their own populations, as the American government likes to pretend is the situation in Indochina.

I note with interest that a recent statement of the Democratic Front (PDFLP) quotes approvingly the following statement attributed to Lenin: "The victorious proletariat cannot impose any 'happiness' on any foreign people without bringing to an end its own victory." The observation is correct. A society must carry out its own revolution, achieve its own "happiness." Revolutionary struggles cannot be exported. They must be indigenous.

It is widely assumed on all sides that a program of social change implemented by Arabs and Israelis acting in concert is impossible. The statement I quoted from the program of the Palestine Resistance Movement was to that effect. If the assumption is correct, there are only two alternatives. The first is a continuation of the national struggle between Jews and Palestinian Arabs, both sides being locked into the losing strategy that I have already discussed. This will lead either to the physical destruction of the Palestinians or to a much wider—probably nuclear—war, with unpredictable consequences. No serious person will succumb to romantic illusions about these matters. It is difficult and dangerous to speak of inevitability in history, but such an outcome is surely of very high probability. In particular, it is a grave, even suicidal error to believe that the situation is in the relevant respects analogous to Vietnam or even to Algeria.

The only other alternative, granted that the assumption is correct, is the establishment of a Palestinian state in the currently occupied areas. Certain groups in Israel and, recently, in the United States government have spoken of such a solution. If such a state were under Israeli military protection (that is, occupation), it would be little other than a kind of Bantustan. I suspect that only extreme pressure from the great powers could lead Israel to accept a truly independent Palestinian state. If this is the end of the matter, the result will be a "Balkanization" of the Levant—an ugly, though conceivably stable, system of small, hostile, suspicious, irredentist societies, very possibly reactionary and repressive as well.

Must we accept the judgment that there is no possibility of a program of social change implemented by indigenous forces in both societies? One can only speculate. However, I think it is premature to accept the counsel of defeat and despair that holds this to be out of the question. What might be the character of such a program, and to whom might it be directed? National states can do very little other than what they are now doing. Such a program could be undertaken only by those in both societies with an interest in some framework other than national conflict. Such groups exist, but they cannot function or gain credibility so long as the fear of "the national enemy" remains paramount within the framework of national conflict.

There may, however, be a different framework. The Jews and the Arabs of the former Palestine claim national rights to the same territory. Each national group demands, with justice, the right of self-government and cultural autonomy. In principle, these demands could be reconciled within a federal framework, perhaps in the form of two federated republics with parity, a guarantee of a high degree of autonomy combined with significant economic integration, highly permeable boundaries, and an ending of all legal ties to outside elements (the world Jewish community and Pan-Arab ties), though, of course, cultural and social connections could remain. Such a program would involve the abandonment of some degree of independence; one must compare it, however, with the abandonment of independence that is an inevitable consequence of national conflict. It would involve an element of risk—how can we trust our adversary?—but this must be compared with the risks inherent in national conflict. There is, of course, no such thing as a riskless policy.

The primary and most crucial difficulty, however, is the absence of a common program. There is, or should be, a common goal: the creation of a democratic, free, socialist society. For the great mass of the population in the Middle East, as elsewhere, this is the natural and proper goal, much as it may be subordinated in the national conflict. Such a program might, in principle, create a common bond between Arab and Jewish left-wing popular forces. One can only hope that sharp national boundaries will crumble as the struggle for a new society takes precedence on an international scale. But it is certain that no such goal can be achieved, or even imagined, if the means proposed is armed struggle by one society against another. It is certain that if any such goal is to be achieved, it will be through the joint efforts of indigenous mass movements in the several societies of the Middle East. To repeat the phrase attributed to Lenin by the PDFLP: "The victorious proletariat cannot impose any 'happiness' on any foreign people without bringing to an end its own victory."

An editorial statement in the Israeli journal *New outlook* proposed that "binationalism could . . . be a banner or a long-range program on which Jews and Arabs could unite and which could make them readier to yield the short-range concessions that more immediate agreements will demand." In part, I agree with the statement. I do not agree with the implicit assumption that the "concessions" away from separate and opposing nationalisms are unwelcome, though perhaps necessary. And I think that binationalism alone, without a program of social reconstruction that can bring Jews and Arabs together in a common cause, will not be a meaningful "banner or a long-range program." But the general point is correct. It would be quite important for left-wing groups within each of the warring national societies to formulate a long-range program that would meet the basic demands of the other and would provide a basis for some degree of common effort. I have suggested that this is not impossible. Such a long-range program must, first of all, mitigate the fear that social destruction—destruction of independent institutions—will be a consequence of relaxing the military confrontation. It should also aim to overcome the paralyzing and destructive tendency of people to identify themselves solely, or primarily, as Jews or as Arabs rather than as participants in a common effort—perhaps still remote—to achieve social justice, freedom, and brotherhood—those old-fashioned ideals that are within reach and can be achieved if only the will is there.

For those of us who are removed from the immediate struggle, it is important to try to open channels through which the goals and aspirations of the people of the Middle East can be expressed and to try to respond to

these expressions with an attitude that is both sympathetic and critical. There has been far too much hysteria
over this issue; although it would be wrong and inhuman
to deny the strong emotions it evokes, it is irresponsible
to yield to these emotions and to fail to consider consequences, prospects, and costs. Far too much is at stake.

Notes

1. John Cooley, *Christian Science Monitor,* Oct. 24, 1970.
2. Quoted by Don Peretz, *Mid East,* June 1970.

CHAPTER 3

Reflections on a National Conflict

I

The present crisis in the Middle East encompasses a range of issues and conflicts. There is a potential conflict between the two great imperial powers. There is, in a sense, a kind of recolonization of the region as the small states lose their independence to their temporary protectors and allies and squander their limited resources in what may be an endless struggle. Israel and the surrounding states are in a state of war. There are tensions, which in 1970 erupted into a bloody war, between Palestinian Arabs and the largely Bedouin forces of Hussein. There are conflicts among the Arab states, in particular, a long-standing rivalry—in a sense, it goes back to the Biblical period—between Egypt and Iraq.

But overshadowing all of these is the conflict between two nations that claim the right of national self-determination in the same territory, which each regards as its historic homeland. The conflict is military, to be sure, but it has a moral dimension as well. The fact is that each of these competing claims is just in its own terms. Furthermore, each claim is in a sense "absolute"—a demand for survival. If this root conflict is not resolved with some semblance of justice, then the other conflicts will continue to simmer, and occasionally explode, and will continue to threaten a catastrophe that may dwarf the repeated tragedies of the past few years. The experience with the Rogers Plan is an example. It excluded the Palestinian Arabs, and in this sense was unjust. This injustice should be rectified. If it is not, there are likely to be further bitter consequences, such as the hijackings and the Jordanian civil wars.

I read not too long ago a formulation of this root problem by Daniel Amit, an Israeli scientist at Brandeis University, that seems to me to put the matter well. He writes:

> As far as the Palestinians are concerned the origin of the conflict is the establishment of a Jewish society and eventually of the State of Israel in Palestine. They consider it a totally immoral act which resulted in the destruction of their society. This claim is to my mind beyond argument. The extenuating circumstance, namely, that European society has become an intolerable place for Jews to live in, can help to defend the moral motivations behind Zionism but cannot shed any doubt on the Palestinian moral grievance. It can also be used to promote understanding between two groups with a history full of suffering.
>
> On the other hand, the destruction of the Israeli society as a way to correct that moral injustice is blatantly immoral. Such a program in no way follows from the recognition of the grievance of the Palestinians. What does, however, follow is the recognition of the following principle:
>
> Palestinian Arabs and Israelis have equal rights in the whole territory of Mandate Palestine.

This principle he suggests as a "moral point of reference," which implies no specific practical steps, but which might serve as a framework for the adjudication of claims and the outline of a long-range program.

In fact, none of the parties in the conflict has accepted this principle, or any meaningful "moral point of reference" that might provide the framework for a just solution. Neither Israel nor any of the Palestinian organizations has unequivocally recognized the national rights of its opponent in this conflict. Neither has recognized unequivocally the right of the other to national self-determination, to independent national institutions, political, social, and cultural, that express the character of their national life as they choose to develop it.

There have been, in the past few years, some moves on each side toward recognition of the fundamental rights of the other. Thus on the Israeli side, Golda Meir, who before had denied the very existence of the Palestinians, revised this position in October 1970 in an important, though, I believe, still unsatisfactory statement. Fatah made some explicit public declarations (November 1969–January 1970), stating in clear terms their acceptance of the right of all present Israelis to remain in the secular state that they envision in Palestine, though this move remains (1) ambiguous, since it appears to be in contradiction to the Palestinian covenant which they still accept, and (2) unacceptable, since it is not coupled with a recognition of the right of Israelis to national self-determination, with the institutions that express this national right.

It is not surprising that such tentative moves meet with cold rejection and hostility on the other side. For one thing, they remain ambiguous and unsatisfactory. For another, it is simpler and more comforting in a situation of conflict to regard one's opponent as the very incarnation of evil. Thus as far as I can discover, there was no mention within Israel of the Fatah declarations, apart from one inexplicit allusion by Arab specialist Shimon Shamir, and American Jews continue to deny their existence, though a more rational approach would be to welcome such moves, while rejecting them as still

unsatisfactory and questioning them as ambiguous. Similarly, there has, to my knowledge, been no departure in
the Palestine Liberation Organization from its uncom-
promising insistence on the destruction of Israeli institutions, a program which is as intolerable from a moral
point of view as it is suicidal from the point of view of
political and military realities.

In fact, each side insists that whatever apparent moves
toward conciliation are made by the other are "for external consumption only"—deceitful propaganda that
conceals the essential aim of domination or destruction.
Those who wish can find statements and declarations to
support this conclusion. One recalls the statements of
Azzam Pasha and Ahmed Shuqeiry calling for the physical destruction of the Jews. And it is claimed—no doubt
correctly—that the Arab press has contained statements
implying that the conciliatory gestures are for propaganda purposes.

There is, in fact, quite an industry devoted to seeking
out horrendous statements from the Arab press that express—allegedly—the true intentions of the Arabs, con-
cealed beneath their occasionally conciliatory rhetoric.
Similarly—and this is something that one forgets too
easily—it would be possible to make a case that Israel is
concealing its true objectives and that Israelis are speaking with one voice within, another without. Suppose, for
example, that one was bent on proving that Israel is a
racist state committed to genocide and indefinite expansion. He might proceed to "prove" this claim by citing, for example, a statement in the journal of the Israeli
Army Rabbinate (*Machanaim*, April 1969), in which
one "Shraga Gafni" cites Biblical authority for driving
the "Canaanite peoples" from the land of Israel. He explains that "not every enemy deserves peace." Specifically:

As to the Arabs—the element that now resides in the land but is foreign in its essence to the land and its promise—their sentence must be that of all previous foreign elements. Our wars with them have been inevitable, just as in the days of the conquest of our possessions in antiquity, our wars with the people who ruled our land for their own benefit were inevitable. . . . In the case of enemies who, in the nature of their being, have only one single goal, to destroy you, there is no remedy but for them to be destroyed. This was the judgment of Amalek.

For details of the judgment of Amalek, see 1 Samuel 15.

The advocate of this position might take note of the fact that the Israeli government did not at first support the Jewish settlement of Hebron in the occupied West Bank, but soon committed £6 million (Israeli) for dwellings for Hebron settlers. Furthermore, General Dayan writes that for one hundred years the Jewish people have been carrying out a process "of colonization to enlarge the borders here—let there not be a Jew to claim that this process is over. Let there not be a Jew to say that we are nearing the end of the road." [1] And Yosef Weitz, former head of the Jewish Agency settlement department, writing in *Davar* shortly after the Six-Day War (September 29, 1967), recalls his diary entry of 1940: "Between ourselves, it must be clear that there is no room in this country for both peoples. . . . The only solution is Eretz Israel, at least the Western Israel, without Arabs, and there is no other way but to transfer the Arabs from here to the neighboring countries—to transfer them all—not one village, not one tribe should be left." And so on. Proceeding with such examples, one could construct a rather grim picture of Israeli intentions.

Such a picture would no doubt be distorted. I would recommend similar skepticism with regard to the widely current descriptions of Arab society and intentions. Although it is natural to think the worst of one's opponents, it is not necessarily correct. It is commonly argued that prudence requires that one assume the worst case, but this too is extremely dubious. What this postulate overlooks is the dynamics of conflict. There are, no doubt, situations in which a conciliatory and sympathetic approach may intensify the aggressiveness of one's opponent. But I think that the opposite is also and perhaps more frequently true.

One should not underestimate the potential dangers that Israel faces in the long term. But at present, it is in a very strong position; with respect to the Palestinian Arabs, it is in a position of overwhelming military dominance. In part, the tragedy of the Palestinians is that they face hostility on all fronts—from the great powers, from the Arab states, and from Israel, which, though small, is an advanced, fundamentally Western society, with a high technological level and, in Middle Eastern terms, tremendous military power. Recall the terrific beating that Egypt was taking prior to the cease-fire of 1970—the cities along the Suez Canal almost totally destroyed by bombardment, perhaps 500 men killed per week along the canal in the two months preceding the cease-fire. In contrast, the Israeli government reports 181 Israeli soldiers killed on all fronts (most on the Suez Canal front) during the year 1970 (Reuters, *New York Times*, January 4, 1971). The comparison gives some indication of the relative military strength at the moment.

Military writers in the Israeli press regularly emphasize the great Israeli military advantage. For example, Reserve General Mattityahu Peled (generally described as a dove) writes in *Maariv* (January 29, 1971) that in the event of a breakdown of the cease-fire, Israel should cross the canal, destroy the Egyptian armies between the canal and the Nile, and drive the Russian fleet from Port Said and Alexandria. "There is no doubt," he writes, that Israeli forces "will succeed from a military point of view" in these actions. (The United States, of course, would have to intervene to prevent an all-out Russian response with strategic weapons.) In *Ha'aretz* (February 4, 1971), B. Amidror explains (under the heading "the Egyptians do not understand that they have ceased to be an independent and serious military power") that strategic bombing can destroy the Aswan Dam, causing catastrophic flooding in the settled areas of Egypt. Quite generally, Israeli experts appear to be very confident of their substantial and growing military advantage over the Arab states. (The guerrillas they describe as at worst a nuisance, from a military standpoint.) As the Israelis see it, the "economic balance" too is developing in their favor, just as the "strategic balance" is. In *Israelis Reply* (March 1970), a bulletin published by Israeli students of Middle East affairs, it is reported that the Israeli GNP will reach that of Egypt in 1971 (Israeli GNP per capita is more than ten times as great) and will rapidly pull ahead, if current tendencies continue.

The situation might alter, but at present Israel appears to be in a strong position. It is difficult to see how its position would be weakened or threatened if it were to recognize, unequivocally, the national rights of the Palestinians; or to permit free political action in the occupied territories—which would entail permitting political, though not military, support for Palestinian guerrilla organizations; or to pursue plans such as those apparently suggested by Dayan and in some form reiterated by Sadat regarding the Suez Canal; or to make explicit commitments concerning withdrawal from the occupied territories, which might be demilitarized in some fashion. Though there are no "riskless policies"—including present policies—it might be argued that such moves would be realistic, from the point of view of perceived security interests, as well as just.

One might imagine a resolution of the fundamental issue—the conflict between Israeli Jews and Palestinian Arabs—that would accord, more or less, with the principle I cited earlier; perhaps a federation of predominantly Jewish and predominantly Arab areas, each preserving national institutions and retaining a high degree of self-government, but moving step-by-step toward closer integration, with parity between the two national communities, if conditions and the growth of mutual trust permit. However, I will not go on to speculate about such possibilities, because they seem to me remote. A rather different outcome seems to be taking shape, for the near future at least, based on a number of important factors.

The first is the Israeli military and technological predominance, already noted, which appears to be considerable and growing. To cite some additional facts, the Israeli aeronautical industry has been growing at greater than 30 percent a year since 1967, and projections are the same for 1971. The general manager of the aeronautical industry expects the industry to do quite well in international sales. Production includes aircraft as well as Gabriel rockets and other electronic systems. (*Davar*, December 28, 1970: TADMIT Newsletter, January 1, 1971.) CIA chief Richard Helms is reported to have informed Congress that Israel has achieved the capacity to manufacture and deliver nuclear weapons (*New York Times*, July 18, 1970). According to the same report, Israel has received two-stage solid-fuel missiles from France that are capable of carrying nuclear warheads and are presumed to be intended for this purpose; and Israel is reported to be manufacturing solid propellants and engines for such missiles and perhaps mobile erector platforms for them along with test facilities. The French MD-660 missiles are reported to be guided missiles with a range of 280 miles (cf. John Cooley, *Christian Science Monitor,* October 24, 1970). Recall that Golda Meir recently warned that the Russians were providing the Egyptians with Frog missiles—unguided missiles, with a range of thirty miles, according to press reports (*ibid.*).

In a careful analysis of the aerial power balance in *New Middle East,* May 1970, Neville Brown writes:

> The conclusion that emerges indisputably is that Israel retains a marked superiority in every class of combat aircraft and airborne weapon system. What is equally certain is that sociological and organizational factors serve to reinforce it. My own view is, however, that too much has been made of differences in "fighting spirit"; already there have been enough instances of Arab pilots joining battle against manifestly hopeless odds. But what is desperately lacking on the Arab side is the combination of administrative and technical professionalism needed to guarantee, for example, high serviceability and sortie rates.

According to Robert D. Beasley (*New Middle East,* August, 1970), the Israelis claim that the Gabriel missile —designed and produced entirely by the Israel aircraft industry—is "possibly the best sea-to-sea missile in the world." One would imagine that it can also be adapted to use as a ground-to-ground missile. Although it is alleged that Egypt has a local superiority in artillery and, of course, troop level at the Suez Canal, Israeli military experts, as noted earlier, seem to feel that this is more than compensated by other factors (unless there is direct Russian intervention, in which case an entirely new situation arises, with a potential escalation to global nuclear war).

If these reports are correct, the Israeli military advantage in offensive weaponry is even greater than previously supposed. Recall that the Israeli Phantom jets are unmatched by any other aircraft in the Middle East (outside of Iran) in their combination of range, speed, and bomb-carrying capacity, according to the information that has so far been made public. Israel is becoming a relatively advanced industrial society. It has, for the moment, a high growth rate and enormous per capita aid from abroad. One can expect that in the near future it will retain and probably increase its advantage relative to the other forces in the region.

A second important factor is that the Palestinian guerrilla movements appear to have been severely weakened, if not virtually destroyed. A report in the London *Times* (January 30, 1971), commenting on the most recent events in Jordan, states that "the guerillas are now officially out of business," having been forced to hand in their arms. The Jordanian prime minister, Wasfi at-Tal, stated over BBC that guerrillas would no longer be allowed to operate from Jordanian territory. The journal of the Fatah central committee has suspended publication as of January 27, 1971. The commander of the Palestine Liberation Army stated in an interview in Beirut that "the PLO is about to be destroyed. Its offices, establishments, and apparatus have been all but paralyzed, and its existence has been rendered only symbolic." (*Christian Science Monitor,* January 28, 1971.)

A third factor is that the Soviet Union appears to have rather limited ambitions in the Middle East, so far as can now be determined. Evidently, it wants the Suez Canal opened, and it will no doubt attempt to maintain its dominant position in Egypt, but there is no indication that it is intending to initiate or support further military action in the Middle East. Apparently, the Soviet Union has been urging for over two years that the canal be opened (*Christian Science Monitor*, October 21, 1970). Opening of the canal would not only reduce the probability of large-scale military aggression but would also presumably stop any "war of attrition" across the Canal. A Russian peace plan announced a few months ago suggests "*de jure* ending of the state of war and the establishment of the state of peace" after the first stage of withdrawal of Israeli troops, and stationing of United Nations forces on both sides of the frontier, along with Big Four or Security Council guarantees (*New York Times*, October 16, 1970). At no time has the Soviet Union supported the political demands of the guerrillas or given any concrete indication of a desire for further military conflict in the region.

Furthermore, although the United States appears to have little interest in the opening of the canal, it too has no wish for a war in the Middle East. The oil is flowing fairly well—even from Algeria, which will be supplying natural gas to the United States, it appears. Problems over oil persist, but they also involve conflicts between the West and such states as Iran, which have been pretty firmly within the Western orbit.

An additional factor of importance is that Israel is gradually carrying out some settlement in the occupied areas. Again, the details are unclear, but I think a pattern is emerging. Here are a few recent examples. I mentioned the settlement plans near Hebron. According to *Davar* (December 24, 1970), Welfare Minister Michael Chazani told Hebron settlers that they will be citizens of Israel. He was presented with a list of industrial projects that private entrepreneurs want to establish in Hebron. (TADMIT Newsletter, January 1, 1971).

On January 5, 1971, the *New York Times* published a Reuters dispatch reporting the first Israeli civilian agricultural settlement in the Sinai desert, between Rafah and El Arish, noting that there are already several para-military villages in the Sinai.

Peter Grose reports (*New York Times*, January 12, 1971) that the Israeli government seems to be moving to make the Jerusalem area predominantly Jewish, so that—critics claim—"any return of conquered territory around Jerusalem . . . would be a practical and a human impossibility." He reports that in northern Jerusalem a new Jewish town of 40,000–50,000 residents is being proposed and cites reports that large Israeli housing projects are under way throughout the area.

John Cooley, in the *Christian Science Monitor*, December 24, 1970, reports that some 4,000 acres of Arab land were expropriated in 1970 within the new and greatly expanded city limits of Jerusalem. Israel plans to double the Jewish population of 200,000 within five years. A new housing project in the Ramat Eshkol area, on 150 acres of seized Arab land, is to include 2,500 housing units, 150 to be allotted to Arabs, according to the Israeli housing minister.

In the Golan Heights area, little of the former Arab population remains, apart from the Druze. There have been reports of new Israeli settlements in the area. I have seen no published confirmation.[2]

What these and other reports suggest is a pattern of slow settlement in the occupied areas that will continue, if the status quo persists. Israel may well try to preserve the status quo and the cease-fire, which are to its short-term advantage. It may accept some token withdrawals and perhaps permit some form of home rule in the West Bank, but it is difficult to foresee any other developments, in the near future at least.

This could be a reasonably stable situation for the near future. How attractive it is depends on one's point of view. It is hardly in doubt that the Arab population will remain second-class citizens in a Jewish state, or in protectorates on its borders, perhaps in parts of the West Bank. This second-class status need not be a matter of law; it may be enforced by administrative decree and local practice. As in the case of American ethnic minorities, it is often not easy to spell out or identify the precise mechanisms by which discriminatory arrangements are preserved. It is frequently claimed—I am in no position to verify or refute these claims—that Jewish urban areas are kept largely free of Arab settlement by the application of laws that require permits for transferring one's residence.

The pattern of land expropriation and resettlement has undoubtedly led to substantial Jewish settlement in formerly Arab areas as the Jewish population has rapidly increased. Lower levels of the military administration over the Arab population were dismantled in 1966 (the military governors retain their authority), but again, it is an open question what that has meant in practice. There are reports that the civilian police administration in effect took over the tasks formerly carried out by the military and that practices were not modified in any significant fashion. I have been able to find very little specific information on this subject. There appear to be only dim prospects for first-class citizenship for the Arab population of Israel. I very much hope that my skepticism about this matter will be proven wrong.

If Israeli control, direct or indirect, extends over 1 million Palestinian Arabs, as appears not unlikely at the moment, then obviously the seeds exist for future troubles, quite apart from the partially unpredictable flux of international politics or the changes that might occur in the surrounding Arab states. What is now happening in Gaza might be a forewarning. The details are still unclear, but it appears that there is a good deal of violence, much of it among Arabs, and harsh repression by the Israeli Border Police. Perhaps Israel will succeed—as it would of course prefer—to institute a liberal occupation policy and create tolerable material conditions for its Arab population. Conceivably, there will be substantial withdrawal and some degree of autonomy for the presently occupied areas, with the establishment of a Palestinian state of some sort. Personally, as I mentioned earlier, I believe that a more desirable outcome might be imagined, but, increasingly, I doubt that it can be achieved.

II

The tendencies noted in the preceding remarks have become more pronounced in the sixteen months that have passed since they were formulated. The Palestinian movements have been crushed. Israeli economic and technological superiority is increasingly evident, as is the Israeli preponderance in offensive military capability.[3]

Steps toward integration of the "administered areas" with Israel are proceeding. At one level, the integration is economic, as Israel increasingly comes to rely on Arab workers in construction and other branches of manual labor. At another level, settlement in these areas is creating the facts of the future. A likely future will see some form of Israeli control over the presently occupied areas, with a scattering of Jewish paramilitary and civilian settlement in the West Bank; a greatly expanded Jerusalem and probably some new Jewish towns; denser settlement in the Gaza strip; only Jewish and Druze settlement in the Golan Heights, now virtually free of other Arabs; and permanent occupation of Sharm al-Sheikh and the communications links to it and very probably much or all of the Sinai peninsula. Very likely, some degree of home rule will be permitted in the West Bank, and perhaps Egypt will be offered the right to carry out civilian administration in parts of the Sinai peninsula, as long as Israeli military control is maintained. These appear to be quite plausible prospects for the foreseeable future.

If Israel succeeds in integrating the "Oriental" Jews successfully into the society now dominated by European (and American) settlers and their descendants, there will be three classes of individuals within the areas that remain under *de facto* Israeli control: Jews, Israeli Arabs, and other Arabs. The Israeli Arabs will be second-class citizens in a Jewish state. The remainder of the Arab population will be effectively deprived of political rights beyond the local level. It is possible that with relative peace and continued economic growth, the treatment of the second- and third-class strata of the society will be fairly decent and that their level of consumption may increase. However, as observers who are by no means unsympathetic to Israel have pointed out: "There is little doubt that this Palestinian minority will become, in the long run, a reservoir of over one million human time-bombs, already ticking away, already becoming a living promise of tears, blood and explosions"; "the Israelis, too, will discover that men who have been deprived of honour and dignity cannot be trusted for ever not to attempt to regain them." [4]

Responding to the Hussein plan for a Jordanian federation on March 15, 1972, Premier Golda Meir stated that

> Israel will continue to pursue her enlightened policy in Judea and Samaria and will maintain the policy of open bridges. She will continue to look after the provision of services to the inhabitants of Judea and Samaria, and will respect every peaceful and law-abiding citizen.

The Israeli Parliament added: "The Knesset has determined that the historic right of the Jewish people to the Land of Israel [understood as including the West Bank] is beyond challenge" (cf. *New Middle East,* May 1972). This declaration is the first official statement to that effect. Strictly speaking, it does not imply that the occupied territories are to be permanently retained; some who speak of the "historic rights of the Jewish people" nevertheless add that these "rights," from two millennia ago, should not be enforced. Taken in context, however, the declaration strongly suggests the intention to stand by these "historic rights." And it has been so understood by knowledgeable and sympathetic correspondents. Walter Schwarz writes:

> In reality, the Israeli statements mean exactly what they say. The Israelis have raised their sights. It is no new phenomenon. Zionism began without insisting on a state at all. At every stage, Arab intransigence has created new situations, invited new claims, and opened up new horizons. All the while, genuine fears for security have been insidiously mixed up with dreams of a bigger country, embracing more, if not all, of the historical borders of ancient Israel.[5]

It is difficult to see in Hussein's proposal, whatever its defects may be, a further sign of "Arab intransigence" which "invites new claims." It would, I think, be more reasonable to interpret the Israeli response as an indication of the intention, perhaps not yet fully conscious or explicit, to maintain Israeli control over "Judea and Samaria." There is no doubt that this response constituted a hardening of the Israeli position with regard to the West Bank. Minister Israel Galili, Premier Meir's political adviser who directs policy on settlement in the administered areas, stated on television that the River Jordan should become Israel's "agreed border—a frontier, not

just a security border." The Allon Plan, hitherto the minimal Israeli position, employed the term "security border"
in referring to the Jordan River, suggesting the possibility of semiindependence for the West Bank. Mrs. Meir
added: "We do not agree that between Israel and Jordan
there should be a Palestinian state." Such a state "could
have only one simple purpose and that is to be a state
which will press against Israel to 'liberate' the Palestinian homeland for the Palestinian people—that is, to
throw the Israelis into the sea."

Given the actual balance of forces, the comment can
only be reasonably interpreted as signifying a refusal to
contemplate any form of independence for a "Palestinian
entity." She went on to say that Israel would "certainly
not encourage any organization or any voice which will
say the West Bank is a separate Palestinian state, because our policy is against it." [6] The phrase "not encourage" is something of a euphemism. With some justice,
the liberal Israeli commentator Amnon Rubinstein sees
in the Israeli government declaration the "increasing influence of the Herut movement [the 'nationalist, anti-
Arab, and extremist religious' right wing of Israeli
politics] over the labor party." [7] This is an important
matter, to which I will briefly return.

Whatever the conscious intentions of the Knesset may
have been in announcing the historic rights of the Jewish
people to the full Land of Israel, some form of indefinite
Israeli occupation is implicit in the dynamics of the post-
1967 situation. A headline in the journal *Maariv* stated
that " 'General Time' is working for the benefit of Israel
in Judea and Samaria" (December 31, 1970). The article
quotes Sheikh Muhammad Ali al-Jaabari who points out
that "as the months pass, Israeli rule will be consolidated
in these territories." In a speech that aroused some controversy, Defense Minister Dayan, by no means an ex-

tremist within the framework of Israeli political life, suggested that Israel should regard itself as the "permanent government" (*memshelet keva*) in the occupied territories. A criticism from the right in the journal of the National Religious Party questioned the public statement of such views, suggesting rather that "whatever has to be done can be implemented without an explicit statement which could be viewed by the world as a proposal for official annexation." [8]

Left-liberal Israeli commentators have pointed out that the consequences of maintaining the present borders are "becoming either a binational state or another Rhodesia." [9] Rejecting these prospects, many have called for withdrawal from the occupied territories and a clear policy of support for United Nations Resolution 242. One may sympathize with them and respect their motives, but in fact, their program is unrealistic. Unless great power pressure is employed—an unlikely as well as ugly prospect—the argument against withdrawal will always be persuasive within Israel. The Arabs, it will be urged, cannot be trusted; security can only be guaranteed through force; we can rely only on ourselves; genocide awaits if we relax our guard. Stability will always seem preferable to the risks of tentative accommodation and compromise. No military force in the region can compel withdrawal or raise the costs of occupation to a significant level, and the great powers have no interest in imposing an alternative solution by force. "General Time" will take care of the longer run.

Under these circumstances, integration of the occupied territories will appear to many to be the humane course, as suggested by Mrs. Meir's remarks, quoted above. After all, the Arabs must exist within some organized structure, and their standard of living may well rise under Israeli administration. Dissidents will be expelled or silenced. Collaborators will be found for local administration. Settlement will proceed in accordance with the long-standing policy of "dunam after dunam," a policy that had progressive content under the British occupation in opposition to the reactionary forces of political Zionism, and that is now second nature to the leaders of Israeli society whose point of view was formed in that period. As General Dayan explained:

> We must devise a pattern of living and of situations which can be tolerated by the Arabs. By this I do not mean arrangements which are to their liking, but those they can live with, if they so wish.[10]

If they do not so wish, they can emigrate, with official blessings. Israel has the capability to develop a program of this sort, and there is every reason to expect that it will continue to receive public support.

Public opinion polls reinforce this natural expectation. The Jerusalem *Post* reported on January 8, 1970, that 41.5 percent of the population believe Israel should integrate the occupied territories into Israel and 86.4 percent favor widespread settlement throughout the areas,[11] surely the prelude to further integration, in the real world. A year ago, the Israpol public opinion survey reported the following response to the question, "What territories should Israel be ready to relinquish in exchange for a peace settlement with the Arab countries?": Sinai—48 percent; Judea and Samaria—21 percent; the Gaza strip—17 percent; Sharm al-Sheikh—3 percent; the Golan Heights—2 percent; Jerusalem—0.6 percent; no territory whatsoever—30 percent.[12] A more recent poll indicates that 31 percent of the population want to retain the whole of Sinai, 56 percent the whole West Bank, 73 percent Gaza, 91 percent Sharm al-Sheikh, and 92 percent the Golan Heights.[13] Surely it is reasonable to expect that these attitudes will harden, if explicit decisions have to be made.

At the time of the Six-Day War in June 1967, I personally believed that the threat of genocide was real and reacted with virtually uncritical support for Israel at what appeared to be a desperate moment. In retrospect, it seems that this assessment of the facts was dubious at best. Some Israeli military experts take a very different view. Reserve General Mattityahu Peled, a member of the Israeli general staff during the Six-Day War, wrote recently that Israel has, in his view, been in no real military danger from Arab attack since 1948 and that there was no threat of destruction in 1967; rather, Israeli forces greatly outnumbered the Egyptians in the Sinai, not to speak of the technological balance.[14] By now it is clear that the potential dangers to Israel, in the short run at least, are not military. They are real, but they lie elsewhere.

One continuing danger, recently emphasized by the brutal massacre at the Lod airport, is that of terror, a weapon of the weak and the desperate which may continue to plague Israeli life. But there are other dangers, more subtle, but no less real, and disturbing to liberal Israelis. Professor Yehoshua Arieli, at the convention of the Movement for Peace and Security in February 1972, warned that current trends would lead to increased dependence on the United States, the consolidation of a "vested interest" of war profiteers, reliance on Arabs for unskilled manual labor, the deterioration of the democratic structure of the country: "If the status quo continues, the internal situation is likely to veer sharply toward nonhomogeneity, nonidentification with the goals of the Jewish State [meaning internal democracy, social justice, and the fundamental values of independent Jewish labor], a lower intellectual level, internal disunity, and fragmentation." [15]

Events in the Gaza region, mentioned briefly at the end of section I, illustrate a continuing danger, not military, but moral. To update these remarks, in recent months it has been reported that families of wanted terrorists from the Gaza strip have been held for a year at a desert camp and permitted to return home only when the hunted man is killed or captured.[16] In the Gaza area, thousands of acres have been fenced off by the Israeli army and thousands of Bedouins evacuated, their wells blocked to prevent return, and some homes and cultivated areas destroyed. The intention appears to be to "dissect the strip," to establish Israeli settlements, urban and rural, paramilitary and civilian, and a new Israeli port town. According to an estimate in the journal of the Labor Party, about one-third of the Gaza strip is to become "state land" (*Davar,* March 20, 1972). The expulsion of the Bedouins was revealed by members of neighboring Mapam Kibbutzim in violation of military censorship, setting off public protests by Israeli peace groups.[17]

Protests may continue, but new facts are being created, in accord with the declaration of Minister Galili in 1969: "It can be said with absolute certainty that the Gaza strip will not be separated from the State of Israel again." [18] Peter Grose reports (see note 17) that the Gaza strip "is gradually being assimilated into Israel" with "a pattern of carrot-and-stick tactics by the occupation administration"; "economic integration with Israel is well advanced, and controversial preparations are under way for new Jewish settlements on land occupied in the 1967 Arab-Israeli war." There is an "apparent program not officially announced—to settle Jews in the rich farmlands of Gaza" and to resettle 3,000 Gaza residents yearly elsewhere in the region, he reports, quoting also a statement by Galili (March 27, 1972) that "Gaza will not again be separated from Israel."

Quite apart from the injustice of such deplorable policies as the use of families as hostages and population expulsion, the impact on Israeli society will surely be significant. In the first place, there will be protest and resistance. There are, for the first time, a number of resisters in Israeli prisons, refusing to serve in occupied areas. In the natural cycle, resistance will lead to repression. As an example, a sixteen-year-old boy, Eytan Grossfeld, has been confined for two months of psychiatric observation for participation in Black Panther demonstrations (*Ha'aretz*, January 30, 1972). It is not impossible that dissident groups within the Oriental Jewish community, such as the Black Panthers, will find some common ground with Arabs in Israel and the occupied territories, in which case Israel will have many more than "one million time bombs" to concern it. This is particularly likely if the state, devoting substantial resources to military purposes, finds itself unable to deal with pressing internal social needs. But far more serious than resistance in its implications for Israeli society would be acceptance of the Gaza pattern as the norm, as an unpleasant necessity. This would surely have a corrosive effect on Israeli democracy and social life.

Israel will have to come to terms somehow with the fact that it is a Jewish state governing a society that is in part non-Jewish. This fact, rarely faced in a serious way, has always been the Achilles' heel of political Zionism. If a state is Jewish in certain respects, then in these respects it is not democratic. That much is obvious. If the respects are marginal and merely symbolic—the color of the flag, the timing of state holidays, and the like—the departure from democratic principle is not serious. If the respects are significant, the problem is correspondingly severe. The problems of achieving democratic goals in a multinational or multiethnic society are not trivial ones. It is pointless to pretend that they do not exist.

It has frequently been suggested that the Jewish state is to be Jewish only in the sense that France is French or England is English. This is patently impossible, however. An immigrant who receives French citizenship is French. If there is some form of institutional discrimination against him, if he is not "truly French" in the eyes of the law or administrative practice, this will be regarded as a departure from the democratic ideal. A citizen of the Jewish state, however, does not become Jewish. This is a matter of principle, not a departure from some ideal norm toward which the society strives. Since it is a matter of principle within a Jewish state, there will be no remedy through slow progress.

The respects in which Israel is a Jewish state are not trivial or merely symbolic, and there is no indication that this situation will change. A non-Jewish citizen suffers various forms of discrimination. He is not permitted to lease or work on state lands or lands owned "in the name of the Jewish people." He is not able to reside in all-Jewish cities, such as Karmiel, built on lands confiscated from Israeli Arabs. To mention a recent case, a Druze, formerly an officer with twenty years service in the Israeli Border Police, was denied the right even to open a business near Karmiel by decision of the Israel Land Authority (*Yediot Ahronot,* February 8, 1971).

According to a publication of the Israeli League for Civil and Human Rights (August, 1971), there are tens of thousands of stateless Israeli Arabs, unable to satisfy the requirements of the Israeli Nationality Law; and the number is increasing, since statelessness is inherited. Arabs born to parents without citizenship, who may not even be aware of this fact until they apply for passports or other documents, do not acquire Israeli citizenship by virtue of the fact that they are born in Israel, in villages where their families may have lived for generations. Arabs do not receive benefits from laws that remunerate families of members of the Israeli armed forces, i.e., virtually all Jewish families and, apart from the Druze, no others. In myriad ways, Arabs will not enjoy the full rights of citizenship. It is for such reasons as these that left-wing elements in the Zionist movement were always wary about the idea of a Jewish state, which did not, in fact, become official Zionist policy until 1942, at the time of the destruction of European Jewry by Nazi terror.

The problem is not a small one, no matter what the size of the Arab population in Israel, but it takes on major dimensions when this population is very large, as it will be if the tendencies noted earlier persist. The High Court of Israel has recently ruled that "there is no Israeli nation apart from the Jewish people, and the Jewish people consists not only of the people residing in Israel but also of the Jews in the Diaspora." The Court so ruled in rejecting the contention of Professor George Tamarin that Israel is separate from the Jewish people, and thus denied his appeal to change the designation "Jew" in his identity card to "Israeli." [19] The ruling no doubt expresses the implicit content of political Zionism. It also reveals that the legal structure of the state, as well as its customary social practices, will be inherently discriminatory. Liberal Americans oppose laws that discriminate against blacks, and would be appalled if New York City should adopt an urban development program to preserve the "white character" of the city. It is unclear why they should react differently when Minister Shimon Peres outlines a plan for development in Jerusalem that is to perpetuate its "Jewish character" [20] or when non-Jews are excluded from the extensive state or national lands, or even from the grant of citizenship.

The fact is that Israel is already a binational state, at least in the sense that it is a state that contains two identifiable national groups, Israeli Jews and Palestinian Arabs. Even this is misleading, in that some may choose to identify themselves differently (like Professor Tamarin), and Arabs may understand their associations in very different terms. While all of this may have seemed a secondary issue before 1967, after the Six-Day War it became a major problem. If the analysis of current trends outlined above is accurate, it is a problem that will become increasingly serious. The operative question, in my opinion, is how Israel will deal with the fact of binationalism.

One approach is to try to change the fact by Israeli withdrawal from the administered territories. As I have mentioned, left-liberal forces in Israel have urged such a policy. I think that they are justified, and should be encouraged in this effort. Though it would not, in my personal opinion, be the optimal solution, it might still be a tolerable one, and for Israelis who actually take part in the internal debate, it is a proper position to uphold. Nevertheless, it seems to me futile, for reasons already mentioned. If I may interpolate a personal note, shortly after the Six-Day War I became convinced, for the reasons cited, that the fact of binationalism was unalterable in the short run at least, that Israeli withdrawal from the occupied territories was a highly unlikely prospect. I have expressed this view since in personal communication with Israeli friends (very few of whom agree), and in public lectures and articles. It now seems to me increasingly apparent that this assessment was correct and that the expectation of Israeli withdrawal and establishment of an independent Palestinian entity of some sort is

illusory. If so, the first approach to the fact of binationalism is not a feasible one.

A second approach is the South African or Rhodesian
model, not necessarily with the brutality or viciousness
of the white racists of Africa, but with a similar institutional structure. Surely this is an intolerable outcome,
though it is far from obvious that it is not a likely outcome. General Dayan, in a recent television interview,
stated:

> First we must be in a position to control the entire West
> Bank absolutely from a military point of view, should
> the need arise. . . . Second, the West Bank is not a
> "bank" but Judea and Samaria, which must be open to
> Jewish settlement. Any agreement must be such that
> allows Jewish settlement everywhere. Third, what is
> needed is an entirely different, much closer tie between
> Israel and the West Bank, if the West Bank areas do
> not remain in our possession. I say "if" for I do not
> think it likely that we'll have to part with them.

Commenting, Israeli journalist Victor Cygielman observes that under this plan, the West Bank would be "a
sort of Israeli protectorate, a reservoir of cheap labor for
the Israeli economy, and a market for Israeli industrial
goods." [21] While Dayan added that "all citizens of Israel,
including Arabs, must be equal citizens," this remains,
in fact, a virtual impossibility in a Jewish state. Dayan,
in the past, has been realistic in his commentary, and
there is no reason not to take his remarks quite seriously.

A third approach would be "population exchange,"
which means, in effect, expulsion of much of the Arab
population. As noted in section I, this has been seriously
suggested. In the article cited above in *Davar*, Yosef
Weitz wrote that the "demographic problem" is the most
serious problem faced by the state, since the "territorial
victory" in the Six-Day War did not lead to the flight of

most of the Arab population. He recalls that many years earlier he had concluded that it would be necessary to transfer all Arabs from the area west of the Jordan ("at least"). Rethinking the matter after the Six-Day War, he observes that a substantial Arab population "is likely to destroy the foundations of our state," a judgment which may well be accurate. Weitz does not go on to consider the implications of his analysis, under the condition of permanent Israeli occupation of the West Bank. It is difficult for me to believe that Israeli public opinion would accept what appears to be the natural conclusion, that the Arab population must, under these conditions, be removed.

A fourth possible approach is the American "melting pot" model. But this is inconsistent with Zionist ideology, and will almost surely not be acceptable within Israel. Mayor Teddy Kollek of Jerusalem has stated that "we have no intention of creating a melting pot for Arabs and Jews along American lines." But he adds, quite properly, that "if, in a few years, the educational and social gaps between Jews and Arabs in Jerusalem do not disappear, some day . . . there will be an explosion." [22] He then goes on to explain that "this year we are building 6,000 dwellings for Jews" and "only 100 housing units for Arabs"—although he would prefer to see 300. He does not go on to comment that the disparity revealed is not a mistake or an oversight, but is rather inherent in the concept of a Jewish state with non-Jewish residents. Furthermore, even in the unlikely event that social, educational, and economic gaps disappear, the "gaps" in political rights are in principle insurmountable, given the legal doctrine that "there is no Israeli nation apart from the Jewish people," which includes the Jews of Israel and the Diaspora.

A fifth approach is the federal model, for example,

along Yugoslav lines, with federated republics, each dominated by one national group, and efforts, one would hope, to achieve social, economic, and political parity. With all of its problems, this approach has possibilities. The inevitable discrimination in a multinational society in which one group dominates might be relieved through the federal structure. One might imagine that a regionally based federation might gradually evolve toward closer linkages, if forms of association along other than national lines prove to be meaningful and firm. A federal approach would imply that in the short run, at least, Palestinian Arabs who wish to return to their former homes within the Jewish-dominated region would have to abandon their hopes; and, correspondingly, that Jews who wish to settle in the Arab-dominated region would be unable to do so. Personally, I feel that among those policies that are at all realistic, given present circumstances, some kind of federal solution is the most desirable.

Other possibilities may be envisioned: for example, parallel national institutions throughout the whole territory with a free option for each individual; and also the option of dissociation from national institutions with retention of full rights of citizenship for those who prefer. I will not sketch out details, though it might be a useful exercise, because it is, for the present, purely an academic exercise. Before such questions can even be faced, it is necessary to come to terms first with certain overriding realities: Israel is a binational society; the concept of a "democratic Jewish state" with non-Jews as citizens (or residents in "administered areas") is inherently flawed.

There is, to be sure, still another approach to these problems: to bury one's head in the sand and pretend that they do not exist. Unfortunately, this approach is characteristic of many Americans who regard themselves as supporters of Israel. Whether or not they are supporting Israel in a meaningful way by adopting this attitude is another question. One of the few articles that even attempts to deal with these problems, by political scientist Michael Walzer,[23] can serve as an illustration. Walzer blandly asserts that "if one could draw the line between an Arab and a Jewish entity, few people would object to making it a dotted line and compromising in small or even in significant ways the absolute independence of the two political systems" in a federal arrangement.

It is, however, quite untrue that "few people would object." As noted earlier, many Israelis object to abandonment of Israeli control over any significant part of the occupied territories, and the Israeli political leadership explicitly rules out any notion of a Palestinian state. To my knowledge, support for compromising Israeli independence is virtually nonexistent in Israel. Of course, it is true that "few people would object" to a dotted line on the Jordan and the Nile (or perhaps even through the mid-Sinai) with no compromise of absolute political independence, but that would leave the essential problem of a Jewish state with a million Arabs unresolved. As to this problem, Walzer has nothing to say, except that the problems can be "smoothed by helping people to leave who have to leave." He considers it sufficient to deride those who "disdain Jewish aspirations to statehood or suggest that Jews (especially) should seek nobler ends" and asserts that "to respond to such people . . . no elaborate argument is necessary."

In Walzer's view, "a democratic secular state called Israel . . . already exists in substance (despite the power of Orthodox Jews)," and he criticizes contemporary advocates of binationalism, who "deny the existence of a *nation* of Jews capable, as Greeks, Poles, and Germans are capable, of rescuing and rehabilitating their fellow nationals." Again, the fallacious argument that Israel will be Jewish only in the sense that France is French. Since he makes no explicit references, it is unclear whose views he has in mind in these comments. But it is evident that he is simply missing the point. Even if the power of Orthodox Jews were to diminish to zero, the real problems of a Jewish state with a non-Jewish minority would not disappear, and it would not in any meaningful sense be a democratic secular state, for obvious reasons already noted.

These problems are serious enough to require an "elaborate argument." They have nothing to do with "disdaining Jewish aspirations" or suggesting that Jews "seek nobler ends," and they are raised precisely by people who recognize the validity of Jewish national goals and associations. Vague and misleading references, in the currently fashionable mode, to "upper-class radicals who are impatient with working-class materialism" also contribute nothing to solving the real problems which Walzer merely evades.

It is, I think, important that some Israelis are seriously facing the facts. After participating in a protest, which he helped to organize, against the expulsions in the Gaza region, Amos Kenan wrote that if, as maximalist groups argue, "one who believes that he has no right to Gaza must also doubt his right to Tel Aviv," then he, Amos Kenan, will "begin to doubt if indeed I have a right to Tel Aviv—at least to Tel Aviv as it now is: a Jewish city, in a Jewish state with a million Arabs deprived of rights" (*Ha'aretz*, April 18, 1972). "Today," he writes, "we are not living in a Jewish state, but in a binational state." The old Israel came to an end in June 1967, and "a colonialist Israel," which he finds "ugly," was born at that time. The "dynamics of Israel 1972 has already left behind it the protestors of the past," those who called for withdrawal. Presently, the state of Israel rules over a million non-Jews who lack the rights of equal citizens and who now "furnish Israel with cheap labor, without which its high standard of living cannot be preserved." These are the bitter comments of a person who has struggled courageously to prevent the permanent occupation that is now taking shape, with its inevitable consequences for a "democratic Jewish state."

I noted earlier Amnon Rubinstein's observations on the increasing influence of Herut on the Labor Party. He adds that Menahem Beigin is correct in claiming that the Government declaration on the "historic right" of the Jewish people to the Land of Israel is an expression of the traditional point of view of the Herut movement and its Revisionist predecessors:

> In fact we observe here a strange process, in which the influence of Herut is growing without any relation to an increase in its electoral strength. This increase strengthens the significance of the Herut movement and the point of view that prevails in it.

The process that Rubinstein describes has historical roots. The Revisionists were forced out of the Zionist movement because of their advocacy of a Jewish state, but their position was officially adopted, years later, in the wake of the holocaust. In both cases, one can point to external factors that led to the growing influence of right-wing nationalist views, though I believe that the present example is far less justifiable than the decision of the 1940s, understandable at the time, to adopt the program of a Jewish state.

Throughout the history of Zionism, there has been a certain tension between radically opposed conceptions, one socialist and "universalist," the other nationalist and exclusive. On the one hand, the Jewish settlement (Yishuv) in Palestine, later Israel, developed the most advanced democratic socialist institutions that exist anywhere, institutions that might be described—without exaggeration, in my opinion—as a model in microcosm for decent human survival. These represent the positive side of a revolutionary development that combined socialism and nationalism.

At the same time, the Zionist movement incorporated expressions of the value of national identification and racial purity that I, at least, find quite objectionable. To cite one case, Joachim Prinz wrote in 1934 [24] that the "German revolution" signifies the end of the liberal era and the decline of parliamentary democracy: "The development from the *unity of man* of the Enlightenment to the *unity of nation* of the present contains within itself the principle of the development from the concept of mankind to the concept of the nation," a development that he appears to regard favorably and which, he states, places the "Jewish question" in a new light. In place of assimilation, natural in the era of liberalism, he proposes the principle of "recognition of the Jewish nation and the Jewish race." "A state which is built upon the principle of the purity of nation and race can have esteem and respect for the Jews only when they identify themselves in the same manner." Jews must therefore identify themselves as people "of one nation and one race."

Putting aside the fact that an emphasis on Jewish nationhood and racial purity would hardly have been likely to awaken respect among the Nazi gangsters, there are unpleasant overtones in these remarks. The Zionist opposition to assimilationist tendencies was, in my opinion, justifiable, but not if it leads to an emphasis on the profound significance of purity of nation and race. Even if it were accurate to claim that the enlightenment view of human unity is disintegrating, I cannot accept the view that this process of disintegration is to be regarded with favor (nor is the "enlightenment view" incompatible with forms of social organization that permit those who wish to retain ties of national identification). Embodied in the political institutions of a Jewish state, concepts of purity of nation and race can prove quite ugly. The legal debate in Israel over "who is a Jew" is an example, in my opinion.[25]

The point is that the tension among competing elements in the Zionist tradition remains unresolved, and has become a matter of fundamental importance under the conditions that now exist in Israel. The problems, of course, can only be faced and dealt with by those who are on the scene. Sympathetic outsiders might be able to be helpful, if it becomes possible to create an intellectual and emotional climate in which rational discourse on the topic is possible.

In the United States, at least, this has hardly been the case. Since the Six-Day War, critics of one or another aspect of Israeli policy have been subjected to ridiculous accusations and childish distortion. They have been portrayed as supporters of terrorism or even genocide, or as opponents of democracy. They are asked why they do not denounce Iraqi and Syrian oppression and atrocities, surely quite real, and are told that only those who prove their good faith by "support of Israel" are permitted to criticize the policies of the state. A generation ago, left-wing critics of the Soviet Union were told that only true supporters of the "revolution" had the right to criticize the Soviet regime and society, and they were asked, "What about the lynchings in the South?" With such defenders as these, Israel hardly needs enemies.

Examples are many. It is, for example, common to

identify binationalism with the PLO position in support of a "democratic secular state." [26] This is a gross error. The PLO (Fatah in particular) has always opposed binationalism in quite explicit terms. This kind of confusion contributes to the unfortunate tendency to identify any critical discussion of current Israeli policy, and any speculation about alternative political arrangements in the Middle East, as "support for terrorism." In chapter 5, I will return to many other examples. In many cases, problems of Israel and the Middle East are incidental to domestic political issues and are cynically exploited as a device for undermining the peace movement and the New Left.

The problems of the Middle East are serious enough in themselves. It is quite improper to infuse them into internal American political debate. There is extensive and quite natural sympathy for Israel within the United States. We can all agree, I presume, that it is no service to Israel or to the search for a just peace when this sympathy is exploited for personal political vendettas.

Surely it is obvious that a critical analysis of Israeli institutions and practices does not in itself imply antagonism to the people of Israel, denial of the national rights of the Jews in Israel, or lack of concern for their just aspirations and needs. The demand for equal rights for Palestinians does not imply a demand for Arab dominance in the former Palestine, or a denial of Jewish national rights. The same is true of critical analysis that questions the existence of the state institutions in their present form.

If one were to propose that the time is ripe for consideration of a South Asian federation, say, linking India, Pakistan, Bangladesh, and Kashmir, it would be appropriate to object on various grounds, but senseless to assert that the person raising this suggestion is "advocating the destruction of India," something which no person of good will can tolerate. If someone were to insist that discussion of the problems of South Asia must proceed on the assumption that "the survival of democratic India is an urgent moral-political necessity," [27] and that anyone who suggests alternative social and political arrangements has therefore removed himself from the domain of moral-political discourse, he would not be demonstrating his sympathy and concern for democracy or for the people of India and their just aspirations, but merely revealing a degree of dogmatism that is of little service to these people.

In every part of the world, there are certainly possibilities other than the system of nation-states; they have their merits and defects, which should be rationally discussed. The problems are particularly acute in multinational societies that are dominated by one national group, with the inevitable violation of democratic principle and practice that results. Neither abuse nor evasion of serious issues makes any contribution to the amelioration of problems that are stubborn and simply will not fade away.

Notes

1. In *Maariv*, July 7, 1968; cited in a publication of the Israeli Group against Oppression, Jan. 1970.
2. Added, March 1971. John Cooley reports in the *Christian Science Monitor* (March 3, 1971) that thirty-five Syrian villages were "totally demolished by the Israeli Army after its final conquest of the Golan plateau" and that "thousands of new Israeli settlers . . . have moved into the new sites," where Arab villages were formerly located. Three settlements are paramilitary, about fifteen other civilian, he reports. On March 11, Ehud Yonay reports in the *Monitor*

that the "master plan" calls for a population of 55,000–60,000 within ten years (including 10,000 Druze), in industrial and agricultural centers including seventeen cooperatives.

3. See E. Luttwak, *New Middle East.* Dec. 1971, for a useful survey.

4. Yigal Laviv, Tel Aviv, April 1972, in *Israel and Palestine*, no. 10, 5-1972, Paris; Peregrine Fellowes, *New Middle East*, May 1972.

5. *Guardian* (Manchester, London), April 3, 1972.

6. Walter Schwarz, *Guardian*, March 22, 1972.

7. "Truly something terrifying," *Ha'aretz*, March 22, 1972.

8. Jay Bushinsky, *Christian Science Monitor*, Aug. 21, 1971.

9. Michael Bruno, in I. Howe and C. Gershman, eds., *Israel, the Arabs and the Middle East*, Quadrangle-Bantam, New York, 1972.

10. Bushinsky, *op. cit.*

11. Cited in *The Arabs Under Israeli Occupation*, published by the Institute for Palestine Studies, Beirut, 1970.

12. *Yediot Ahronot*, May 23, 1971; TADMIT Newsletter, June 1, 1971.

13. David Hirst, *Manchester Guardian Weekly*, May 6, 1972.

14. "The claim that Israel was under the threat of destruction—'a bluff,'" *Ha'aretz*, March 13, 1972. General Ezer Weizmann, former head of the Israeli air force, added his agreement, stating further that the remainder of the Sinai (Port Fuad, specifically) was not conquered only through oversight; *Ha'aretz*, March 20, 1972. For futher details, see Amnon Kapeliouk, *Le Monde hebdomadaire*, June 8–14, 1972. He quotes also former army chief of staff Haim Bar-Lev in support of Peled and Weizmann, and states that "no serious argument has been advanced to refute the thesis of the three generals." The American press seems to have ignored this very important discussion within Israel, apart from a report by John K. Cooley, *Christian Science Monitor*, July 17, 1972.

15. *Yediot Ahronot*, Feb. 2, 1972; TADMIT Newsletter, Feb. 15, 1972.

16. *Ha'aretz*, Dec. 5, 1971.

17. *Ha-Olam Ha-Ze*, in TADMIT Newsletter, March 15, 1972; *Israel and Palestine*, no. 10, 5-1972; "Robbery in Rafiah." *Information Bulletin* of the Israeli Communist Party, April 1972; also same journal, March 1972, citing several Israeli journals; Simha Flapan, *New Outlook*, March–April 1972; Peter Grose, *New York Times*, April 25, 1972.

18. Cited by Amnon Rubinstein, *Ha'aretz*, July 30, 1971; TADMIT Newsletter, Aug. 1, 1971.
19. *Al-Hamishmar*, Jan. 21, 1972; TADMIT Newsletter, Feb. 1, 1972.
20. Cited from the Jewish Telegraphic Agency Daily Bulletin, May 19, 1970, in *The Arabs Under Israeli Occupation*, 1970 (see note 11).
21. *New Outlook*, March–April 1972.
22. *Maariv*, Sept. 1971; TADMIT Newsletter, Oct. 1, 1971.
23. In Howe and Gershman, eds., *op. cit.*
24. Joachim Prinz, *Wir Juden*, Berlin, 1934, pp. 150–157.
25. See B. Shefi, "Israel: the Jewish Religion Abused," *Middle East International*, Dec. 1971, for some examples cited from judicial opinions and other sources.
26. See, e.g., C. Gershman, *Commentary*, Aug. 1970.
27. From the editors' introduction to Howe and Gershman, *op. cit.*, with "Israel" replaced by "India." The problems involved in "survival of a democratic Israel" are never mentioned. It is merely asserted that "the survival of Israel is a major priority for everyone who cares about democracy." It is tacitly assumed that the only alternatives are the survival of Israel or the destruction of Israel. If correct, then the former would be a major priority for any decent person. But there are other alternatives: namely, the evolution of Israel in a way that will enable it to be a true democracy, hence not (except possibly in symbolic respects alone) a Jewish state, and a variety of possible arrangements, some mentioned earlier, in the former Mandate Palestine.

CHAPTER 4

The Fourth Round

When Syrian and Egyptian armies invaded Israeli-occupied territories on October 6, 1973, the reaction in Israel and the West was one of amazement and disbelief. The visible military preparations had been discounted, as were the extensive maneuvers, including amphibious operations, a few months earlier. The prevailing assumption was that it would be suicidal for the Arab states to provoke the Israeli juggernaut—"lunacy," as Golda Meir put it. "Action against Israel is clearly out of the question," the well-informed correspondent of the *Guardian* wrote shortly before the war broke out,[1] expressing a virtually unanimous view. General "Arik" Sharon, commander of the Southern Front and now a leading figure in the right-wing coalition Likud, informed an Israeli political meeting last July that Israel is more powerful than any European NATO force and is capable of conquering the area from Khartoum to Baghdad to Algeria within a week, if necessary.[2] When Israeli Chief of Staff David Elazar announced in his first press conference that the tide had already turned and that Israeli forces would soon "break the bones" of their enemies, few doubted the accuracy of his prediction.

Events proved otherwise. Israel reconquered the Golan Heights and moved deeper into Syria, but the Syrian army was not destroyed and conducted vigorous counterattacks until the cease-fire. Correspondents in

Syria detected no sense of urgency and wrote of "astoundingly high" morale and "relatively few" casualties, more civilian casualties than military in one Damascus clinic.[3] In Egypt, reports indicate that "the demoralization, not to say decomposition, of Egyptian society which the endless no-war no-peace situation had produced has been replaced by a true cohesion," so that now "Sadat can ask of his people sacrifices which were inconceivable before the war broke out."[4] Earlier this year, David Hirst comments, a war budget had to be withdrawn under popular pressure. No longer. The Suez battle remained a stand-off until the last days before the cease-fire, when Israeli armor succeeded in breaking through the Egyptian lines and crossing the Suez Canal. It was only after the cease-fire that Israeli troops surrounded the Egyptian III Corps, threatening a military catastrophe that led Sadat to call on the great powers to enforce the cease-fire, provoking a carefully stage-managed superpower confrontation.

Israel plainly was unable to "trample Arab faces in the mud," as its Arabic-language broadcasts promised.[5] Still less did it prove that it could conquer most of the Middle East and North Africa within a week. Rather, as one Israeli officer stated, "we have learned that given Soviet supplies to the Arabs, we cannot fight a two-front war simultaneously against the Egyptians and the Syrians"—"a very sad lesson," he added.[6] Without a massive United States military supply effort continuing without let-up after the cease-fire,[7] Israel might have been compelled to abandon parts of the occupied territories, and Israeli urban centers might have been exposed to bombardment—as Damascus and other Arab cities were—by the still intact Arab air forces. The United States government was sufficiently concerned to dispatch combat marines aboard two helicopter carriers to the Sixth Fleet.

Merely a "normal replacement," Defense Secretary Schlesinger explained as he attempted to convince the public that the world-wide alert of conventional and nuclear forces was justified by the ambiguous indications that the Russians were preparing to dispatch airborne troops.[8] To be sure, the severity of the confrontation was not great, since the world understood that it was largely contrived for domestic political purposes in the United States and that the local issue was enforcement of the cease-fire before the destruction of the trapped Egyptian forces. But American concern over the fortunes of the Israeli military was real enough.

Sadat's "Operation Spark" seems to have been a successful gamble. New forces were set in motion in the Arab world, and the United States may be impelled to reassess its policy of *de facto* support for permanent Israeli occupation of the territories gained in 1967. Earlier efforts by Egypt and other Arab states to achieve this end had failed, but it may be a result of the October fighting. Certainly, the basic assumptions of United States policy have been shaken, if not undermined. The oil producers and the great powers were compelled to involve themselves directly in the conflict. A potentially serious rift was exposed between the United States and its NATO allies. By disrupting regional stability and posing a threat to the fundamental interests of the superpowers, Egypt and Syria may have set the stage for an imposed settlement much along the lines of their earlier demands.

Israeli policy since 1967, and American support for it, have been based on the premise that Israel is a military superpower by the standards of the region and that its technological predominance will only increase. Though Sharon's bravado was excessive, his basic point was a commonplace. The Syrian minister of information observed that "America has based its Middle East policy on the assumption of overwhelming Israeli military superiority," and the leading paper of Kuwait warned that, in the light of Arab military successes, "America should realize that Israel is no longer a suitable protector" for its interests. In emphasizing that "Israel (and the United States) will never seriously consider concessions unless the Arabs show Israel is incapable of keeping the lid on the Middle East," [9] Arab commentators were offering their own version of principles expressed as well by Israeli spokesmen. Thus General Yitzhak Rabin assured his countrymen that "Americans have given us weapons . . . so that we should use them effectively when necessary," adding that the West is coming to understand that "if some medieval-type rulers really mean to endanger the oil needs of hundreds of millions of people in the civilized world, then the West is permitted to take tough steps to prevent this." [10] The implications of these —possibly prophetic—remarks seem obvious.

Confident in its power, Israel pursued the policy of gradual incorporation of the occupied territories already described.[11] With the August 1973 electoral program (the "Galili Protocols"), the dominant Labor Party took a position that implied virtual annexation of the occupied territories. It thus outflanked the rightist opposition from the right, as the liberal Israeli commentator Amnon Rubinstein noted, by adopting in effect Dayan's principle that Jews and Arabs can live together only under Israeli military occupation. According to Rubinstein, Dayan's statement to this effect had been received "with deafening applause" at the graduating ceremony of Tel Aviv University.[12] It is hardly likely that such programs can have been adopted without United States government backing.

Until October, American policy seemed a qualified suc-

cess. The major military powers in the region, Israel and
Iran, were firmly in the American camp, as were Jordan
and Saudi Arabia. In important respects, the policy of
reliance on Israel as a threat to radical nationalism represented a point of convergence of the interests of these
powers, as was clear when the Palestinians were crushed
in September 1970. Furthermore, Egypt had expelled
Russian advisers and was appealing for American support. Even during the war, final negotiations continued
with the Bechtel Corporation and Kidder Peabody Investment bankers over an oil pipeline that is to be the
biggest Egyptian undertaking since the Aswan Dam.[13]
In Egypt, the leftist opposition had been eliminated.
Syria had closed down the Palestinian radio station. A
de facto settlement favorable to American interests
seemed to be taking shape, a settlement which also coincided with domestic political needs of the Nixon administration.

It is important to bear in mind, however, that the
United States has other policy options, which it will not
hesitate to pursue if its basic interests are endangered.
It might attempt to organize reactionary Arab regimes
explicitly in an alliance that might well incorporate an
Israel compelled to abandon its 1967 territorial gains.
These were the implications of the Rogers Plan, dis-
carded in favor of tacit support for permanent Israeli
occupation. The latter policy is no law of nature, however, and the famous Jewish vote and Zionist lobby will
be no serious barrier to reversing it if circumstances so
require, just as they did not prevent Eisenhower from
forcing Israeli withdrawal from the Sinai in 1956 or the
Democratic administrations from giving twice as much
aid to Egypt as did the Soviet Union during the Five-
Year Plan of 1960–1965.[14]

The policy of supporting Israeli occupation carried

serious risks, despite its appearance of success. It was unacceptable to Syria and Egypt, and there was always a danger—now quite real—that the Saudi Arabian regime might be compelled by nationalist pressures to withdraw its tacit acquiescence and to modify its close association with the United States. The United States government is not prepared to see the world's largest petroleum reserve slip from the control of American oil companies. Sadat's military success called forth gestures of support from Saudi Arabia and the Gulf oil producers. They have already cut back production and restricted export to the United States. Taking their pronouncements at face value, Aramco profits would be seriously reduced and the East Coast of the United States faced with a severe oil shortage. The matter would be still more serious if the oil producers were to expand state control or shift allegiance to Japanese or Western European state and corporate power. There is little indication of any such moves, and if they were to take place on any significant scale, this would signal a major conflict within the capitalist world, with unpredictable consequences.

There is little doubt that the regimes of the major oil-producing states would prefer to remain in the American orbit (as, it appears, would Sadat). If the United States comes to the conclusion that the major premise of its policy is now "inoperative," it can move toward an alternative policy option, and, with Russian support, impose a settlement along the lines of United Nations Resolution 242 of November 1967. There is every reason to expect Russian cooperation. The major goal of the Soviet Union remains an international arrangement (détente), under which it is free to control its imperial domains and suppress internal dissidence while benefitting from badly needed trade and investment and adapting itself, in general, to the requirements of American global policy. If the United States moves in this direction, Israel will have no choice but to submit, abandoning the policy of creeping annexation.

To establish the validity of the premise that was the foundation of its policy and American support for it, Israel had to win a quick and decisive victory. This it failed to do. The United States might therefore conclude that "Israel is no longer a suitable protector." One can imagine an imposed solution with a return of civil control to Egypt and perhaps Syria in occupied territories and a superpower guarantee of demilitarization, and perhaps a federation of parts of the West Bank (a "Palestinian entity") with Jordan, along the lines of Hussein's proposals.[15] For the Palestinians, the most tragic victims of the endless conflict, such a solution offers little. But it has long been clear that the rights and interests of the Palestinians are the concern of none of the contestants, apart from some inconsequential rhetoric. Every organized force in the region and the great powers as well will be more than pleased if the Palestinian plea for justice is stilled.

Such an outcome, essentially of the Latin American variety, seems not too unlikely. The basic logic of the approach would be support for reaction throughout the Arab world and continued suppression of the Palestinians and other disruptive forces. What would be the effect within Israel of such a shift in American policy? Loss of the post-1967 élan would be the most likely immediate effect. Just before the Six-Day War, the outlook within Israel was not overly optimistic. There was substantial emigration and an economic recession, largely overcome since by the expansion of war-related industry and the availability of a cheap Arab labor force. Arrangements of this sort might persist even after an imposed "Rogers Plan," and it is possible that with a shift to the

right in Israeli politics, which should be welcome to the
Nixon administration, Israel could be incorporated into
an American-dominated alliance in the region as part of
a general "peace settlement."

It remains true that Israel is the most advanced technological society and the major military force in the region. Within Israel, in the short run, the hawks will
appear to have won a major political victory. But it is
hard to believe that it will last. Implicit in the Israeli
policy of gaining security through strength is the expectation of repeated military confrontations, in each of
which Israel is likely to prevail. Plainly, in the long run,
the policy is suicidal, since Israel can lose only once;
and the need to rely on a single superpower and to accept increasing international isolation is no less risky
from the standpoint of security. Recent events simply
show that "the long run" may not be so long as antici-
pated. The war was very costly and much more of a
close call than anyone expected. The isolation of Israel
and the United States was remarkable. Even Ethiopia
broke diplomatic relations with Israel. Turkey is reported to have permitted Russian overflights; Greece and
Spain refused to permit the use of bases for resupply;
and other NATO powers were so uncooperative as to call
forth a rebuke from the United States government. The
handwriting seems to be on the wall, and only the hopelessly irrational will ignore it.

There are, in fact, some indications that Israel has be-
gun to lose its advantage in technical rationality—a very
serious matter. General Sharon's comments, cited above,
are only one of many indications that have been noted
with dismay by sympathetic observers.[16] I believe that
the growing irrationality and arrogance within some circles in Israel may be traced to the problem of living with
the eternal contradiction of a "democratic Jewish state"

with non-Jewish inhabitants, and since 1967, with a sub-ject population in territories that were being gradually assimilated. Under such circumstances, it is natural that a doctrine of historic national mission will arise, accom-panied by some form of colonialist ideology and the be-lief that the natives are better off under external control, incapable of acting in any effective way on their own. The recent war may well provide a shock to any such system of belief, just as it seems to have already had the complementary effect of reviving Arab confidence.

The war leaves the three societies that were directly engaged battered and wounded. Even more than before, they are subject to the will of external powers and dom-inated by reactionary forces within. It is likely that, in the short run at least, articulate groups will be still more firmly committed to the belief that only through military strength can their minimal demands be met. The domes-tic consequences of this commitment are plain. Unless other tendencies develop or the superpowers impose a solution by force, the stage will be set for another more brutal episode with still more awesome weapons and still greater destruction. Even now, the contending states may well be better armed than before the outbreak of the conflict. Western analysts seem to agree that Israel has the capability to produce nuclear weapons; the head of the French Institute of National Defense Studies as-serts that it "certainly" possesses nuclear weapons.[17] Is-rael has long-range missiles that can carry nuclear warheads, and Sadat has claimed that Egypt possesses missiles of comparable range and probably similar char-acter. In a moment of desperation, such weapons may well be used.

Quite apart from these dangers, the constellation of forces and the prevailing tendencies offer grim prospects for the people of the former Palestine. Yet their interests are perhaps not irreconcilable, and there is, perhaps, a slender hope that they may come to realize that the pursuit of their common interests, possibly in conflict with other regional or global powers, offers the best long-term hope for survival, as well as for a settlement that will satisfy the just demands of both peoples. This can only mean a program of socialist binationalism, which might take various forms. Realists on both sides will dismiss such possibilities, insisting that nations must organize themselves in a system of competing states for the purposes of mutual destruction and oppression. People who are willing to face reality may not be so sure.

Notes

1. Anthony McDermott, *Middle East International*, Sept. 1973. United States and Israeli intelligence insisted that there was virtually no chance of an Arab attack, according to Henry Kissinger. Benjamin Welles, *Christian Science Monitor*, Oct. 29, 1973.
2. *Yediot Ahronot*, July 26, 1973.
3. John Cooley, *Christian Science Monitor*, Oct. 27, 1973.
4. David Hirst, *Guardian Weekly* (Manchester-London), Oct. 20, 1973.
5. Joseph Fitchett, *Christian Science Monitor*, Oct. 13, 1973.
6. William Tuohy, *Los Angeles Times–Boston Globe*, Oct. 26, 1973.
7. John Finney, *New York Times*, Oct. 17, 1973; Dana Adams Schmidt, *Christian Science Monitor*, Oct. 26, 1973.
8. Dana Adams Schmidt, *Christian Science Monitor*, Oct. 27, 1973. "Under questioning, Mr. Schlesinger acknowledged that the alert of the Soviet airborne forces had been ordered five or six days ago and was known by United States officials before yesterday's crisis developed" (John Finney, *New York Times*, Oct. 27, 1973).
9. Joseph Fitchett, *Christian Science Monitor*, Oct. 16, 13, 1973.
10. *Ha'aretz*, July 22, 1973.
11. Cf. chapter 3, pp. 115–16, 125; introduction, pp. 15–16.

12. *Ha'aretz*, Sept. 26, 1973. Translated in *Israleft*, no. 25, Oct. 2, 1973, P.O. Box 9013, Jerusalem.

13. Joseph Fitchett, *Christian Science Monitor*, Oct. 16, 1973.

14. Warren Young, *New Outlook*, Jan. 1970.

15. A recent version appeared in the London *Times*, Feb. 3, 1973. The text is reproduced in IDOC, *Controversy in the Middle East*, Sept. 1973. A possible general settlement of this sort is outlined by Michel Tatu, *Le Monde*, Oct. 23, 1973.

16. See the comments by Michael Brecher, Canadian specialist in Israeli foreign policy, in an interview in *New Outlook*, June 1973. He speaks of the "retreat from reason" and the "growing weight being given to mystic identities and irredentist aspirations in government decisions," the "quasi-religious roots" of the new expansionism, and the "revival of identification with mystic roots of a regenerated Jewish nation."

17. Drew Middleton, *New York Times*, Oct. 17, 1973.

CHAPTER 5

The Peace Movement and the Middle East

In November 1969, *Liberation* published a symposium on the Middle East. The editor's introduction had this to say:

> The peace movement and the American left have generally adopted a stance of pained indifference to the conflict in the Middle East. The apparent hopelessness of finding a just resolution is almost overwhelming. Moreover, many of us, without necessarily supporting the Arab or Palestinian position, have recoiled from the pro-Israeli chauvinism of the American Jewish community. The strenuous efforts by Zionist fund-raisers to picture Israel as a "free-world bastion" exploits and reinforces cold war idiocies. The celebration of the "fighting Jew" further alienates those of us who are not thrilled by Prussian efficiency.

A few months later, I was asked to discuss the topic "Israel and the New Left" at a Zionist conference.[1] I gave a fairly extensive review of "New Left" literature expressing a wide range of attitudes and concluded that there is no identifiable "New Left doctrine" on the Middle East. "Rather, there is confusion, unhappiness, some —though limited—debate, and a great deal of sympathy, often at a rather intuitive and barely articulated level, for socialist elements within the Jewish and Arab na-

tional movements, combined with a general fear that
national movements can do enormous harm if they sub-
ordinate the struggle for social reconstruction to purely
national aims." I cited the remarks just quoted from *Liberation* as accurate, to my knowledge, in expressing attitudes widely held in the peace movement and the left,
and also in pointing out that such anti-Israel feeling as
exists "is in part in reaction to the behavior of the American Jewish community . . . which has always been predominantly on the right, in the spectrum of world Zionism."

In the same symposium, other commentators drew a
very different picture of New Left doctrine on Israel.
Irving Howe wrote that "Jewish boys and girls, children
of the generation that saw Auschwitz, hate democratic
Israel and celebrate as revolutionary the Egyptian dictatorship." Taken in their context, these remarks imply
that such is "the ideology of the New Left." He gave no
examples of any celebration of the Egyptian dictatorship. In fact, he did not refer at all to the scanty New
Left literature on the subject he was discussing. Nathan
Glazer went still further: "It is clear," he asserted, "that
the New Left has an overwhelming and unbendable
tendency to support the Arabs and to oppose Israel."
Glazer presented no evidence whatsoever to support this
categorical judgment and was unperturbed when presented with substantial evidence showing that it was
false.[2]

Still more interesting was the contribution of Seymour
Martin Lipset. He contributed to the symposium a
slightly revised version of an article that had appeared
in *Encounter* (December 1969), the contents of which
I have discussed elsewhere.[3] The revisions give a particularly clear insight into just what Lipset is up to in
this study of left-wing anti-Semitism. In the original,

Lipset identified I. F. Stone and me as "older left-wing critics of Israel [who] cannot be accused of ignorance concerning the Israeli socialist movement or its radical institutions." Stone and I, according to Lipset, have

> a commitment which currently involves defining the Al Fatah terrorists as "left-wing guerrillas" and Israel as "a collaborator with imperialism," if not worse. One doubts whether even the most sophisticated presentation of Israel's case could ever regain their support.

Note the quotation marks around the phrases "left-wing guerrillas" and "a collaborator with imperialism," the implication being, presumably, that these phrases were taken from our writings. Lipset also stated that

> Chomsky, in fact, was a long-time member of Hashomer Hatzair, the left-wing Zionist youth movement, which prided itself on its Marxism-Leninism and its loyalty to communist ideals.

All of this is complete fabrication. The alleged quotations do not exist. I had discussed Fatah, not identifying it as a left-wing movement, which would be nonsensical, but pointing out that it contains left-wing elements, as, of course, it does. I had quoted Chaliand's observation that Fatah appears to be analogous to the early Kuomintang and that it might be supplanted by more revolutionary groups, as in China, if it fails (cf. chapter 1, note 26.) Neither Stone nor I have ever written anything expressing the commitment Lipset attributes to us (without reference), though it is easy enough to find explicit refutations of these views.

As for my long-time membership in an organization priding itself on its Marxism-Leninism, I was never a member of Hashomer Hatzair, precisely because I was opposed to its various Stalinist and Trotskyist tendencies. But, as Lipset knows, a little red-baiting is always helpful in a pinch.

In a letter published in *Encounter,* I pointed out these errors, and Lipset duly revised his article—in a revealing way. In the revision published in the symposium, Lipset withdrew without comment his inventions with regard to my personal background. He then reformulated the commitment that Stone and I allegedly share as follows:

> [They] are today committed supporters of the international revolutionary left. And that left currently defines the Al Fatah terrorists as "left-wing guerrillas," and Israel as "a collaborator with imperialism," if not worse. One doubts whether even the most sophisticated presentation of Israel's case could ever regain their support.

It is conceivable that the false statements that appeared in the original article were the result of carelessness. The revisions introduced in response to my letter cannot be explained in this way. Knowing that he cannot support his allegations, Lipset attempted to insinuate what he knew very well to be false. Thus, if Stone and I are committed supporters of the international revolutionary left, which defines al-Fatah as "left-wing guerrillas" and Israel as "a collaborator with imperialism," if not worse, then it will be concluded by Lipset's readers that Stone and I accept these positions of the movement to which he claims we are committed. Naturally, Lipset makes no attempt to document his false allegations.

It would be interesting to learn just what Lipset takes "the international revolutionary left" to be, or to learn how Stone and I have demonstrated our committed support for this international movement and its doctrines. But perhaps it is pointless to pursue these fantasies any further.

Irving Howe took up the cudgels again a few months

later.[4] "Anyone who keeps an eye on our intellectual life," he wrote, "must know that the turn against Israel reflects a complex of values and moods verging on the pathology of authoritarianism." Specifically, the "turn in sentiment [against Israel] among portions of our 'left' academics" results from two factors: anti-Semitism and "the growing distaste, the downright contempt, a portion of the New Left intellectuals shows towards the very idea of democracy." Those who "yearn for a charismatic-authoritarian Maximum Leader . . . will despise Israel not because of her flaws but because of her virtues," that is, because Israel offers "as good a model as we have for the democratic socialist hope of combining radical social change with political freedom." Again, no facts, no argument. If everyone "must know" these truths, then presumably it is unnecessary to establish them. Rather, in an attempt at parody, Howe explains how Israel might regain "the favor of the campus Guevarists, Trotskyists, Maoists, and Panthers who lead the assault against her." The method would be to institute a fascist dictatorship in a bloody revolution. Then, Howe writes, we would observe the following response:

> Everywhere the New Left rejoices. Brigades of youth from Scarsdale, Evanston, and Palo Alto race to Israel to help with "the planting." The *New York Review* plans a special issue. And Jean-Paul Sartre and Mme. de Beauvoir take the next plane to Israel, prepared to write a thousand pages in four weeks on *The Achievements of the Israeli Revolution* (while getting the street names of Tel Aviv wrong).

These are the kinds of slanders that one does not even bother to refute. I am quite certain that Howe knows that his insinuations are outrageously false. But he also understands very well a convention of American political discourse. When the target is activist elements of the peace movement or the left, slander and abuse are permissible, argument and evidence are superfluous. In this particular diatribe, Israel and the Middle East are really quite irrelevant, as are the facts. Howe is simply exploiting the natural and overwhelming sympathy for Israel in the United States to attack his political enemies. How convenient to have these enemies committed to the destruction of Israel and bloody, fascist revolutions, irrespective of the facts.

Howe returns to this theme in a recent lament that "intellectual prominences are silent" while Israel faces destruction.[5] "Some leaders of the Vietnam opposition, with trained capacities for public speech, have not said a word in behalf of Israel," while others denounce Israel. One might ask why, in an article that is ostensibly about Israel and its problems, there should be so much ado about "young professors and academics . . . whose minds are filled with the notions of Fanon, Guevara, and Mao" and who are "contemptuous of Israel" precisely because it is a democracy advancing toward socialism. Such people, if they exist, are politically irrelevant in the United States, as Howe very well knows—just as Lipset knows what merit there is in his claim that "the most important political event affecting Israel in Western politics in recent years has been the rise of the New Left." [6] In both cases, Israel and the Middle East are incidental to private political feuds.

It is difficult to imagine any other reason why Howe, with the familiar sneer, should bring up fund-raising parties for the Black Panthers—how much more civilized was his response when Fred Hampton and Mark Clark were assassinated by the Chicago police. And it may explain why he deplores the "self-denying tradition" among "prosperous or suburban Jews" and "some Jewish New Left students soliciting help for Al-Fatah." Wealth

. . . suburbs . . . New Left. Is the reader perhaps intended to conjure up the image of the suburban New Left, always one of Howe's favorites? Recall his earlier parody on the New Left "from Scarsdale, Evanston, and Palo Alto" rejoicing over a fascist revolution in Israel, while the democratic socialists soberly continue their work in Harlem, Gary, and Watts.

Howe writes that "to be deeply involved with the fate of Israel is no longer very chic," especially "at Elaine's in Upper Manhattan," though "Israel may be strong in the lower-middle class neighborhoods of Brooklyn and Queens." It would be interesting to see the data on which this sociological observation is based. It would be interesting to test this claim against the experience of fund raisers for Israel. I suspect that, as a statement of fact, it is about on a par with Howe's insinuation that New Leftists regard Saudi Arabia (no less) as a progressive Third World regime and that they oppose Israel precisely because of its democratic and socialist structures. The rhetoric is useful for Howe's domestic political purposes; facts can be cheerfully ignored.

The same motivation can perhaps explain why Lipset and Glazer are unperturbed when their assertions and judgments are demonstrated to be false. These judgments express a deeper truth: they provide an ideological weapon that is useful for current political battles. So much the worse for the facts.

All of this is at about the same level of intellectual integrity as Joseph Alsop's allegation that people who attack "America's will and America's power" (I am cited as the prime, though extreme, example) are virtually inviting the Russians to destroy Israel. To enliven the story, Alsop even invented a meeting in which an unofficial emissary of the Israeli government attempted to explain to me the relation between "the defense of the

United States" and "the defense of Israel." (I dismissed this out of hand as part of the Alsopian fable.) Alsop then turns to that other notorious anti-Semite, I. F. Stone, who, he claims, "hurled the first stone at Israel from the New Left,[7] in a slimy article on the Six-Day War that was closely comparable to his book on the Korean war." The reference is to an article of Stone's in the *New York Review* (August 3, 1967), in which Stone, speaking from the point of view of someone "closely bound emotionally with the birth of Israel," describes the conflict as a "tragedy," "a struggle of right against right"; expresses his faith in Israeli "zeal and intelligence" while giving no word of support to the Palestinian Arab movements; argues that "Jewry can no more turn its back on Israel than Israel on Jewry"; and urges that Israel should find "acceptance as a Jewish state in a renascent Arab civilization." Not even Alsop's imagination can construct a comparison between this article and Stone's book on the Korean War. The point, of course, is not to present a rational argument, but rather to plant a useful association: "slimy" attack on Israel, skepticism about the Korean War, assault on America's will and power. With a skillful exploitation of the general sympathy for Israel and a few well-chosen innuendos and misrepresentations, Alsop can finally end by warning Senator Jacob Javits to stop "whacking away at our own national defense."[8]

These examples illustrate a phenomenon of some generality. Left-liberal criticism of Israeli government policy since 1967 has evoked hysterical accusations and outright lies. Anyone associated with the peace movement or the American left who has opposed expansionist or exclusivist tendencies within Israel has been reviled, without documentary evidence, as a supporter of terrorism and reactionary Arab states, an opponent of democracy, an anti-Semite, or if Jewish, a traitor afflicted with self-hatred. In some instances, the explanation is transparent. Thus Joseph Alsop will apparently grasp at any straw to try to undermine opposition to the policies of militarism and intervention that he supports. Similarly, one need not search very far to explain the denunciation of Daniel Berrigan by John Roche, "intellectual in residence" at the White House in the latter part of the Johnson administration and one of the last defenders of the American war in Vietnam. As such, Roche has little affection for "that gentle Christian, Daniel Berrigan, S.J.," who, Roche alleges, "delivered himself of some of the most venomous remarks on Israel that I have seen outside of the Arab and anti-Semitic press." Particularly disturbing is the "premise" that Roche alleges is "fundamental," namely, "the premise that the Israelis have been sitting around, like Spartans, for the last 25 years conspiring to enslave the 70-odd million Arab neighbors." Roche does not reveal where Berrigan expressed this fundamental premise, but "as one Irishman to another," he informs Berrigan that his views on the Middle East "may be politely defined as ten pounds of dung in a five-pound sack." To refute Berrigan's alleged errors, Roche treats us to such historical insights as the observation that the Jews in the Arab states "had lived in virtual slavery for a millennium or more." Plainly, Berrigan has much to learn from this eminent political scientist.[9]

It is also not very difficult to explain why Abba Eban should present the following analysis of Israel's problems with the New Left:

> Let there be no mistake: The New Left is the author and the progenitor of the new anti-Semitism. One of the chief tasks of any dialogue with the Gentile world is to prove that the distinction between anti-Semitism and anti-Zionism is not a distinction at all. Anti-Zionism

is merely the new anti-Semitism . . . I do not believe
that any argument, however sophisticated, can probably
change the convictions of Noam Chomsky or of I. F.
Stone, whose basic complex is one of guilt about Jewish
survival.[10]

Naturally, Abba Eban will seek to identify anti-Zionism
and anti-Semitism. Then any criticism of the policies of
the state he represents can be dismissed at once. Resort
to this device is common enough. Lipset claims that, at a
private meeting he attended, Martin Luther King ad-
monished black students that criticism of Zionism is
simply anti-Semitism; this he found "an experience which
was at once fascinating and moving." Howe attributes
Israel's dangerous international isolation to "skillful manipulation of oil" and that "sour apothegm: *In the warm-
est of hearts there's a cold spot for the Jews.*" If this is
all there is to it, it is unnecessary to consider the impact
of Israel's policies of annexation, as many Israeli commentators do.[11] As for Eban's comments on the infamous
duo Stone-Chomsky, I doubt that he knows anything at
all of our expressed views; the rhetoric suggests that he
is simply paraphrasing Lipset, and it is possible that he
regards Lipset as a responsible scholar. But whatever
the facts, his analysis is again convenient. If criticism of
Israeli policy by Jews is simply a neurotic complex, then
it too can be dismissed with amateur psychoanalysis of
the Lipset variety, and all criticism is neutralized: Non-
Jews are anti-Semites; Jews are guilt-ridden neurotics.

Eban's remarks are of interest only because he is regarded as an Israeli dove. Perhaps it is true that Eban
represents a less militant and more conciliatory position
within the Israeli government, but it must be understood
that he is the kind of "dove" who argues, before the
Knesset, that:

To raise the question of a Palestinian identity different from the people living in Jordan would be a distortion of history and the facts. . . . Most of the Palestinians are Jordanian citizens, and most of the Jordanians are Palestinians. Moreover, the dissociation of the concepts of "Palestinians" and "Jordanians" is meaningless. . . .

The views of Eban, the dove, are indistinguishable in this respect from those of Golda Meir, who is quite sure that "there is no Palestinian people wandering in the world without knowing where to go." [12] The Labor Party insists that there is no Palestinian people and no issue of Palestinian national rights (cf. above, introduction, pp. 19–20), and it is natural therefore that Eban should try to dismiss any concern for this mythical entity.

Abuse directed against the peace movement and the left with regard to Middle East problems can easily be explained when it originates from spokesmen for the Israeli government or for American militarism. It is more interesting when the source is left-liberal American opinion, as in several of the examples I have discussed. Had there been any effort to support the remarkable allegations I have cited or any concern over the obvious falsehood of many of the charges, we would be within the domain of rational discourse over factual issues and complex problems that can be variously interpreted and understood. But this is not the case. Therefore, it is appropriate to seek some explanation.

I have already suggested a plausible one. The problems of Israel and the Middle East are incidental; the overwhelming sympathy for Israel since 1967 is simply being exploited by certain embattled liberals and "democratic socialists" in an effort to regain a position of credibility that was seriously threatened in the late 1960s by the mass popular opposition to the Vietnam war and to American militarism. This development was deeply troubling to many left-liberals, who were unwilling to associate themselves with this movement, and who lost their position as the critics of American society from the left. Their own ambiguous attitudes toward the American war in Vietnam [13] became a serious embarrassment by the late 1960s. Particularly disturbing were the developments that placed the movement against the war in opposition to state power, often in direct resistance. To deal seriously with the issues was not easy. It was much more convenient to denounce one's enemies as totalitarians, radical-chic suburbanites, anti-Semites, or backers of Arab genocide.

Furthermore, with the right in disarray over Watergate,[14] there are new opportunities for those segments of the liberal intelligentsia that naturally gravitate toward state power. I will not discuss here whether this is a good or bad thing, or what the impact on state policy is likely to be.[15] It is sufficient to remark that the prospects for a political success are quite real.

A few ingredients are missing, however. If Camelot is to be rebuilt, it will be necessary to achieve a new élan, a sense of moral purpose and legitimacy. To this end, a few adjustments in the historical record will be helpful. The war in Vietnam was a ghastly failure, and too many people think of it as the liberals' war. Thus, it will be necessary to create a new past in which everyone really abhorred and opposed the war, from the start. The Berrigan brothers, latecomers to the general cause, opposed the war in one way; and the Bundy brothers—who were not simply bent on martyrdom and self-glorification— opposed the war in their more serious and effective way. So did McNamara, the Americans for Democratic Action, and democratic socialists pondering the question whether the "value of peace" outweighs our commitment to democracy. The Jason scientists struggled against the war under their slogan "Gravel Mines for Peace." Government consultants ruminating on "forced-draft urbanization" opposed the war, along with crusading editors and liberal historians who prayed that Joseph Alsop would be right, but feared that he would not. Everyone opposed the war, although the serious efforts to bring it to an end were often impeded by the tantrums of that part of the "peace movement" that was actually visible, and confusion was sown in the minds of the guilt-ridden upper middle class by moralists who do not understand the awesome dilemmas faced by responsible leaders.

Since the intelligentsia are the custodians of history, we can anticipate that the 1960s will be reconstructed to meet the need.[16]

It is in this context, I believe, that one can understand much of the vilification of the New Left under the guise of discussion of the Middle East. In the late 1960s, I. F. Stone was a proper target for slanderous attacks; his criticism of the Vietnam war was beyond the limits of responsible opinion.[17] And in 1973, who could be a more appropriate target than Daniel Berrigan, the very symbol of resistance to the state?

As I write, there is much furor over an address that Daniel Berrigan delivered before an Arab-American audience on "sane conduct" in the Middle East, on October 19, 1973, in the last days of the fourth Arab-Israeli war.[18] It is instructive to investigate with some care the responses to Berrigan's address.

Berrigan announced himself to be no expert. He predicted that "the present course . . . leads to the same dead end for both sides" and that the local antagonists are in danger of becoming clients of the superpowers, thus losing the independence for which they have fought. He condemned both sides in harsh terms. He refused to "take sides" and urged nonviolence. He paid "tribute to the great majority of the Jewish community" in the United States who did not let "their acute and legitimate concern for Israel" become "a weapon against Vietnamese survival," thus rejecting the bait that Nixon had offered them. He stated terms that he found "reasonable" for a cease-fire: "a declaration of de facto respect [by the Arab states] for the existence of Israel, a de facto state . . . a return to the boundary lines which existed before the 1967 war, and some justice for the Palestinian people." He expressed his personal dismay that Jews, who had taught him a "vision . . . of human conduct in a human community," should resort to "the violence and repression of the great (and little) powers, a common method, a common dead end."

Predictably, these remarks provoked a storm of protest. I have yet to read protest against Berrigan's unmitigated condemnation of the Arab states for "their capacity for deception, which is remarkable even for our world . . . their contempt for their own poor . . . their willingness to oil the war machinery of the superpowers . . . their cupidity masked only by their monumental indifference to the facts of their world." Hardly a balanced analysis. The recent history of Kuwait, Syria, and Egypt, for example, is not simply a record of "contempt for their own poor." But Berrigan's rhetorical excesses in this regard passed unnoticed.[19] That is not surprising. Such characterizations are common enough in American political discourse,[20] so much so that James Wechsler could write in the *New York Post* that "in its totality, the lecture had the quality of a simplistic Arab propaganda tract delivered before a fan club."

But Berrigan's remarks about Israel evoked the usual response. He has been denounced as an anti-Semite, a Father Coughlin, a totalitarian, and so on through the familiar litany. Still, the predictability of the response does not in itself justify dismissing it as simply another outbreak of the deplorable fanaticism of the past few years. Perhaps, for once, the criticism is well taken and the charges accurate. I will not attempt to review the full range of responses to Berrigan. Rather, I will consider in some detail two of the more serious examples, which are, I think, typical and instructive both for the insight they provide into the critical reaction to involvement of the "peace movement" with Middle East problems, and for the illustrations they provide of some of the misconceptions that underlie much of the current discussion of the Arab-Israeli conflict.

One of the first and most widely quoted responses to Berrigan was by Rabbi Arthur Hertzberg, president of the American Jewish Congress.[21] Hertzberg describes himself as an early and vigorous opponent of the Vietnam war; thus he is no Alsop or Roche. He also describes himself as "slightly notorious also for being a 'dove' on the Israel-Arab conflict." Hertzberg sees Berrigan's remarks as "old-fashioned theological anti-Semitism," a severe charge that deserves a careful analysis. Consider now Hertzberg's reasoning.

Hertzberg attributes to Berrigan the claim "that the Arabs were right and the Jews were wrong" and urges that he "not malign Israel with unique venom." But he nowhere mentions Berrigan's condemnation of the Arab states, already cited, or his condemnation of the Arab resistance for its "rhetorical violence and blind terrorism." Nowhere does Berrigan suggest that the Arabs were right and the Jews wrong. Rather, he consistently adheres to his refusal to "take sides." We can therefore dismiss this charge as simply another fabrication.

According to Hertzberg, Berrigan's recognition of the injustices to the Arab refugees leads him to "assert . . . that an end be made of the state of Israel." Discussing

Berrigan's "horror stories," Hertzberg alleges that concern over the refugees has led some (by implication, Berrigan) to argue that "only Israel must be refused the right to exist at all," though "moral hysterics" over other refugee displacements have long since ceased. Again, fabrication. Berrigan nowhere suggests that an end be made of the State of Israel. Rather, he insists that the Arab states at once declare "de facto respect for the existence of Israel, a de facto state."

Hertzberg does not tell us, incidentally, whether the concern of the Zionist movement over the displacement of Jewish refugees two thousand years ago was also an example of "moral hysterics."

Hertzberg then accuses Berrigan of misrepresenting the relation between the American Jewish community and its leaders:

> Berrigan asserts that the great majority of the American Jewish community "refused the bait offered by Nixon and peddled by their own leaders"—that is, they resisted Zionism. This distinction of his has absolutely nothing to do with the truth.

What has absolutely nothing to do with the truth is Hertzberg's rendition of Berrigan's statements. Berrigan nowhere suggests that American Jews resisted Zionism. On the contrary, immediately after paying tribute to the Jewish community in the remarks Hertzberg cites, Berrigan went on as follows (emphasis mine):

> Their *acute and legitimate concern for Israel* never became a weapon against Vietnamese survival. They refused that immoral choice offered them by a leader who would make a price of the safety of one people, the extinction of another.

Thus Hertzberg attributes to Berrigan the exact opposite of what he clearly stated in remarks that Hertzberg partially quotes.

To Berrigan's statement that Israel is deficient in "the Jewish passion for the poor and forgotten," Hertzberg offers the following rebuttal:

> What does he think that Israel's hospitality since 1948 to hundreds of thousands of refugees from the Arab lands has represented? For that matter, why are Israel and the world Jewish community fighting so hard with Soviet Russia about the right of emigration?

Surely this is too much. Israel's acceptance (indeed, encouragement) of Jewish immigration is hardly evidence for "the Jewish passion for the poor and forgotten." Rather it was an effort, justified or not, to establish a Jewish majority in a Jewish state. Before the establishment of Israel, the Zionist movement gave no encouragement to resettlement of Jewish refugees outside of Palestine. That is an understatement. "For Zionists a national homeland in Palestine was so clearly the answer that to divert money and energy to resettlement elsewhere was akin to heresy. . . . The bitter truth seems to be that in order for mass rescue [of European Jews] to have succeeded, the effort in Palestine would not only have had to be supplemented by other resettlement ventures but also by mass infiltration into established states," [22] and to this project the Zionist movement was always opposed. The same is true today. The world Jewish community is fighting hard to compel Russia to permit Jews to emigrate and is expending considerable resources to bring Russian Jews to Israel and settle them there. Millions of dollars of United States government aid have been specifically allocated by Congress to this purpose. I imagine that there might be some Russian Jews interested in coming to the United States, and "passion for the poor and forgotten" would certainly motivate some concerted efforts on their behalf. I am aware of none.

I suspect that a Palestinian Arab who had been evicted from his home might find Hertzberg's rebuttal a bit cynical on this score.

On the matter of the flight of refugees, Hertzberg has the following to say:

> As a matter of fact, the Arab refugee problem began in the war of 1948 in large part because the Arabs . . . chose to leave as part of a tactical maneuver.

The evidence for this claim, at present, is slight indeed. Earlier claims were thoroughly demolished by Erskine Childers, who also exposed numerous propaganda fabrications in the process.[23] No doubt the case is not settled, but Hertzberg's "matter of fact" might better be labeled "a highly dubious claim" or "a probable fabrication."

Hertzberg objects to Berrigan's unremitting denunciation of Israeli society and his failure to find any good in it—in particular, his assertion that Israel has failed "to create new forms of political and social life for her own citizens." In this case, Hertzberg's criticism is justified. He is quite right to refer to the Kibbutz as an outstanding example of new forms of political and social life, as is commonly done in literature of the New Left.[24] Berrigan does not give a balanced appraisal of Israeli society, any more than he gave a balanced account of the policies of the Arab states.

But when Hertzberg gets down to specifics, his criticism again falls wide of the mark. He objects to Berrigan's discussion of "the price in Israeli coinage" for the policies of the past years: the "creation of an elite of millionaires, generals and entrepreneurs," with the price "being paid by Israel's Oriental Jews, the poor, the excluded, prisoners." These observations, however, are not only reasonably accurate, but also commonplace.[25]

The remainder of Hertzberg's accusations are too vague for comment. On the whole, his response is careless and inaccurate and supports none of his conclusions. Rather, it falls squarely within the tendencies described earlier. Since there is no reason to suspect that Hertzberg is motivated by domestic political concerns, one can only conclude that he, like Eban, simply hopes to stifle discussion.

The conclusion is strengthened by a look at Hertzberg's ideas on an appropriate policy for Israel. Berrigan advocates a peace treaty with recognition of Israel within its 1967 borders; it seems that he supports something like the Rogers Plan. Hertzberg's position is quite different. Speaking in Israel at a meeting of Jewish organizations, Hertzberg warned that Nixon and Kissinger "now need an impressive diplomatic victory" because of Watergate and are therefore putting pressure on Israel:

> We—and now I refer to Israel and American Jewry—are unable to accept this pace and this arrangement under pressure and ultimatum. Kissinger proposes as a first step Israeli withdrawal to the Mitla and Giddi passes, and the Arabs want this to take place tomorrow. From a historical and psychological point of view—not to speak of other considerations—the matter cannot be handled in this way. A government that agrees to this would be overturned and assassinated at once. Jews in the Diaspora who agree to this will be called traitors. And from the psychological point of view, this is correct.[26]

Interesting views for a "slightly notorious dove," assuming that he was not badly misquoted. In rather similar language, the right-wing Likud opposed the January 18 Egyptian-Israeli agreement that called for Israeli withdrawal to the Mitla and Giddi passes. Comparing Hertzberg's position with Berrigan's, we see that there is indeed a difference worth discussing. Hertzberg would have done a service had he made this clear. But this would presuppose a willingness to have these crucial issues aired, and I suggest that to prevent this is precisely the purpose of personal attacks and distortions of the kind I have been discussing.

I have suggested that much of the commentary on Israel and the New Left is motivated by domestic American concerns and by a desire to forestall debate that might reach serious issues. Hertzberg's attack on Berrigan as an old-fashioned theological anti-Semite falls into the second category. Irving Howe's comments, discussed earlier, fall within the first. It is therefore interesting to consider his response to the Berrigan address.[27]

Howe denounces Berrigan as "arrogant," "elitist," with "little taste for mere 'formal' liberty," moved only by "his own persuasion of righteousness." Berrigan's address is, furthermore, "an extreme instance"—of what, Howe does not make clear. A charitable interpretation of Howe's critique would make Berrigan an extreme instance of erosion of support for Israel. But since the preceding paragraph refers to unnamed New Leftists "whose minds are filled with the notions of Fanon, Guevara, and Mao" and who therefore are "contemptuous of Israel" precisely because of its "advanced social legislation, progress towards socialism, the kibbutz experiments, ebullient democracy," perhaps Howe is trying to tell us that Berrigan, with his distaste for mere "formal" liberty, is an extreme instance of this type. Whatever Howe may have in mind exactly, these are plainly serious accusations, not to be made lightly. Let us consider then the evidence that Howe adduces to support these charges.

Howe's argument rests on two observations. First, "it does not stir the heart" of Father Berrigan "that, in a moment when the whole country feels itself in the utmost peril, the Israelis set an example of democratic openness and debate, running an election with God alone knows how many parties (including two Communist parties, one of which has long been pro-Arab)." Second, while Berrigan preaches resistance against the state, "to get himself arrested, to maneuver himself into the condition of 'resistance' [in Israel], he would have to do something really extreme, like providing military help to Egypt or Syria."

Howe's second observation is false outright; his first suffers from important omissions. But even if correct, Howe's two observations would not substantiate his charges. They would simply show that Berrigan ignored positive features of Israeli society, which is true, just as he ignored positive developments in the Arab states. When Howe denounces Egypt as a "rigid dictatorship," overlooking entirely all constructive programs undertaken by Nasser, are we to conclude austerely that Howe has little taste for mere human needs (subsistence, education, welfare)? Adopting his style of argument, that is exactly what we would conclude. What is more serious, the deficiencies in Howe's two observations, as we shall see directly, are traceable to a single cause: he has little concern for the condition of Arabs in the Jewish state. Are we to conclude, then, reasoning in Howe's style, that Howe is simply a racist? That would hardly be just, though to ignore substantive evils while engaging in fulsome praise of a regime is a serious fault—far worse than overlooking much that is praiseworthy while condemning substantive evils.

Now a look at Howe's premises. Take first the matter of resistance. Uri Davis spent five months in prison, not for providing military help to Egypt or Syria, but for entering a "military zone" without a permit. The "military zone" consisted of land expropriated from Arabs on the pretext of "security" and then converted into an all-Jewish settlement area from which Arabs are officially excluded. Even a Druze veteran of the Israeli Border Patrol, in a recent scandal, was denied the right to open a business there.[28] It would take a vivid imagination to interpret Davis's act of resistance as a case of providing military help to Egypt or Syria or the like.

Davis was apparently the first Jew to be arrested under the Emergency Regulations of 1945, previously applied only to Arabs (since 1948). These regulations were described in 1946 by Y. S. Shapira, later to be attorney general of Israel and minister of justice, as "unparalleled in any civilized country; there were no such laws even in Nazi Germany." They are still in effect, although the first Knesset, in 1951, declared them "incompatible with the principles of a democratic state." [29]

Davis is not the only example of a resister who managed to get himself arrested without approaching the extremes that Howe suggests are necessary in Israel. Since 1967, a number of people have been imprisoned as resisters for their refusal to serve in the armed forces in the occupied territories. Are they guilty, by Howe's standards, of giving military help to Egypt or Syria or the like? Or consider the case of Rami Livneh, sentenced in 1973 to ten years in prison for failing to report to the authorities a meeting with a Palestinian alleged by the prosecution to be a "foreign agent." No proof was offered that Livneh had given military aid to Egypt, Syria, the Palestinians, or anyone else. The court stated in its decision that "replacement of the present structure of the state by an Arab-Jewish regime (as was the central purpose of the organization [to which the defendants belonged]) constitutes an attack on the sovereignty of Israel." Since Israel was established as a Jewish state, the court held, advocacy of a Jewish-Arab state is equivalent to advocacy of overthrow of the state.[30]

Howe regards Berrigan's remarks on resistance in Israel as so ridiculous that he asks, "Does he know what he has in mind?" I suspect that Berrigan knows all too well some things that Howe has yet to learn, not only about Israel but about state power and propaganda in general. We have already noted Howe's scorn for Sartre and de Beauvoir for their alleged superficiality and factual inaccuracy. They would have little difficulty in returning the compliment, with ample evidence.

Consider next Howe's comment on elections. True, Israel is a Western democracy, with relatively high standards of freedom and justice—for its Jewish citizens. Arabs may take part in political life, but under certain understood conditions. On one occasion, an Arab nationalist group (the al-Ard group) attempted to form an Arab political party (all-Jewish parties, e.g., the governing Labor Party, have been the rule). This attempt was blocked by the district governor on grounds that it had the object of "prejudicing the existence and security of the State of Israel." Upholding the ban, the High Court held that "it has never happened in history that in countries where there is a sound democratic regime, monopolistic fascist movements have been allowed to operate against the state, using the rights of freedom of speech, freedom of the press and freedom of association, in order to organise destructive activities under cover of these freedoms." [31] Since the Court invoked the analogy of Weimar—a slight exaggeration, perhaps—it might be useful to recall the record of the judiciary under the Weimar Republic:

> It is impossible to escape the conclusion that political justice is the blackest page in the life of the German

Republic. The judicial weapon was used by the reaction with steadily increasing intensity.[32]

In Israel, Arab-Jewish communist parties are permitted to function, but not Arab parties that might prove effective in rallying popular support for Arab rights.

Howe assures us that one of the communist parties (Rakah) is "pro-Arab," a testimonial to Israeli democracy. It is always useful in such cases to listen to those who are suffering from discriminatory practices. The well-informed Israeli Arab lawyer Sabri Jiryis, who was himself restricted to Haifa for over a year under the Emergency Regulations, though charges were never brought against him, and who now lives in Beirut, describes Rakah as "the Communist sector of the Israeli establishment." Nevertheless, "most of the Arab members of the party's leadership, including the members of its Political Bureau, its newspaper editors and correspondents, and its village branch secretaries and youth leaders, are subject to various restrictions" under the Emergency Regulations. But "these restrictions have never once been imposed on Jewish members of the Party." From these and many similar examples, Jiryis concludes, judiciously and I think plausibly, that in the area of democratic freedoms:

> ... the authorities do not practise discrimination against individuals or groups on the basis of purely national or communal considerations. It is when ethnic differences are combined with opposition to their basic political and social concepts that they allow themselves to be influenced by racial differences.[33]

In short, by no means South Africa, but not quite an "ebullient democracy" either.

This is within Israel proper. In the occupied territories, no serious form of political organization has been tolerated. Dissidents are quickly taken care of. To cite only the most recent case, on December 10, 1973, Israeli troops expelled eight prominent Palestinians, marching them blindfolded into Jordan. This provoked a protest at a junior college (Bir Zeit) in the occupied West Bank. Israeli troops closed the college, giving the students and staff six hours to leave.[34] The incident was described as follows in the Israeli press:

> The last straw was a demonstration, which took place in the institution, last week, protesting the deportation of 8 Arab notables to Jordan. Once more the teachers and students were warned that they are exploiting freedom of speech in Israel too far, and when they did not comply with the warnings, it was decided to silence them and close other channels of activity by less delicate means.[35]

If Howe would attend to the issues instead of simply berating his enemies, he would perceive at once that his unqualified praise for Israeli democracy could not possibly be accurate. Israel is a Jewish state with non-Jewish citizens. By law and administrative practice it must be—and is—a state based on discrimination and exclusivism.[36] It will not do simply to assert that "there is no perfection in this world, and the case for Israelis rests on no claim that they are perfect," while describing this "ebullient democracy" progressing toward socialism [37] as being "about as good a model as we have for the democratic socialist hope of combining radical social change with political freedom." Howe must be aware that there are Arabs, as well as those who might not choose to identify themselves as Jews, in the Jewish state. But nowhere does he face the problem of their status.

One might argue that the essentially flawed democracy of a Jewish state (equivalently, an Arab state) is the least unjust solution available, given the objective realities. That is a rational position, one that can be respected and discussed. But Howe attempts no such argument. His method, with regard to this issue at least, is to try to bury difficult and uncomfortable facts in a heap of invective.

I do not mean to suggest that New Left positions on the Middle East, or criticisms of Israel expressed by people associated with the peace movement, are beyond criticism—far from it. In fact, I find myself in strong disagreement with much of the peace movement and the left over these issues (see chapter 2). Reasonable criticism can only be welcomed. But the examples I have discussed here and in the references cited do not fall within this category. I think that they are to be explained by a combination of the two factors mentioned: fear of critical analysis, and the desire to exorcise the heresies of the 1960s so that "respectable" left-liberalism can regain its position of moral authority.

The authors of the denunciations I have discussed describe themselves as supporters of Israel against those who seek its destruction. I happen to think that many of them bear a measure of responsibility for the October 1973 tragedy and for further conflicts that are likely, if the policies they advocate are pursued (see introduction, pp. 11–12, 22, 25). I do not therefore castigate them as "supporters of Arab genocide," though their stand may well contribute to the ultimate destruction of Israel. But I do reject their claim that they "support Israel" against its enemies. Contrary to their belief, this self-characterization requires an argument, not merely declamation, no less than their accusations against their political enemies.

In fact, a rational person will be wary about such phrases as "support for Israel." Are Sakharov and Solzhenitsyn enemies of the Soviet people when they denounce atrocities committed by the Russian state? Or

Daniel Berrigan, when he supports Russian dissidents, who, no doubt, are quite isolated from the mainstream of Russian opinion? Was A. J. Muste supporting or attacking the United States when he called for American withdrawal from Vietnam, virtually alone, at a time when democratic socialist *Dissent* was explaining that American withdrawal "would mean something quite as inhumane" as the policy of "hopeless attrition of the Vietnamese people"? [38] Were American resisters and deserters enemies of the United States, or were they defending the interests of the American people and their professed ideals? The semantic trap is obvious. Apologists for state power are always quick to identify opposition and resistance to state policy as an attack on the society and its people. In the case at hand, support for policies of the Israeli state may or may not be "support for Israel" in any reasonable sense of this notion, and criticism of these policies must also be analyzed on its merits.

The matter is not academic. Quite apart from questions of right and justice, it is far from obvious that Israeli policy since 1967 has been motivated by considerations of security, though these are, of course, invoked in Israel as elsewhere for the purposes of the state. It is not very surprising that Moshe Dayan should bitterly attack the professorial doves who have been pointing out, with some accuracy, just where his policies of annexation are leading. For Dayan, the role of the professors is to "contribute to faith and strengthening," not to "humiliation and depression," as they have been doing by discussing the likely consequences of his policies. "Were they a lion cub?" Dayan asks rhetorically, "or a worm of Jacob?"—adding, "I don't mean just the worm of Jacob Talmon." [39]

I have given my own views on the matter of security,

and referred to those of some Israeli doves, including those denounced by Dayan (cf. introduction, pp. 24–8). These views are surely debatable and are perhaps incorrect, but it is striking to see how the relevant questions are ignored in some of the eloquent pleas that we raise our voices in support of Israel. Irving Howe is again a case in point. He asks a question that "haunts us: why is it that some people—Jews, liberals, intellectuals, persons conspicuous for developed political and moral sensibilities—refrain from expressing such anxieties" over the fate of Israel? The silence of opponents of the Vietnam war is particularly troubling to him, almost as troubling as the antagonism to Israel on the part of the two people he specifically names: Daniel Berrigan and me.

When Berrigan speaks of the Israelis as "a people in danger," of the "acute and legitimate concern for Israel" on the part of American Jews, of the "dead end" to which Israeli policy is leading, of the possibilities for a peaceful solution involving recognition of Israel by the Arab states, could it be that he is, in fact, expressing anxieties over the fate of Israel? Howe makes the familiar point that "the Israelis need only suffer one serious defeat in order to face extinction." I have been writing the same thing for years and arguing that the policies of the Israeli state are leading in that very direction. Could it be that, in so doing, I am expressing the anxieties that Howe feels? Such questions are apparently incomprehensible to him. One finds absolutely no awareness in his writings of the problems of security and the many discussions of them. He simply takes it for granted that his views, whatever they may be, constitute "support for Israel." Anything else must be a form of radical chic, "romantic authoritarian delusion," or the "radiant sincerity" of ideologists blind to fact. Argument and evidence are, as always, quite beside the point.

I wrote, "his views, whatever they may be." The reason is that it is not easy to determine what these views are. An examination of Howe's treatment of the issue—or better, nontreatment—gives some insight into the attitudes toward Israel of substantial segments of the left-liberal intelligentsia. We know what Howe rejects. Judging by his comments on Berrigan, we may conclude that he rejects Berrigan's suggestion that Israel be recognized by the Arab states within its 1967 boundaries. Howe writes that he sympathizes with the proposal that Israel should give up "most of the occupied territories, provided that secure borders followed," but it must have "the kinds of borders that would allow the Israelis to establish their own guarantee" of security. Just what borders would suffice for this purpose? Evidently, the borders of September 1973 did not. With these borders, Israel suffered serious losses and came perilously close to disaster. Still wider borders, perhaps? But Howe supports withdrawal from most of the occupied territories. It is impossible to make sense out of such inconsistencies.

Howe adds that unless Israelis are in a position to guarantee their own security, "they will be left in a state of economic decline and political debacle, and gravely wounded in national morale," facing destruction. Perhaps he means to suggest that with a settlement of the sort that Berrigan advocates or the very similar principles of the Rogers Plan, the situation in Israel will revert to something like 1966, a period of serious economic and psychological crisis, with emigration exceeding immigration—the "most serious crisis" in Israel's history, when its "entire social, economic and ideological structure was at risk." [40] But if this is the reason for opposing withdrawal, then let us say so directly and not invoke the problem of security.

Howe's few remarks explaining why he objects to compelling Israeli withdrawal from the occupied territories are remarkably like those heard from extremist right-wing and chauvinist elements within Israel. Eliezer Livneh, an Israeli writer who is one of the spokesmen for the expansionist Greater Israel Movement, explains his opposition to United Nations Resolution 242 "or any other formulation of the Kissinger plan" on the following grounds. The result will be, he says,

> a militaristic Israeli society, a state in siege. It will not have sufficient manpower and resources to absorb immigrants. The realization of Zionism will be strangled at the height of its impetus. The breaking up of Israel and the heavy curbs on her development will erode the impulses for immigration. Just as victory in the Six Day War and the restoration of large areas of the homeland gave tremendous impetus to the desire for immigration from the Soviet Union, so the retreat from the liberated areas will bring about a Zionist depression. And is it not possible that the reverse movement, that of emigration from Israel, will be renewed, if the Zionist lever, which gives purpose and sense to Israeli society, is broken? [41]

Left-liberal commentators in Israel and conservative doves have taken pains to refute Livneh's argument, which is virtually the same as Howe's. Howe's remarks on security and morale also recall to mind those of General Ezer Weizmann, air force commander in 1967 and a leading right-wing political figure. Speaking of the 1967 war, Weizmann stated that he would

> accept the claim that there was no threat of destruction against the existence of the State of Israel. This does not mean, however, that one could have refrained from attacking the Egyptians, the Jordanians and the Syrians. Had we not done that, the State of Israel would have ceased to exist *according to the scale, spirit and quality*

she now embodies. . . . We entered the Six-Day War
in order to secure a position in which we can manage
our lives here according to our wishes without external
pressures. . . .[42]

In fact, it is obvious that neither Israel nor any other
small country can guarantee its own security. Talk of
"guaranteeing one's own security" is either a sign of
serious confusion or a euphemism.[43] Security is not
strictly a military concept. Its foundations are political.
It rests on international opinion, regional settlement, and,
ultimately, on the interests of the superpowers, much
as we may deplore the fact. Howe derides the "U.S.
'guarantee' of [Israel's] future survival," and with some
justice, though again he seriously misunderstands the
basic problem. It is foolish indeed to place one's fate in
the hands of a great power—as Israel has done, and will
continue to do if it follows Howe's prescription. The
escape from this predicament lies not in a mythical capability to guarantee one's own security, but in local and
regional accommodation. But this path leads to consideration of social and political policy that Howe, like so
many "supporters of Israel," always ignores. With his
insistence that Israel be in a position to establish its own
guarantee of security, Howe lends his support, not to
Israel, but to the most dangerous and ultimately self-
destructive tendencies in its recent policy: the displacement of politics by reliance on power. Howe says that
he sympathizes with Israeli doves, but it is precisely this
tendency in Israeli policy that they have most insistently
condemned. They have insisted, and rightly so, that the
policy of annexation favored by General Weizmann does
not "secure a position in which we can manage our lives
here according to our wishes without external pressures."
This policy does not guarantee security, but only further
conflict. It leads precisely to "political debacle," as Israel

becomes isolated internationally and thus compelled to rely on a "U.S. 'guarantee' of future survival." It does not preserve "national morale," at least in any sense congenial to those who value Israeli democracy, which cannot survive the annexation of territories inhabited by Arabs—the famous "demographic problem" that I have discussed before. (See introduction, p. 19, and chapter 3, pp. 117–18 126 ff.)

Whatever Howe may have in mind exactly, his remarks on security and its basis, while vague and confused, nevertheless tend in the direction of extremist right-wing elements in Israel. As in the case of Rabbi Hertzberg, once again we have an American dove who sounds, by Israeli standards, strangely like a hawk. Again we see an illustration of the association of American Zionism to right-wing and chauvinist tendencies within Israel—and formerly, world Zionism (cf. chapter 1, p. 52, and this chapter, p. 171).

Howe urges that we "keep our voices in readiness" and continue with "the work of politics, pressure, persuasion." We are to persuade those in power that . . . That what? That Israel not be destroyed? But on this issue I am aware of no disagreement in the United States, except for the most marginal and inconsequential groups. There are real disagreements over security and how it is to be achieved. But on these matters, Howe is silent.

There are also real disagreements over the question of what would constitute a just and proper solution to the multitude of problems that arise in the Arab-Jewish conflict. But like many others who ask us to raise our voices in support of Israel, Howe has no more to say about these questions than about the problem of security. There are a number of possibilities that might be considered, each with several variants (see chapter 3, section II): (1) an Arab state with those Jews who are permitted to remain granted second-class citizenship as a tolerated minority (Qaddafi); (2) a Jewish state with Arabs as second-class citizens, after population transfer (right-wing Zionism); (3) a Jewish and a Palestinian state, side by side in cis-Jordan, perhaps part of a broader federation (some Zionist doves); (4) a democratic secular state (PLO); (5) an Arab-Jewish binational state (the Zionist left until 1947; Ihud; Ben-Gurion and other Zionist leaders in the early 1930s); (6) a Jewish state in most of cis-Jordan with Arabs as second-class citizens, with some areas returned to Jordanian administration and a division of Sinai with Egypt (doves of the Eban variety, if we consider the actual meaning of their proposals). Evidently, Howe rejects (1), (2), and (4). Alternative (3) seems ruled out by his vague remarks about the need for Israel to guarantee its own security. He makes it clear, with the obligatory insults and with arguments that deserve no comment, that he regards socialist binationalism of the sort I have discussed as an absurdity. Thus, (5) is ruled out. We are left, by elimination, with (6): that is, Israel is to remain a Jewish state in most of cis-Jordan, hence necessarily a discriminatory state with a substantial class of second-class Arab citizens—given current demographic trends, a very substantial class, and perhaps even a majority before too long (or does Howe support the population-transfer concept of his fellow "democratic socialist" Michael Walzer [44] and the outright Jewish Qaddafis?).

But can this be? After all, Howe insists, "I have never been a Zionist; I have always felt contempt for nationalist and chauvinist sentiments." Furthermore, as a democratic socialist Howe is surely committed to the universality of such values as democracy and equal rights. The circle seems complete. An explanation would be helpful, but instead we are treated only to denuncia-

tion and abuse and to the plea that we speak out for
Israel.

Like many other left-liberal American Zionists whose
writings I have discussed, Howe always skirts the crucial
questions: What is the relation between "security" and
annexation of the occupied territories? How can a Jewish state with non-Jewish citizens be a "democratic
state," let alone a socialist society? How are American
liberals or socialists to respond to the blatantly discriminatory legal and administrative structures that are the
foundation of the state of Israel? These are nontrivial
questions. The ostrich approach is decidedly unhelpful.

Given that Howe has "always felt contempt for nationalist or chauvinist sentiments," we search with interest
for his expression of concern for the Palestinians, let us
say, those who have been expelled from their lands to
make room for all-Jewish settlement. We find these ring-
ing declarations of principle: "I think Golda Meir inadequate on the Palestinian question. . . . I believe that some
of the Arab claims, especially in regard to the Palestinian problem, have an element of validity." That is all.
It is good to learn that Golda Meir's position—that the
Palestinians do not exist—is "inadequate." [45] It would be
still more interesting to learn how the "element of validity" in Palestinian claims is to be dealt with.

For example, is there an "element of validity" in the
claims of the villagers of Aqraba on the West Bank,
whose fields were defoliated in 1972 and then turned
over to a nearby Jewish settlement? Or the villagers of
Kaffr Kassem, whose claims we discover in the following
news item (emphases in the original):

> Kaffr Kassem, east of Petah Tiqva, was the place where
> a trigger-happy army killed some women and peasants
> that had returned from the fields, where they had
> neither been told that the *Sinai war* (1956) had broken

out, nor that a curfew had been imposed on their village. This week, the mayor of the small Arab town
came to the Knesset to protest against the *confiscation of
most of the land* cultivated by his village. The New
Force Party has taken up the problem.[46]

According to the Palestinian historian and geographer
Aref el-Aref of Ramallah, 475 Arab villages existed before
1948 within the 1967 borders of Israel. Today, 90 remain.
In many cases, there is no record of what has happened,
and even the sites are now unknown.[47] Is there, perhaps,
some "element of validity" lurking in the background
here? Of these matters too, we hear nothing.

Israeli leftists and civil libertarians are deeply concerned over these issues. There have been protests and
demonstrations in particular instances, though the impact on state policy has been negligible. The protestors
do not thereby become "enemies of Israel," whatever
Moshe Dayan may think. Or Glazer, Lipset, Howe, *et al*.

Unfortunately, much of the discussion of the Middle
East conflict in the United States not only overlooks such
critical issues as those I have mentioned here and in the
preceding essays, but also seriously misrepresents others.
This is true even on the part of commentators from
whom one has come to expect a much higher degree of
accuracy and clarity. Thus Hans Morgenthau writes:

> Four times the Arabs tried to eliminate Israel by war.
> . . . it is an undisputed historic fact that none of the
> violent encounters in the Middle East between the
> Arabs and the Jews—from the 20s to the Six Day War—
> had anything to do with the boundaries of the Jewish
> State. They concerned first the presence of Jewish set-
> tlers in Palestine, and then the existence of a Jewish
> state in the midst of the Arab world.[48]

Surely one cannot characterize the 1956 Israeli-British-
French aggression against Egypt in these terms. Earlier

terrorist incidents also relate directly, in some cases at least, to the boundaries of the Jewish state (cf. introduction, note 20). As for the 1967 war, the situation was far more complex. Israeli Chief of Staff Rabin observed that "there is a difference between concentrating forces in order to get into a war and making a move that, while it might end up in war, is not aimed at war but at something else. . . . [Nasser] preferred the danger of war to backing down." [49] I have already cited Rabin's analysis of the 1973 war (cf. introduction, note 48). The interaction over the years has been far more complex than Morgenthau's remarks indicate. If there is to be useful analysis and discussion of the complex and painful problems of the conflict between Jews and Arabs, it must proceed on firmer grounds than these.

In past years, many people in the peace movement felt that problems of the Middle East should, to preserve the unity of popular opposition to the war in Vietnam, be given a wide berth. I am sure that this is one reason for the "stance of pained indifference" noted by the editors of Liberation (cf. above, p. 153). Furthermore, it was always obvious that opponents of the movement against the war, including some who were unhappy about the course the war had taken, would eagerly seize upon any departure from Zionist orthodoxy (with its predominant right-wing character in the United States) as a means to undermine the mass popular opposition that developed. Perhaps it was justifiable to keep away from the problem on these grounds, but it is no longer.

I think that Israel has suffered, and will continue to suffer, from efforts in the United States to stifle discussion, slander critics, and exploit Israel's problems cynically for domestic political purposes, as it suffers from the general tendency in the United States to support the more chauvinistic and militaristic elements in Israeli society. We should, at the very least, be able to duplicate here the range of discussion and debate that exists in Israel itself. We should, in fact, be able to do better, a step removed from the immediate conflict. In Israel, the "peace list" (Reshimat Shalom) was known as "the Professors' Party." In the United States, the American Professors for Peace in the Middle East (APPME) publishes statements that, to me at least, suggest the rhetoric of the Greater Israel movement, and often appears to be serving virtually as an organ of Israel state propaganda.[50] The contrast is striking and reflects a most regrettable situation.

The United States, with its vast military and economic aid [51] to several countries in the region and with the massive investments of American corporations in petroleum and increasingly other projects, is deeply involved in affairs of the Middle East. The structure of international capitalism and relations with the state socialist system depend crucially on how the problems of this region evolve. In no other region of the world are the problems so likely to lead to devastating regional conflict and possible global war. Furthermore, for Israeli Jews and Palestinian Arabs, problems of justice and even national survival are posed in stark and threatening terms. I have suggested that these problems have only been aggravated by the irrationality and intolerance that has dominated discussion in the United States. It will be most unfortunate if this state of affairs persists.

Notes

1. Papers submitted to, or resulting from, the conference, and some others, appear in Mordecai S. Chertoff, ed., *The New Left and the Jews*, Pitman, New York 1971. The timing of

the conference was appropriate, in that the New Left had no organized existence or expression after this time.

2. Many examples to the contrary are cited in my paper, "Israel and the New Left," in Chertoff, ed., *op. cit.* Note that what is at issue is Glazer's categorical judgment, not the fact (also illustrated in my review) that there are cases to which his characterization applies. In my review, I barely mentioned "Old Left" groups or "the Black Liberation movement," whose attitudes toward the Middle East must be interpreted in terms of domestic American problems and developments." But I did comment on the zeal with which some American Zionist sociologists seek out statements in obscure periodicals to "prove" that the black groups are anti-Semitic, and I noted the exaggerated conclusions that are drawn as to the significance of these instances. One might almost think, reading some of these analyses, that American Jews are standing at the gates of the crematoria, barely fending off the Black Panthers. I might add that my personal contacts with black groups that are alleged to be anti-Semitic, while not very extensive, are surely far more extensive than is the case for those who see Nazis around every corner. I have yet to see any instances of anti-Semitism or even antiwhite "reverse racism", even at moments of considerable crisis and tension—for example, at the public funeral of Fred Hampton and Mark Clark. Surely there is nothing that compares with what I experienced personally growing up in a pure white (but non-Jewish) neighborhood in suburban Philadelphia, and nothing that compares with what one would have found at elite universities not too many years ago.

3. *Ibid.*

4. "The Campus Left and Israel," *New York Times*, Op-Ed page, March 13, 1971. Reprinted in Irving Howe and Carl Gershman, *Israel, the Arabs, and the Middle East*, Bantam Books, New York 1972.

5. "Thinking the Unthinkable About Israel: A Personal Statement," *New York* magazine, Dec. 24, 1973.

6. Or in his claim that "self-hatred is becoming a major problem for the American Jewish community." Cf. also note 24. I discuss some of Lipset's examples of "black anti-Semitism" in "Israel and the New Left."

7. People who were active in the New Left in the 1960s will be as interested as Stone himself to learn that he was one of the spokesmen for the New Left.

8. *Boston Globe*, Feb. 12–13, 1970.

9. John Roche, *Baltimore News-American*, Nov. 23, 1973. For some examples of Roche's scholarly analysis of the war in Vietnam, see my *For Reasons of State*, Pantheon Books, New York, 1973, p. 137.

10. Speech delivered July 31, 1972. Reprinted in *Congress Bi-Weekly*, March 30, 1973.

11, Cf. the analyses by Salpeter and Talmon cited in the introduction, pp. 16, 24.

12. The statements by Eban and Meir appear in Pierre Rondot, "Les Palestiniens et la négociation," *Le Monde diplomatique*, Dec. 1973, citing earlier reports in *Le Monde*.

13. What these attitudes actually were I have discussed extensively elsewhere, most recently in *For Reasons of State* and (with Edward S. Herman) *Counterrevolutionary Violence: Bloodbaths in Fact and Propaganda*, Warner Modular, Andover, Mass., 1973. Cf. also note 38.

14. The response to Watergate is unprincipled in many respects. Outrage has been caused more by the choice of enemies than the choice of means. See my articles "The Watergate Illusion," *New York Review*, Sept. 20, 1973; "The President and the Presidency," *Liberation*, Nov. 1973. As an illustration, consider the following report of a news conference held by Elliot Richardson: "The 'fatal flaw' of the Nixon administration—not yet corrected—is the proclivity of the White House to perceive critics and opposition as 'enemies' and the willingness to 'adopt tactics used against an enemy' in handling such criticism" (Guy Halverson, *Christian Science Monitor*, Jan. 23, 1974). It is of little concern to Richardson or the mass media when these tactics, or worse, are used against legitimate enemies of the state. Thus, the FBI was recently compelled by court order to release a May 1968 directive by J. Edgar Hoover initiating a program "to expose, disrupt, and otherwise neutralize the activities of the various New Left organizations, their leadership, and adherents" and to "frustrate every effort of these groups and individuals to consolidate their forces or to recruit new or youthful adherents," if necessary "disrupting the organized activity of these groups" and "capitaliz[ing] upon organizational and personal conflicts of their leadership." This program represents a use of the political police to attack dissent that goes well beyond anything exposed in the Watergate investigations, but one will find virtually no comment in the liberal press.

15. For discussion of what the impact has been in the case of Vietnam, and for a possible explanation of the specific contributions of the technical intelligentsia, see my *For Reasons of*

State, introduction and chapter 1; also my "Science and Ideology," *Jawaharlal Nehru Memorial Lectures, 1967–1972,* New Delhi, 1973.

16. For some of the remarkable successes of the past, see my *American Power and the New Mandarins,* Pantheon, New York, 1969, particularly chapters 1 and 6; also, my *Problems of Knowledge and Freedom,* Pantheon, New York 1971, chapter 2; "American Historians as 'Experts in Legitimation,'" *Social Scientist,* New Delhi, Feb. 1973; and the references of note 13. For some of the contributions of the press as an agency of state propaganda, see my "Reporting Indochina: The News Media and the Legitimation of Lies," *Social Policy,* Sept.–Oct., 1973.

17. Later, Stone achieved respectability and even some acclaim. This was after general opinion had turned against the war as a failed venture (and also after Stone had suspended regular publication of his *Weekly*).

18. The text appears in *American Report,* Oct. 29, 1973.

19. Virtually unnoticed, to be more precise. A letter in the Marxist-Leninist *Guardian,* New York, Jan. 30, 1974, by two people who attended the conference that Berrigan addressed, states that some people in the audience "were at the point of leaving because he attacked the Arabs and Palestinians too much."

20. The anti-Arab bias of the American press (with rare exceptions—notably, the *Christian Science Monitor*) is notorious. Arabs are regularly portrayed as sadistic terrorists. Racist caricatures are not uncommon. Furthermore, atrocities committed against them often pass without notice. Thus, there has been much justifiable outrage over the savage treatment of Israeli prisoners captured by the Syrians, many of whom are reported to have been tortured or murdered (see, e.g., William Novak, *New York Times,* Op-Ed, Jan. 26, 1974). Less is heard in the United States of the 700 civilians reported killed in the Israeli bombing of Damascus (David Hirst, *Guardian Weekly,* Manchester-London, Jan. 26, 1974), or the blocking by Israeli troops of a Red Cross convoy bringing urgently needed medical supplies to Suez— "20 or 30 men will die tonight [in the Suez hospital] because the Israelis won't let us through," according to the Swiss doctor leading the convoy (UPI, *International Herald Tribune,* Nov. 12, 1973; reprinted in *Middle East International,* Dec. 1973). This is not the first such report. After the Six-Day War, Israel reportedly blocked a Red Cross rescue operation for five days, while thousands of

Egyptian soldiers died in the Sinai desert (London *Times*, June 15, 1967; cited in *Who are the Terrorists?* Institute for Palestine Studies, Beirut, 1972, a detailed factual record reversing the general bias of American reports); also Kennett Love, *Suez*, McGraw-Hill, New York, 1969, p. 689. Bernard Avishai, an Israeli dove, writes in *New York Review* (Jan 24, 1974) that although the Israeli government now "recognizes that no settlement can be possible without accommodating sensible Palestinian national demands, it understandably cannot contrive the amnesia to overlook Arafat's murderous escapades." Such escapades were real enough, but it is well to recall that the Palestinians also have a slight problem of "contriving amnesia" on this score. See, for example, note 46.

21. *American Report*, Nov. 12, 1973.
22. Henry L. Feingold, *The Politics of Rescue*, Rutgers University Press, New Brunswick, N.J., 1970, pp. 300–1. Further inquiry into this matter indicates that there may be some ugly stories buried here. For one report, see my article "Daniel in the Lion's Den: Berrigan and His Critics," *Liberation*, Feb. 1974, from which much of this discussion of the response to Berrigan's address is taken.
23. See his essay "The Wordless Wish: From Citizens to Refugees," in Ibrahim Abu-Lughod, ed., *The Transformation of Palestine*, Northwestern University Press, Evanston, Ill., 1971.
24. I cited a few examples in my "Israel and the New Left." I also noted that Lipset is wrong in still another of his charges against the New Left, that it has been unaware of the Kibbutz. The charge might be leveled with greater accuracy against Lipset's generation of socialists.
25. Compare the rather similar remarks in Jon Kimche, *There Could Have Been Peace*, Dial Press, New York 1973, pp. 274–6.
26. *Maariv*, Nov. 26, 1973.
27. See note 5.
28. Cf. Chapter 3, p. 127.
29. Sabri Jiryis, *The Arabs in Israel*, The Institute for Palestine Studies, Beirut, 1968, pp. 4, 35. To be accurate, certain provisions of the Emergency Regulations have indeed been repealed, according to Jiryis, whose books provide a detailed account of these laws and their application in practice: "At the very moment of the establishment of Israel, on the evening of May 14, 1948, after the Declaration of the Establishment of the State had been read, the Provisional

Council of State immediately decided to repeal certain articles of the Regulations. These were the articles relative to
the Zionist institutions in Palestine, those which dealt with
methods of expropriating and confiscating land and those
which restricted Jewish immigration into the country. The
rest were left unchanged." Sabri Jiryis, *Democratic Freedoms in Israel*, Institute for Palestine Studies, Beirut, 1972,
pp. 29–30.

30. Haifa District Court, Criminal Record 64/73, pp. 541–5.
Substantial parts of the court record are reprinted in *Mish-
patam shel: Rami Livneh, Meli Lerman* (Siah publication,
Sept. 14, 1973; P.O. Box 8253, Jerusalem). Livneh was
sentenced to ten years under a paragraph of the criminal
code that states that "anyone who knowingly makes contact with a [foreign] agent without a legitimate explanation
may be sentenced to 15 years in prison." The court held
that "the contention that the purpose [of the contact] was
only exchange of political ideas of the two organizations does
not serve as a legitimate explanation" (p. 503; no evidence
was presented showing that the contact went beyond exchange of political ideas.) This paragraph of the criminal
code is a 1967 revision of a 1955 law that related such contact to transfer of official secrets. The logic of the revision is
that contact alone is a crime, and the court's decision implies that political discussions with foreign agents are also
a crime. Professor Teodor Shanin, testifying for the defense,
observed that punishment for expression of revolutionary
ideas (as is implicit in the full charge) is unknown outside
of such states as Greece, Spain, and Portugal. Perhaps one
might argue that under present circumstances Israel must
resort to the Draconian measures legitimized by the court
decision. I disagree, but that is not the question at issue
here. Rather, the point is that this remarkable court decision
alone suffices to refute Howe's contention. One might also
note that the court decision would appear to rule illegal any
contacts between Israelis and Palestinians for the purpose of
exchanging ideas on possible resolution of the conflict—in
particular, any discussions relating to binational arrangements.

31. Jiryis, *The Arabs in Israel*, p. 134. The two books by Jiryis
give a detailed record of these events, and discuss the program of the group.

32. Franz Neumann, *Behemoth*, Victor Gollancz, London, 1943,
p. 29.

33. Jiryis, *Democratic Freedoms in Israel*, pp. 58, 94, 95.

34. *Christian Science Monitor*, Dec. 31, 1973. The college was re-opened a few weeks later.

35. *Yediot Ahronot*, cited in *Israleft*, Dec. 30, 1973.

36. Cf. chapter 3, section II, for a few examples.

37. The socialist structures of the Yishuv prior to the establish-ment of the State of Israel were, indeed, remarkable in many respects, and they have retained their vigor and, in my opinion, their promise. But it is quite untrue that Israel is progressing toward socialism. There has been a relative de-cline in the importance of the genuine socialist institutions as the state has developed. It may be true that (apart from the fundamental discriminatory system and the theocratic intrusions on personal freedom) Israel provides about as good a model as we have for democratic socialism, but if so, this is, I am afraid, primarily a comment on existing models.

38. *Dissent*, Summer 1964. For discussion, see Bertrand Russell, *War Crimes in Vietnam*, Monthly Review Press, New York, 1967. To the editors of *Dissent*, withdrawal seemed as in-humane as a war of attrition because it would leave the country under communist control "and there would almost certainly follow a slaughter in the South of all those . . . who have fought against the Communists." They seemed oblivious to the likely consequences of a United States–Saigon victory, though the story of Diem's murderous assault on the opposition (with American backing) in the post-1954 period was already well known. See my *For Reasons of State* for some discussion. Particularly striking is the un-spoken assumption that the United States has the authority to intervene in Vietnam to impose its concept of "humanity." To support their position in this regard, some democratic socialists have found it necessary to credit American propa-ganda on policies in North Vietnam even after these had been exposed as fabrications. For a striking example, again from *Dissent*, see *Counterrevolutionary Violence*, note 201.

39. *Yediot Ahronot*, Dec. 26, 1973, cited in Israleft, Jan. 15, 1974. Dayan was particularly incensed by Jacob Talmon's articles, cited in the introduction, note 51. Shulamit Har-Even re-torted aptly: "Professor Jacob Talmon in his famous article in *Ha'aretz* acted as a historian. Not as a battalion comman-der, not as a political commissar, and not as a defense minister, but as a historian. As such, he is not obliged to find golden rays of light joyfully playing in every act of ministers" (*Ha'aretz*, Dec. 31, 1973, cited in *Israleft*, Jan. 15, 1974).

40. Kimche, *op. cit.*, p. 243.

41. *Ha'aretz*, Nov. 21, 1973, cited in *Jewish Liberation Information Service*, P.O. Box 7557, Jerusalem.

42. Cited in John K. Cooley, *Green March, Black September,* Frank Cass, London, 1973, p. 162, from *Ha'aretz*, March 20, 29; my emphasis. Cooley gives extensive quotes. Cf. chapter 3, section II, note 14, for further discussion.

43. Often, for expansionism. Cf. the remarks of Peled and Bar-Zohar, cited in the introduction, pp. 24–7.

44. See chapter 3, section II, p. 133.

45. See introduction, p. 20; chapter 3, section I, p. 107; this chapter, p. 163, above.

46. *Newsletter* of Ha'olam Haze–Koah Hadash (New Force Party), Feb. 8, 1973, represented at the time in the Knesset by Uri Avneri. A detailed account of the incident, with extensive quotes from Israeli court records, appears in Jiryis, *The Arabs in Israel*, ch. 3. The perpetrators of the massacre did not go unpunished. Three soldiers were given prison sentences; a series of pardons reduced the longest to just over a year. The officer in charge was found guilty of a "merely technical" error and fined one Israeli piaster. A few months after his release, Lieutenant Joubrael Dahan, who had been sentenced for the murder of forty-three unarmed Arab men, women, and children, was appointed by the municipality of Ramle as "Officer responsible for Arab affairs in the city." Americans will find all of this rather familiar.

47. El-Aref was a major source for Kimche (*op. cit.*). His findings are presented in a report by Dr. Israel Shahak. Shahak's courageous work as chairman of the Israeli League for Human and Civil Rights deserves special comment—as does the response to it, both in Israel and here. In November 1972, some two hundred people appeared at a meeting of this small civil rights group, insisted on being registered as members, took over the meeting, and forced out the leadership. The Israeli courts, quite properly, declared the results of the meeting null and void (Judge Lovenberg, Nov. 26, 1972). The Labor Party (Youth Department) then circulated a leaflet headed "internal, not to be published," requesting party members to join the league as a "state duty . . . for the purpose of enabling our party to have a predominant influence in the League . . .", offering to pay membership dues. There was no mention of civil liberties in this call. Judge Lovenberg ruled (April 8, 1973) that the League must accept mass membership organized in this

fashion, while reaffirming his earlier ruling. Obviously, no open organization can survive such tactics on the part of the dominant political party.

On the basis of these events, the New York-based International League for Human Rights, in a most astonishing decision, suspended the Israeli League. In April 1973, Shahak visited the United States. In an interview with the *Boston Globe* (April 18), he identified himself, quite accurately, as chairman of the Israeli League. This interview, dealing with topics rarely discussed here, elicited an abusive response from Harvard law professor Alan Dershowitz, who claimed, among other falsehoods, that Shahak "was overwhelmingly defeated for re-election" as chairman in November 1970 (*sic*) and that the courts had "ruled that the election was legal and that Shahak had been validly defeated" (*Globe*, April 29, May 25; see also my responses, May 17, June 5, citing the court records). The incident illustrates again the lengths to which American Zionists will go in their efforts to silence discussion and discredit political opponents. Dershowitz offered no factual evidence at any point. His assertions are directly refuted by the court records, which are not, of course, normal reading fare here. Still more interesting was Dershowitz's reaction when the Labor Party tactics were brought to his attention. He wrote that he saw nothing wrong with the Labor Party effort to take over the League (May 25). One can imagine his reaction if the Watergate investigations were to reveal a comparable attempt by the Republican Party to take over the ACLU. Dershowitz has done admirable work in defense of civil rights in the United States, but—typically—all standards disappear when the scene shifts to Israel.

48. Hans J. Morgenthau, "The Geopolitics of Israel's Survival," *New Leader*, Dec. 24, 1973. Morgenthau's dire prognosis provides the framework for Howe's "Thinking the Unthinkable About Israel."

49. *Ha'aretz*, Dec. 22, 1967. A lengthy excerpt appears in Arie Bober, ed., *The Other Israel*, Doubleday Anchor Books, New York 1972, pp. 79–80. Cf. also references of note 42.

50. Reports in the Israeli press suggest that this perception is quite accurate. Thus Yehudit Winkler describes a meeting between a delegation of the APPME and Michael Elitsur, head of the Office of North American Affairs of the Israeli Foreign Office, in which Elitsur explained his views on United States–Soviet détente and the Middle East. Within days, she reports, the APPME published material in the

United States reflecting these views (*Ha'aretz*, Dec. 13, 1973). One can have no objection to a group of Americans organizing themselves for one or another purpose, but it is unfortunate—and indicative of the actual situation in the United States—that the one academic group organized to deal with "peace in the Middle East" should serve as a channel for the expression of this particular narrow range of views.

51. As far as I know, Israel is the only country to which American citizens can give tax-free contributions, thus imposing on others a subsidy to Israel, in addition to the direct official aid and loans.

About the Author

Professor Noam Chomsky, an eminent and revolutionary scholar in the field of linguistics, has in recent years
become a figure of national attention through his leadership in Resist, a national movement founded to support draft resistance and radical social change, and
through his brilliant criticism of American political life.
He received his B.A., M.A., and PH.D. from the University of Pennsylvania and was a Junior Fellow of the
Society of Fellows at Harvard from 1951 to 1955. In
1955 he was appointed to the faculty of the Massachusetts Institute of Technology, where he is now Ferrari
Ward Professor of Linguistics. In addition he has served
as John Locke Lecturer at Oxford; as a visiting professor at the University of California, Los Angeles, and at
Berkeley; and as a Research Fellow at the Institute for
Advanced Study at Princeton and the Center for Cog-
nitive Studies at Harvard.

Among the many works Professor Chomsky has written in his field are *Syntactic Structures, Aspects of the
Theory of Syntax, Cartesian Linguistics, Language and
Mind,* and with Morris Halle, *Sound Pattern of English.*
Recently his articles on political and historical themes
have attracted widespread attention. Professor Chomsky is a member of the National Academy of Sciences
and the American Academy of Arts and Sciences, as
well as of numerous professional societies and of the
Council of the International Confederation for Disarm-
ament and Peace. His most recent books are *American
Power and the New Mandarins, Problems of Knowledge
and Freedom: The Russell Lectures,* and *For Reasons
of State.*

VINTAGE POLITICAL SCIENCE
AND SOCIAL CRITICISM

V-428   ABDEL-MALEK, ANOUAR   *Egypt: Military Society*
V-625   ACKLAND, LEN AND SAM BROWN   *Why Are We Still in Vietnam?*
V-196   ADAMS, RICHARD N.   *Social Change in Latin America Today*
V-568   ALINSKY, SAUL D.   *Reveille for Radicals*
V-286   ARIES, PHILIPPE   *Centuries of Childhood*
V-604   BAILYN, BERNARD   *Origins of American Politics*
V-334   BALTZELL, E. DIGBY   *The Protestant Establishment*
V-335   BANFIELD, E. G. AND J. Q. WILSON   *City Politics*
V-674   BARBIANA, SCHOOL OF   *Letter to a Teacher*
V-198   BARDOLPH, RICHARD   *The Negro Vanguard*
V-60   BECKER, CARL L.   *The Declaration of Independence*
V-199   BERMAN, H. J. (ed.)   *Talks on American Law*
V-81   BLAUSTEIN, ARTHUR I. AND ROGER R. WOOCK (eds.)   *Man Against Poverty*
V-513   BOORSTIN, DANIEL J.   *The Americans: The Colonial Experience*
V-358   BOORSTIN, DANIEL J.   *The Americans: The National Experience*
V-621   BOORSTIN, DANIEL J.   *The Decline of Radicalism: Reflections on America Today*
V-414   BOTTOMORE, T. B.   *Classes in Modern Society*
V-44   BRINTON, CRANE   *The Anatomy of Revolution*
V-234   BRUNER, JEROME   *The Process of Education*
V-590   BULLETIN OF ATOMIC SCIENTISTS   *China after the Cultural Revolution*
V-684   CALVERT, GREG AND CAROL   *The New Left and the New Capitalism*
V-30   CAMUS, ALBERT   *The Rebel*
V-33   CARMICHAEL, STOKELY AND CHARLES HAMILTON   *Black Power*
V-664   CARMICHAEL, STOKELY   *Stokely Speaks*
V-98   CASH, W. J.   *The Mind of the South*
V-272   CATER, DOUGLASS   *The Fourth Branch of Government*
V-290   CATER, DOUGLASS   *Power in Washington*
V-555   CHOMSKY, NOAM   *American Power and the New Mandarins*
V-640   CHOMSKY, NOAM   *At War With Asia*
V-538   COX COMMISSION   *Crisis at Columbia*
V-311   CREMIN, LAWRENCE A.   *The Genius of American Education*
V-638   DENNISON, GEORGE   *The Lives of Children*
V-746   DEUTSCHER, ISAAC   *The Prophet Armed*
V-747   DEUTSCHER, ISAAC   *The Prophet Unarmed*
V-748   DEUTSCHER, ISAAC   *The Prophet Outcast*
V-617   DEVLIN, BERNADETTE   *The Price of My Soul*
V-671   DOMHOFF, G. WILLIAM   *The Higher Circles*
V-603   DOUGLAS, WILLIAM O.   *Points of Rebellion*
V-645   DOUGLAS, WILLIAM O.   *International Dissent*
V-390   ELLUL, JACQUES   *The Technological Society*
V-692   EPSTEIN, JASON   *The Great Conspiracy Trial*
V-661   FALK, RICHARD A., GABRIEL KOLKO, AND ROBERT JAY LIFTON   *Crimes of War: After Songmy*
V-442   FALL, BERNARD B.   *Hell in a Very Small Place: The Siege of Dien Bien Phu*
V-667   FINN, JAMES   *Conscience and Command*

V-413   FRANK, JEROME D.   *Sanity and Survival*

V-382   FRANKLIN, JOHN HOPE AND ISIDORE STARR (eds.)   *The Negro in 20th Century America*

V-368   FRIEDENBERG, EDGAR Z.   *Coming of Age in America*

V-662   FRIEDMAN, EDWARD AND MARK SELDEN (eds.)   *America's Asia: Dissenting Essays in Asian Studies*

V-378   FULBRIGHT, J. WILLIAM   *The Arrogance of Power*

V-688   FULBRIGHT, J. WILLIAM   *The Pentagon Propaganda Machine*

V-475   GAY, PETER   *The Enlightenment: The Rise of Modern Paganism*

V-668   GERASSI, JOHN   *Revolutionary Priest: The Complete Writings and Messages of Camillo Torres*

V-657   GETTLEMAN, MARVIN E. AND DAVID MERMELSTEIN (eds.) *The Failure of American Liberalism*

V-451   GETTLEMAN, MARVIN E. AND SUSAN, AND LAWRENCE AND CAROL KAPLAN   *Conflict in Indochina: A Reader on the Widening War in Laos and Cambodia*

V-174   GOODMAN, PAUL AND PERCIVAL   *Communitas*

V-325   GOODMAN, PAUL   *Compulsory Mis-education and The Community of Scholars*

V-32   GOODMAN, PAUL   *Growing Up Absurd*

V-417   GOODMAN, PAUL   *People or Personnel* and *Like a Conquered Province*

V-606   GORO, HERB   *The Block*

V-633   GREEN, PHILIP AND SANFORD LEVINSON (eds.)   *Power and Community: Dissenting Essays in Political Science*

V-457   GREENE, FELIX   *The Enemy: Some Notes on the Nature of Contemporary Imperialism*

V-618   GREENSTONE, J. DAVID   *Labor in American Politics*

V-430   GUEVERA, CHE   *Guerrilla Warfare*

V-685   HAMSIK, DUSAN   *Writers Against Rulers*

V-427   HAYDEN, TOM   *Rebellion in Newark*

V-453   HEALTH PAC   *The American Health Empire*

V-635   HEILBRONER, ROBERT L.   *Between Capitalism and Socialism*

V-450   HERSH, SEYMOUR M.   *My Lai 4*

V-283   HENRY, JULES   *Culture Against Man*

V-644   HESS, KARL AND THOMAS REEVES   *The End of the Draft*

V-465   HINTON, WILLIAM   *Fanshen: A Documentary of Revolution in a Chinese Village*

V-576   HOFFMAN, ABBIE   *Woodstock Nation*

V-95   HOFSTADTER, RICHARD   *The Age of Reform: From Bryan to F.D.R.*

V-9   HOFSTADTER, RICHARD   *The American Political Tradition*

V-317   HOFSTADTER, RICHARD   *Anti-Intellectualism in American Life*

V-385   HOFSTADTER, RICHARD   *Paranoid Style in American Politics and other Essays*

V-686   HOFSTADTER, RICHARD AND MICHAEL WALLACE (eds.)   *American Violence, A Documentary History*

V-429   HOROWITZ, DE CASTRO, AND GERASSI (eds.)   *Latin American Radicalism*

V-666   HOWE, LOUISE KAPP (ed.)   *The White Majority: Between Poverty and Affluence*

V-630   HOROWITZ, DAVID   *Empire and Revolution*

V-201   HUGHES, H. STUART   *Consciousness and Society*

V-241   JACOBS, JANE   *Death & Life of Great American Cities*

V-584   JACOBS, JANE   *The Economy of Cities*

V-433   JACOBS, PAUL   *Prelude to Riot*

V-332   JACOBS, PAUL AND SAUL LANDAU (eds.)   *The New Radicals*

V-459   JACOBS, PAUL AND SAUL LANDAU, WITH EVE PELL   *To Serve the Devil: Natives & Slaves*, Vol. I

V-460   JACOBS, PAUL AND SAUL LANDAU, WITH EVE PELL   *To Serve the Devil: Colonials & Sojourners*, Volume II

V-456   JONES, ITA   *The Grubbag*

V-369   KAUFMANN, WALTER (trans.)   *The Birth of Tragedy* and *The Case of Wagner*

V-401   KAUFMANN, WALTER (trans.)   *On the Genealogy of Morals* and *Ecce Homo*

V-337   KAUFMANN, WALTER (trans.)   *Beyond Good and Evil*

V-582   KIRSHBAUM, LAURENCE AND ROGER RAPOPORT   *Is the Library Burning?*

V-631   KOLKO, GABRIEL   *Politics of War*

V-361   KOMAROVSKY, MIRRA   *Blue-Collar Marriage*

V-675   KOVEL, JOEL   *White Racism*

V-215   LACOUTURE, JEAN   *Ho Chi Minh*

V-367   LASCH, CHRISTOPHER   *The New Radicalism in America*

V-560   LASCH, CHRISTOPHER   *The Agony of the American Left*

V-280   LEWIS, OSCAR   *The Children of Sánchez*

V-421   LEWIS, OSCAR   *La Vida*

V-634   LEWIS, OSCAR   *A Death in the Sánchez Family*

V-637   LIBARLE, MARC AND TOM SELIGSON (eds.)   *The High School Revolutionaries*

V-474   LIFTON, ROBERT JAY   *Revolutionary Immortality*

V-384   LINDESMITH, ALFRED   *The Addict and The Law*

V-533   LOCKWOOD, LEE   *Castro's Cuba, Cuba's Fidel*

V-469   LOWE, JEANNE R.   *Cities in a Race with Time*

V-659   LURIE, ELLEN   *How to Change the Schools*

V-193   MALRAUX, ANDRE   *Temptation of the West*

V-480   MARCUSE, HERBERT   *Soviet Marxism*

V-502   MATTHEWS, DONALD R.   *U. S. Senators and Their World*

V-577   MAYER, ARNO J.   *Political Origins of the New Diplomacy, 1917-1918*

V-575   MCCARTHY, RICHARD D.   *The Ultimate Folly*

V-619   MCCONNELL, GRANT   *Private Power and American Democracy*

V-386   MCPHERSON, JAMES   *The Negro's Civil War*

V-615   MITFORD, JESSICA   *The Trial of Dr. Spock*

V-539   MORGAN, ROBIN (ed.)   *Sisterhood Is Powerful*

V-274   MYRDAL, GUNNAR   *Challenge to Affluence*

V-573   MYRDAL, GUNNAR   *An Approach to the Asian Drama*

V-687   NEVILE, RICHARD   *Play Power*

V-377   NIETZSCHE, FRIEDRICH   *Beyond Good and Evil*

V-369   NIETZSCHE, FRIEDRICH   *The Birth of Tragedy* and *The Case of Wagner*

V-401   NIETZSCHE, FRIEDRICH   *On the Genealogy of Morals* and *Ecce Homo*

V-642   O'GORMAN, NED   *Prophetic Voices*

V-583   ORTIZ, FERNANDO   *Cuban Counterpoint: Tobacco and Sugar*

V-128   PLATO   *The Republic*

V-648   RADOSH, RONALD   *American Labor and U.S. Foreign Policy*

V-309   RASKIN, MARCUS AND BERNARD FALL (eds.)   *The Viet-nam Reader*

V-719   REED, JOHN   *Ten Days That Shook the World*

V-644   REEVES, THOMAS AND KARL HESS   *The End of the Draft*

V-192   REISCHAUER, EDWIN O.   *Beyond Vietnam: The United States and Asia*

V-548   RESTON, JAMES   *Sketches in the Sand*

V-622   ROAZEN, PAUL   *Freud: Political and Social Thought*

V-534   ROGERS, DAVID   *110 Livingston Street*

V-559   ROSE, TOM (ed.)   *Violence in America*

V-212   ROSSITER, CLINTON   *Conservatism in America*

V-472   ROSZAK, THEODORE (ed.)   *The Dissenting Academy*

V-431   SCHELL, JONATHAN   *The Village of Ben Suc*

V-375   SCHURMANN, F. AND O. SCHELL (eds.)   *The China Reader: Imperial China, I*

V-376   SCHURMANN, F. AND O. SCHELL (eds.)   *The China Reader: Republican China, II*

V-377   SCHURMANN, F. AND O. SCHELL (eds.)   *The China Reader: Communist China, III*

V-649   SEALE, BOBBY   *Seize the Time*

V-279   SILBERMAN, CHARLES E.   *Crisis in Black and White*

V-681   SNOW, EDGAR   *Red China Today*

V-222   SPENDER, STEPHEN   *The Year of the Young Rebels*

V-388   STAMPP, KENNETH   *The Era of Reconstruction 1865-1877*

V-253   STAMPP, KENNETH   *The Peculiar Institution*

V-613   STERNGLASS, ERNEST J.   *The Stillborn Future*

V-439   STONE, I. F.   *In a Time of Torment*

V-231   TANNENBAUM, FRANK   *Slave & Citizen: The Negro in the Americas*

V-312   TANNENBAUM, FRANK   *Ten Keys to Latin America*

V-686   WALLACE, MICHAEL AND RICHARD HOFSTADTER (eds.)   *American Violence: A Documentary History*

V-206   WALLERSTEIN, IMMANUEL   *Africa: The Politics of Independence*

V-543   WALLERSTEIN, IMMANUEL   *Africa: The Politics of Unity*

V-454   WALLERSTEIN, IMMANUEL AND PAUL STARR (eds.)   *The University Crisis Reader: The Liberal University Under Attack, Vol. I*

V-455   WALLERSTEIN, IMMANUAL AND PAUL STARR (eds.)   *The University Crisis Reader: Confrontation and Counterattack, Vol. II*

V-323   WARREN, ROBERT PENN   *Who Speaks for the Negro?*

V-405   WASSERMAN AND SWITZER   *The Random House Guide to Graduate Study in the Arts and Sciences*

V-249   WIEDNER, DONALD L.   *A History of Africa: South of the Sahara*

V-557   WEINSTEIN, JAMES   *Decline of Socialism in America 1912-1925*

V-585   WEINSTEIN, JAMES AND DAVID EAKINS (eds.)   *For a New America*

V-605   WILLIAMS, JOHN A. AND CHARLES HARRIS (eds.)   *Amistad 1*

V-660   WILLIAMS, JOHN A. AND CHARLES HARRIS (eds.)   *Amistad 2*

V-651   WILLIAMS, WILLIAM APPLEMAN   *The Roots of the Modern American Empire*

V-545   WOOLF., S. J. (ed.)   *The Nature of Fascism*

V-495   YGLESIAS, JOSE   *In the Fist of the Revolution*

V-483   ZINN, HOWARD   *Disobedience and Democracy*